Privilege, Power, and Difference

Third Edition

Allan G. Johnson, Ph.D.

McGraw Hill Education

PRIVILEGE, POWER, AND DIFFERENCE, THIRD EDITION

Published by McGraw-Hill Education, 2 Penn Plaza, New York, NY 10121. Copyright © 2018 by McGraw-Hill Education. All rights reserved. Printed in the United States of America. Previous editions © 2006 and 2001. No part of this publication may be reproduced or distributed in any form or by any means, or stored in a database or retrieval system, without the prior written consent of McGraw-Hill Education, including, but not limited to, in any network or other electronic storage or transmission, or broadcast for distance learning.

Some ancillaries, including electronic and print components, may not be available to customers outside the United States.

This book is printed on acid-free paper.

2 3 4 5 6 7 8 9 LCR 21 20 19

ISBN 978-0-07-340422-6
MHID 0-07-340422-5

Chief Product Officer, SVP Products & Markets: *G. Scott Virkler*	Content Project Managers: *Jennifer Shekleton, Katie Klochan*
Vice President, General Manager, Products & Markets: *Michael Ryan*	Buyer: *Susan K. Culbertson*
	Design: *Studio Montage, Inc.*
Managing Director: *David Patterson*	Content Licensing Specialists:
Brand Manager: *Jamie Laferrera*	*Lori Hancock*
Product Developer: *Jamie Laferrera*	Cover Image: *The Studio Dog/Getty Images*
Marketing Manager: *Meredith Leo*	Compositor: *Aptara®, Inc.*
Program Manager: *Jennifer Shekleton*	Printer: *LSC Communications*

All credits appearing on page or at the end of the book are considered to be an extension of the copyright page.

Library of Congress Cataloging-in-Publication Data

Cataloging-in-Publication Data has been requested from the Library of Congress

The Internet addresses listed in the text were accurate at the time of publication. The inclusion of a website does not indicate an endorsement by the authors or McGraw-Hill Education, and McGraw-Hill Education does not guarantee the accuracy of the information presented at these sites.

mheducation.com/highered

Contents

For Jane Tuohy

About the Author

Allan G. Johnson is a nationally recognized sociologist, nonfiction author, novelist, and public speaker best known for his work on issues of privilege and oppression, especially in relation to gender and race. He is the author of numerous books, including *The Gender Knot: Unraveling Our Patriarchal Legacy, 3e* (2014), *The Forest and the Trees: Sociology as Life, Practice, and Promise, 3e* (2014), and a memoir, *Not From Here* (2015). His work has been translated into several languages and is excerpted in numerous anthologies. Visit his website at www.agjohnson.com and follow his blog at agjohnson.wordpress.com.

Also by Allan G. Johnson

Nonfiction

Not from Here: A Memoir
The Gender Knot
The Forest and the Trees
The Blackwell Dictionary of Sociology

Fiction

The First Thing and the Last
Nothing Left to Lose

Introduction

I didn't make this world. It was given to me this way!

Lorraine Hansberry, *A Raisin in the Sun*[1]

It isn't news that a great deal of trouble surrounds issues of privilege, power, and difference, trouble based on gender and race, sexual orientation and identity, disability, social class. Or that it causes a great deal of injustice, anger, conflict, and suffering. We seem unable, however, to do anything about it as it continues from one generation to the next. We are, as individuals, as a society, stuck in a kind of paralysis that perpetuates the trouble and what it does to people's lives.

We are, each of us, part of the problem, because, in one way or another, and for all our differences, we have in common the fact of our participation in a society we did not create. We can also make ourselves a part of the solution, but only if we know how. That there are choices to be made is true for everyone, no matter how we are located in the world, and the effectiveness of those choices can be no better than our understanding of how it works. What we bring to that is shaped by our position and experience of the world—as male or female, for example, of color or white, working or middle class. But no matter who we are and what we know because of it, we still need tools for making sense of reality in ways that connect us with the experience and lives of others. Because it is only then that we can come together across lines of difference to make something better than the legacy that was passed to us.

I wrote this book to help us get unstuck, by sharing a way of thinking about privilege and oppression that provides a framework that is conceptual and theoretical on the one hand and grounded in research and the experience of everyday life on the other. In this way it allows us to see not only where the trouble comes from but also how we are connected to it, which is the only thing that gives us the potential to make a difference.

ix

When people hear "how we are connected to it," they often react as if they're about to be accused of doing something wrong. It's especially common among men and whites, but it also happens with women and people of color who anticipate being blamed for their own oppression. Either way, it is a kind of defensive reaction that does more than perhaps anything else to keep us stuck.

As a white, male, heterosexual, nondisabled, cisgender, upper-middle-class professional, I know about such feelings from my own life. But as a sociologist, I also know that it's possible to understand the world and myself in relation to it in ways that get past defensiveness and denial to put us on a common ground from which we can work for change. My purpose here is to articulate that understanding in ways that are clear and compelling and, above all, useful.

Because my main goal is to change how people think about issues of privilege, I have been less concerned with describing all the forms that privilege can take and the problems associated with them. In choosing, I've been drawn to what affects the greatest number of people and produces the most harm, and, like any author, I tend to stick to what I know best. As a result, I focus almost entirely on gender, race, social class, disability status, and sexual orientation.

In the second edition, I added issues of disability, and I think it's important to say something about how that came about. Why was it not included before? The main reason is that I, as a person without disabilities, was unable to see the reality of disability status as a form of privilege. After the first edition was published, I heard from several readers—most notably Marshall Mitchell, a professor of disability studies at Washington State University—who urged me to reconsider. What followed was many months during which I had to educate myself and listen to those who knew more about this than I did. I had to come to terms with what I didn't know about privilege and what I *thought* I knew, which is to say, I had to do for myself what I wrote this book to help others do.

Simple ignorance, however, is not the whole story, for the difficulties that people without disabilities face in seeing their privilege and the oppression of people socially identified as disabled is rooted in the place of disability in human life. Unlike gender, race, and sexual orientation, disability status can change during a person's lifetime. In fact, almost everyone will experience some form of disability during their lives, unless they die first.

People with disabilities, then, are a constant reminder of the reality of the human experience—how vulnerable we are and how much there is in life that we cannot control.

For many nondisabled people, this can be a frightening thing to contemplate. Treating people with disabilities as if they were invisible, designing buildings as if everyone was nondisabled, seeing people with disabilities as inferior or abnormal, even less than human—all these oppressive practices enable nondisabled people to deny a basic feature of the human condition.

Accepting that condition is especially difficult for nondisabled people in the United States, where the cultural ideal of being autonomous, independent, young, strong, and needing no one's help is deeply rooted. As any student of social life knows, however, this is based on an illusion, because from the time we are born to the moment we die, we all depend on other human beings for our very existence. But being an illusion does not lessen the power of such ideas, and I had to come to terms with how they affected my writing of this book.

You might be wondering why I use the word "nondisabled" to refer to people without disabilities. Wouldn't "abled" be simpler and more direct? It would, but it would also cover up the reason for including disability issues in a book on privilege.

Consider this: if I have use of my eyes and you cannot see, it is reasonable to say that I have an ability and you have an inability. Or, put differently, when it comes to using eyes to see, I am abled and you are disabled. I might point out that my condition gives me certain advantages, and I'd be right, although you might counter that your condition gives you access to experiences, insights, and sensitivities that I would be less likely to have. You might even assert that your way of seeing is just different from mine and that you don't consider yourself disabled at all. Still, if we're looking at the specific ability to use the eyes to see, I think most people would agree that "abled" and "disabled" are reasonable ways to describe this particular objective difference between us.

The problem—and this is where privilege comes in—is that not being able to use your eyes to see brings with it disadvantages that go beyond sight itself, whereas having the use of your eyes brings with it unearned advantages that go beyond the fact of being able to see. This happens, for example, when the inability to see leads to being labeled a "blind person" or a "disabled person" who is perceived and judged to be nothing more than that—a helpless, damaged, inferior human being who deserves to be treated accordingly. But not being able to see does not mean that you are unintelligent or helpless or inferior or unable to hold a decent job or make your own decisions. It just means you cannot see. Even so, you might be discriminated against, giving others—people who can see and therefore are not perceived as "disabled"—an advantage they did not earn.

So, "nondisability privilege" refers to the privilege of *not* being burdened with the stigma and subordinate status that go along with being identified as disabled in this culture. Admittedly, it is an awkward way to put it, but as is so often the case, systems of privilege do not provide a language that makes it easy to name the reality of what is going on.[2]

You may also have noticed that I don't include social class as an example of privilege, power, and difference. I made this choice not from a belief that class is unimportant, but because the nature and dynamics of class are beyond the scope of what I'm trying to do. My focus is on how differences that would otherwise have little if any inherent connection to social inequality are nonetheless seized on and turned into a basis for privilege and oppression.

Race is perhaps the most obvious example of this. Biologists have long agreed that what are identified as racial differences—skin color being the most prominent—do not define actual biological groups but instead are socially defined categories.[3] More important is that for most of human history, such "differences" have been regarded as socially insignificant. When Europeans began to exploit indigenous peoples for territorial conquest and economic gain, however, they developed the idea of race as a way to justify their behavior on the grounds of supposed racial superiority. In other words, by itself, something like skin color has no importance in social life but was turned into something significant in order to create, justify, and enforce privilege.[4]

Social class, of course, has huge effects on people's lives, but this is not an example of this phenomenon. On the contrary, social class differences are inherently about privilege. It is also true, however, that class plays an important role in the forms of privilege that are the focus of this book, which is why I devote an entire chapter to the capitalist system that produces social class today. Although racism is a problem that involves all white people, for example, how it plays out in their lives is affected by class. For upper-class whites, white privilege may take the form of being able to hire women of color to do domestic service work they would rather not do themselves (such as maids and nannies) or, on a larger scale, to benefit from investments in industries that make use of people of color as a source of cheap labor. In contrast, in the working class, white privilege is more likely to take the form of preferential treatment in hiring and promotion in skilled trades and other upper-level blue-collar occupations, or access to unions or mortgages and loans, or being less vulnerable to the excessive use of force by police.

In similar ways, the effect of race on people of color is also shaped by social class differences. Blacks and Latinos, for example, who have achieved wealth or power—such as Barack Obama, Sonia Sotomayor, or Ben Carson— are more protected from many overt and extreme forms of racism. In similar ways, the children of elite black families who attend Ivy League colleges may be spared the most extreme expressions of racist violence and discrimination, while experiencing more subtle microaggressions.[5]

Without taking such patterns into account, it is difficult to know just what something like "white privilege" means across the complexity of people's lives.

To some degree, this book cannot help having a point of view that is shaped by my social location as a white, heterosexual, cisgender, nondisabled, upper-middle-class male. But that combination of social characteristics does not simply limit what I bring to this, for each provides a bridge to some portion of almost every reader's life. I cannot know from my own experience, for example, what it's like to be female or of color or LGBT in this society. But I can bring my experience as a white person to the struggle of white people—including white women and working-class white men—to deal with the subject of racism, just as I can bring my experience as a man to men's work—including gay men and men of color—around the subject of sexism and male privilege. In the same way, I can bring my perspective and experience to the challenges faced by people who are heterosexual or nondisabled, regardless of their gender or race or class.

What I cannot know from my own experience I have tried to supplement by studying the experience and research and writings of others. This has led me, over the course of my career, to design and teach courses on class and capitalism, the sociology of gender, feminist theory, and, with a female African American colleague, race in the United States. I have written on male privilege and gender inequality (*The Gender Knot*), I've been active in the movement against men's violence against women, and I've given hundreds of presentations on gender and race across the United States.

In these and other ways, I've spent most of my life as a sociologist and a writer and a human being trying to understand the world we live in, how it's organized and how it works, shaping our lives in so many different ways. None of this means that what I've written is the last word on anything. If, however, I have succeeded in what I set out to do here—and only you will know if I have done that for you—then I believe this book has something to offer anyone who wants to deal with these difficult issues and help change the world for the better.

If, however, you come to this with the expectation of not liking what you're about to read, I suggest you go next to the Epilogue before turning to Chapter 1.

CHAPTER 1

We're in Trouble

In 1991, a black motorist named Rodney King suffered a brutal beating by police officers in Los Angeles. When his assailants were acquitted and riots broke out in the city, King uttered a simple yet exasperated plea that echoed across the long history and deep divide of racism in the United States. "Can we all get along?"

Fast forward more than twenty-five years to mass protests against police shootings of unarmed black people,[1] and King's question still resonates with our racial dilemma—what W. E. B. Du Bois called, more than a century ago, "the problem of the color line."[2] It is a question that has haunted us ever since the Civil War ended slavery, and, like any serious question, it deserves a serious response.

In the 21st century, in spite of Barack Obama's two terms as president, the evidence is clear that however much we might wish it otherwise, the answer to Rodney King's question is still no.[3] Whether it is a matter of can't or won't, the truth is that we simply do not get along. In addition to police violence, people of color are disproportionately singled out for arrest, prosecution, and punishment for types of crimes that they are no more likely than whites to commit. Among illegal drug users, for example, whites outnumber blacks by more than five to one, and yet blacks make up sixty percent of those imprisoned for that offense.[4] Segregation in housing and schools is still pervasive and, in many parts of the country, increasing.[5] The average net wealth of white families is twenty times that of blacks, with the 2008 financial collapse being far more devastating for people of color than it was for whites.[6] At every level of education, whites are half as likely as blacks and Latinos to be unemployed or to have incomes below the poverty line. The average annual income for whites who work year round and full time is forty-four percent greater than it is for comparable African Americans. It is sixty percent greater than for Latinos. The white income advantage exists at all levels of educational attainment and only increases at higher levels.[7]

The damage caused by everyday racism is everywhere, and is especially galling to middle-class blacks who have believed what whites have told them that if they go to school and work hard and make something of themselves, race will no longer be an issue. But they soon discover, and learn anew every day, that nothing protects them from their vulnerability to white racism.[8]

As I write this, I'm aware that some readers—whites in particular, and especially those who do not have the luxury of class privilege—may already feel put off by words like "privilege," "racism," "white," and (even worse) "white privilege" or "white racism." One way to avoid such a reaction is to not use such words. As the rest of this book will make clear, however, if we can't use the words, we also can't talk about what's really going on and what it has to do with us. And that makes it impossible to see what the problems are or how we might make ourselves part of the solution to them, which is, after all, the point of writing or reading a book such as this.

With that in mind, the most important thing I can say to reassure those readers who are wondering whether to continue reading is that things are not what they seem. The defensive, irritable, and even angry feelings that people in dominant groups often experience when they come across such language are usually based on misperceptions that this book will try to clarify and set straight, including, in Chapter 2, the widely misunderstood concept of privilege.

It is also important to keep in mind that the reality of privilege and oppression is complicated, and it will take much of this book to outline an approach that many have found useful—especially men and whites trying to understand not only how it all works, but what it has to do with them. It is an approach that isn't widely known in our society and, so, as with any unfamiliar way of thinking, it helps to be patient and to give the benefit of the doubt until you've followed it to the end.

Problems of perception and defensiveness apply not only to race but to a broad and interconnected set of social differences that have become the basis for a great deal of trouble in the world. Although Du Bois was correct that race would be a defining issue in the 20th century, the problem of "getting along" does not stop there. It is also an issue across differences of gender, gender identity, sexual orientation, disability status,* and numerous other divides.

Since 1990, for example, and Hillary Clinton's nearly successful candidacy for the presidency notwithstanding, there has been little progress in the struggle for gender equity. The average man working full time earns almost thirty percent more than the average woman. In spite of being a majority among college graduates, most employed women are still confined to a narrow range of lower status, lower paid occupations, and those women who have made inroads into previously male-dominated professions, such as medicine and law, are more likely than men to be in lower ranked, lower paid positions. At the same time, men entering occupations such as nursing and elementary school teaching are more highly paid than comparable women and are more likely to advance to supervisory positions. In universities, science professors, both male and female, widely regard female students as less competent than comparable males and are less likely to offer women jobs, or to pay those they do hire salaries equal to those of men. In politics, women make up less than nineteen percent of the U.S. Congress and hold less than a quarter of all seats in state legislature and statewide office, in spite of being a majority of the population. In families, women do twice as much housework and child care as men, even when also employed outside the home.[9]

There is also a global epidemic of men's violence, including war, terrorism, and mass murder, as well as sex trafficking, rape, and battery directed primarily at girls and women.[10] Official responses and public conversations show little understanding of the underlying causes or what to do, including the fact that the overwhelming majority of violence is perpetrated by men. Worldwide, thirty percent of women report having been sexually or physically assaulted by a partner, and women are more at risk of being a victim of

---

*Throughout this book, I use the word "status" to indicate a position or characteristic that connects people to one another through social relationships, such as student, female, parent, or white.

rape and domestic violence than of cancer, car accidents, war, and malaria *combined.*[11] In the United States, one out of every five female college students is sexually assaulted during their college careers, and sexual assault is so pervasive in the military that the greatest threat to women comes not from the hazards of military service but from sexual assault by male service members.[12] In addition, harassment, discrimination, and violence directed at LGBT* people are still commonplace, in spite of signs of growing social acceptance, as with the legalization of same-sex marriage. It is still legal in most states, for example, to discriminate against LGBT people in employment, housing, and public accommodations.

In addition to issues of gender, race, and sexual orientation, the estimated fifty-four million people with disabilities in the United States are vulnerable to abuse both within and outside their homes. They are routinely stereotyped as damaged, helpless, and inferior human beings who lack intelligence and are therefore denied the opportunity to develop their abilities fully. The physical environment—from appropriate signage to entrances to buildings, buses, and airplanes—is typically designed in ways that make it difficult if not impossible for them to have what they need and to get from one place to another. Because of such conditions, they are far less likely than others to finish high school or college and are far more likely to be unemployed; and, when they do find work, to be paid less than the minimum wage. The result is a pervasive pattern of exploitation, deprivation, poverty, mistreatment, and isolation that denies access to the employment, housing, transportation, information, and basic services needed to fully participate in social life.[13]

Clearly, across many dimensions of difference, we are not getting along with one another, and we need to ask why.

For many, the answer is some variation on "human nature." People cannot help fearing the unfamiliar, for example, or women and men are so different that it's as though they come from different planets, and it's a miracle that we get along at all. Or there is only one natural sexual orientation (heterosexual)

---

*LGBT is an acronym for lesbian, gay, bisexual, and transgender. Some activists expand it to include "queer" (LGBTQ), a general term that refers to those who, in various ways, reject, test, or otherwise transgress the boundaries of what is culturally regarded as normal in relation to gender, gender identity, or sexual orientation and expression. Some regard it as an umbrella term for the other four components of LGBT. "Queer" is also routinely used as an insult directed at LGBT people. A cisgender person is one who was assigned a sex at birth that culturally matches their self-identified gender, such as someone identified as female at birth who self identifies as a woman.

and gender identity (woman or man) that must culturally match the sex we are assigned at birth (making us cisgender), and all the rest are unacceptable and bound to cause conflict wherever they show up. Or those who are more capable will get more than everyone else—they always have and always will. Someone, after all, has to be on top.

As popular as such arguments are, they depend on ignoring most of what history, psychology, anthropology, sociology, biology, and, if we look closely, our own experiences reveal about human beings and how we live. We are not prisoners to some natural order that pits us hopelessly and endlessly against one another. We are prisoners to *something,* but it is more of our own making than we realize.

The Trouble We're In

Every morning I walk with our dogs in acres of woods behind our house, a quiet and peaceful place where I can feel the seasons come and go. I like the solitude, a chance to reflect on my life and the world, and to see things in perspective and more clearly. And I like to watch the dogs chase each other in games of tag, sniff out the trail of an animal that passed by the night before. They go out far and then come back to make sure I'm still there.

It's hard not to notice that everything seems pretty simple to them—or at least from what I can see. They never stray far from what I imagine to be the essential nature of what it means to be a dog in relation to everything around them. And that is all they seem to need or care about.

It's also hard not to wonder about my own species, which, by comparison, seems deeply troubled most of the time. I believe we do not have to be, because even though I'm trained as a sociologist to see the complexity of things, I think we are fairly simple.

Deep in our bones, for example, we are social beings. There is no escaping it. We cannot survive on our own when we're young, and it doesn't get that much easier later on. We need to feel that we belong to something bigger than ourselves, whether it's a community or a whole society. We look to other people to tell us that we measure up, that we matter, that we're okay. We have a huge capacity to be creative and generous and loving. We spin stories, make music and art, help children turn into adults, save one another in countless ways, and ease our loved ones into death. We have large brains and opposable thumbs and are clever in how we use them. I'm not sure if we're the only species with a sense of humor—I think I've known dogs to laugh—but we have made the most of it. And we are highly adaptable, able to live just about anywhere under almost any conditions. We can take in the strange and unfamiliar and learn to understand and embrace it, whether it's a new language or the person sitting next to us on the crosstown bus who doesn't look like anyone we've ever seen before.

For all of our potential, you would think we could get along with one another. By that I don't mean love one another in some idealistic way. We don't need to love, or even like, one another to work together or share space in the world. I also don't mean something as minimal as tolerance. I mean treating one another with decency and respect and appreciating, if not supporting, the best we have in us.

It doesn't seem unreasonable to imagine a community, for example, where parents don't have to coach their children on how to avoid being shot by police on the way home from school, or raped on a date. Or a workplace where all kinds of people feel comfortable showing up, secure in the knowledge that they have a place they don't have to defend every time they turn around, where they're encouraged to do their best, and valued for it. We all like to feel that way—accepted, valued, supported, appreciated, respected, belonging. So you would think we'd go after it like dogs on the trail of something good to eat. We would, that is, unless something powerful kept us from it.

Apparently, something powerful does keep us from it, to judge from all the trouble there is around issues of difference and how far we are from anything like a world where people feel comfortable showing up and good about themselves and one another. And yet, for all the trouble, we don't know how to talk about it, and so we act as though it's always somewhere other than where we are.

It reminds me of sitting in a restaurant with an African American woman, as we talk about a course on race and gender that we want to teach together. And while we talk about what we want our students to think about and learn, I'm feeling how hard it is to talk about race and gender in that moment—about how the legacy of racism and sexism shapes our lives in such different ways, how my whiteness and maleness are sources of privilege that elevate people like me not above some abstract groups, but above people like her, my friend.

The simple truth is that when I go shopping, for example, I will probably get waited on faster and better than she will. I will benefit from the cultural assumption that I'm a serious customer who doesn't need to be followed around to keep me from stealing something. The clerk won't ask me for three kinds of ID before accepting my check or credit card. But all these indignities, which my whiteness protects me from, are part of her everyday existence. And it doesn't matter how she dresses or behaves or that she's an executive in a large corporation. Her being black and the clerk being white in a racist society is all it takes.[14]

She also cannot go for a walk alone at night without thinking about her safety a lot more than I do—planning what to do in case a man approaches her with something other than goodwill. She has to consider what he might think if she smiles in a friendly way and says hello, or what he'll think if she does not. She has to decide where to park her car for safety, to remember to have her keys out as she approaches it, to check the back seat before she gets in. In other words, she has to limit her life in ways that almost never occur to me, and her being female is the reason why.[15]

As these thoughts fill my mind, I struggle with how to sit across from her and talk and eat our lunch while all of this is going on all the time. I want to say, "Can we talk about this and *us?*" But I don't, because it feels too risky, the kind of thing both of you know but keep from saying, like a couple where one has been unfaithful and both know it, but they collude in silence because they know that if either speaks the truth of what they both already know, they won't be able to go on as if this awful thing between them isn't there.

It's not that I have *done* something or thought bad thoughts about her because she is black and female. No, the problem is that in the world as it is, race and gender shape her life and mine in dramatically different ways. And it isn't some random accident that befell her while I escaped. A tornado didn't blow through town and level her house while leaving mine alone. No, her misfortune is connected to my good fortune. The reality of her having to deal with racism and sexism every day is connected to the reality that I *do not*. I did not have to do anything for this to be true and neither did she. But there it is just the same.

All of that sits in the middle of the table like the elephant that everyone pretends not to see.

The "elephant" is a society and its people—for whom a decent and productive social life that is true to the best of our human selves—continues to be elusive. In its place is a powerful kind of trouble that is tenacious, profound, and seems only to get worse.

The trouble we are in is the privileging of some groups at the expense of others. It creates a yawning divide in levels of income, wealth, dignity, safety, health, and quality of life. It promotes fear, suspicion, discrimination, anger, harassment, and violence. It sets people against one another. It weaves the corrosive effects of oppression into the daily lives of tens of millions of women, men, and children. It has the potential to ruin entire generations and, in the long run, to take just about everyone down with it.

It is a trouble that shows up everywhere and touches every life in one way or another. There is no escape, however thick the denial. It is in families and neighborhoods, in schools and churches, in government and the courts, in colleges and the workplace, wherever people experience people unlike themselves and what this society makes of such differences.

The hard and simple truth is that the "we" who are in trouble includes everyone, us, and it will take most of us to get us out of it. It is relatively easy, for example, for white people to fall into the safe and comfortable rut of thinking that racism is a problem that belongs to people of color. But such thinking assumes that we can talk about "up" without "down" or that a "you" or a "them" can mean something without a "me" or an "us."

There is no way that a problem of difference can involve just one group of people. The "problem" of race cannot be just a problem of being black, Asian, Arab, Sioux, or Latino. It has to be more than that, because there is no way to separate the "problem" of being, say, Native American from the "problem" of *not* being white. And there is no way to separate not being white from *being* white. This means privilege is always a problem both for those who do not have it and those who do, because privilege is always in *relation* to others. Privilege is always at someone else's expense and always exacts a cost. Everything that is done to receive or maintain it—however passive and unconscious—results in suffering and deprivation for someone else.

We live in a society that attaches privilege to a variety of characteristics regardless of social class. If I do not see how that makes me part of the problem of privilege, I also will not see myself as part of the solution. And if people in privileged groups do not include themselves in the solution, the default is to leave it to women and Asians, Latinos/as, blacks, Native Americans, LGBT people, people with disabilities, and the lower and working classes to do it on their own. Although these groups are not powerless to affect the conditions of their own lives, they do not have the power to singlehandedly do away with entrenched systems of privilege. If they could do that, there wouldn't be a problem in the first place.

The trouble we are in cannot be solved unless people who have privilege feel obligated to make the problem of privilege *their* problem, and to do something about it. For me, it means I have to take the initiative to find out how privilege operates in the world, how it affects people, and what that has to do with me. It means I have to think the unthinkable, speak the unspeakable, break the silence, acknowledge the elephant, and then take my share of responsibility for what comes next. It means I have to *do* something to create the possibility for my African American woman friend and me to have a conversation about race, gender, and us, rather than leave it to her to take all the risks and do all the work. The fact that it's so easy for people in dominant groups not to do this is the single most powerful barrier to change. Understanding how to change that by bringing them into the conversation and the solution is the biggest challenge we face.

My work here is to help us meet that challenge by identifying tools for understanding what is going on and what it's got to do with us without being swallowed up in a sea of guilt and blame, of denial and angry self-defense. It is to share a way of thinking about difference and what has been made of it. It is to remove barriers that stand between us and serious, long-term work *across* difference, and effective action for change that can *make* a difference.

We Can't Talk about It If We Can't Use the Words

Dealing with a problem begins with naming it, so that we can think and talk and write about it, so that we can make sense of it by seeing how it's connected to other things that explain it, and point toward solutions. The language we need usually comes from people working to solve the problem, typically those who suffer most because of it, and who rely on words like privilege, racism, sexism, anti-Semitism, Islamophobia, heterosexism, heteronormativity, classism, ableism, dominance, subordination, oppression, and patriarchy.

Naming something draws attention to it, making us more likely to notice it as significant, which is why people often have a negative reaction to words like sexism or privilege. They don't want to look at what the words point to. Men don't want to look at sexism, nor whites at racism, especially if they've worked hard to improve their own class position. People don't want to look because they don't want to know what it has to do with them, and how doing something about it might change not only the world but themselves and their own lives.

One means of escape is to discredit the words or twist their meaning or turn them into a phobia or make them invisible. It has become almost impossible, for example, to say "men's violence" or "male privilege" without men being uncomfortable and defensive, as if saying the words is to accuse them of something. The same is true of all the other "isms." Since few people like to see themselves as bad, the words are taboo in "polite" company, including many training programs in corporations and universities. So, instead of talking about the sexism and racism that plague people's lives, the focus is on "diversity" and "tolerance" and "appreciating difference," all good things to talk about, but not at all the same as the isms and the trouble they're connected to.

More than once I have been asked to talk about the consequences of domination and oppression without saying "dominant," "subordinate," or "oppression." At such times, I feel like a doctor trying to help a patient without mentioning the body or naming what is wrong. We cannot get anywhere that way, with our collective house burning down while we tiptoe around, afraid to say "fire."

The bottom line is that a trouble we cannot talk about is a trouble we can't do anything about. Words like "privilege" and "oppression" point to difficult and painful parts of our history that continue to shape everyday life today. That means there is no way to talk about it without difficulty or the possibility of fear or pain. It is possible, however, to talk about it in ways that make the struggle worth it. To do that, however, we have to reclaim these lost and discredited words so that we can use them to name and make sense of the reality of how things really are.

Reclaiming words begins with seeing that they rarely mean what most people think they mean. "Patriarchy" is not code for "men," for example, just as "racist" is not another way to say "bad white people." Oppression and dominance name social realities that we can participate in without being oppressive or dominating people. And feminism is not an ideology organized around being lesbian or hating men. But you would never know it by listening to how these words are used in the media, popular culture, and over many a dinner table. You would never know such words could be part of a serious discussion of how to resolve a problem that belongs to us all.

I use these words freely in this book because I am writing about the problems they name. I don't use them as accusations. If I did, I would have a hard time looking in the mirror. Nor do I intend that anyone take them personally. As a heterosexual, nondisabled, white, upper-middle-class male, I do know that in some ways these words are about me. There is no way for me to avoid playing a role in the troubles they name, and that is something I must be willing to look at. But it's also important to realize how the words are *not* about me, because they name something much larger than me, a system I did not invent or create, but that was passed on to me as a legacy when I was born into this society.

Like everyone else, if I am going to be part of changing that legacy, I need a way to step back from my defensive sensitivity to such language. Then I can look at the reality of what that language points to, what it has to do with me and, most importantly, what I can do to make a difference.

CHAPTER 2

Privilege, Oppression, and Difference

The trouble around difference is privilege and oppression, and the unequal distribution of power that keeps it going. It is a legacy we all inherited, and while we're here, it belongs to us. It is not our fault, but it is up to us to decide what we're going to pass on to generations to come.

Talking about power and privilege isn't easy, especially for dominant groups, which is why it is so often avoided, from politics to workplaces to college classrooms. Part of the difficulty comes from a fear of anything that might make dominant groups uncomfortable, angry, or otherwise cause conflict,[1] even though (as we will see) groups are already pitted against one another by the system of privilege that organizes society as a whole. But a deeper reason is a misunderstanding of the problem itself, which is what this chapter is about.

Difference Is Not the Problem

Difference can, of course, be a problem when it comes to working across cultures and their varied ways of thinking and doing things, but human beings have been bridging such divides for thousands of years.

Related to this is the idea that difference makes us afraid of one another because we naturally fear the strange and unfamiliar, the unknown, what we do not understand. What we fear we do not trust, making it difficult to get along in our diversity.

For all its popularity, the notion that difference is inherently frightening is really a cultural myth, one that justifies keeping outsiders on the outside, and treating them badly if they happen to get in. The mere fact that something is new or strange is not enough to make us afraid. When Europeans first came to North America, for example, they were not afraid of the people they encountered, and the typical response of Native Americans was to welcome these astonishingly "different" people and help them to survive.[2] Scientists, psychotherapists, inventors, novelists (and their fans), explorers, philosophers, spiritualists, anthropologists, and the just plain curious are all drawn to the mystery of what they do not know. Even children seem to love the unknown, which is why parents are always worrying about what new thing their toddler will get into next.

What does frighten us is how we *think* about the strange, the unfamiliar, the unknown—what might happen next or what's behind that door or in the mind of the weird-looking guy on the empty train. And those ideas, those fears, are not something we are born with. We acquire them just as we learn to talk or tie our shoes. Marshall Mitchell, for example, an expert in disability studies, tells of young children who "approach me in my wheelchair with no hesitation or fear. But, each year that they get older, they become more fearful. Why? Because then they are afraid of what they've been taught and think they know."[3]

Mapping Difference: Who Are We?

Issues of difference cover a large territory. A useful way to put it in perspective is with a "diversity wheel" see figure on page 15 based on the work of Marilyn Loden and Judy Rosener.[4] In the hub of the wheel are seven social characteristics: age, race, ethnicity, gender, sex, physical ability and qualities (such as height), and sexual orientation. Around the outer ring are several others, including religion, marital and parental status, and social-class indicators such as education, occupation, and income.

Anyone can describe themselves by going around the wheel. Starting in the hub, for example, I identify myself as a male and a man. I was assigned as male when I was born, and since my gender identification is as a man, the two are a cultural match, making me cisgender. Not so long ago, it did not occur to most people to separate sex and gender, based on the assumption that if you know how someone identifies in relation to gender (woman or man) then you also know what kind of body they have (female or male). In fact, however, human beings come in all kinds of sex and gender combinations, assigned, for example, as male when they were born but identifying themselves as women now, or as neither man nor woman, or as some combination of the two. Or they might be intersex, born with a combination of biological characteristics that cannot be easily classified as either male or female.

Continuing on, I am also English-Norwegian (as far as I know), white (again, as far as I know), seventy years old, heterosexual, and nondisabled (so far). In the outer ring, I am married, a father and grandfather, and an upper-middle-class professional with a Ph.D. I've lived in New England most of my life, but I've also lived in other countries. If I had to identify my spiritual life with a particular tradition, I would lean toward Buddhism and earth-based practices. I served a brief stint in the U.S. Army reserves.

It would be useful to stop reading for a moment and do what I just did. Go around the wheel and get a sense of where you fit.

As you reflect on the results of this exercise, it might occur to you (as it did to me) that the wheel does not say much about the unique private individual you know yourself to be, your personal history, the content of your character, what you dream and feel. It does, however, say a lot about the social reality that has shaped your life in powerful ways.

Imagine, for example, that you woke up tomorrow and found that your race was different from what it was when you went to bed (the plot of a 1970 movie called *Watermelon Man*). Or imagine that your sex had changed (as happens to the central character in Virginia Woolf's novel, *Orlando*) or you realized one day that you were not heterosexual, or you suddenly lost the ability to hear or see. How would that affect how people perceive and treat you? How would it affect how you see yourself? How would it change the material circumstances of your life, such as where you live or how much money you have? In what ways would the change make life better? In what ways worse?

In answering these questions, try to go beyond the obvious consequences to ones that are perhaps more subtle. If you are heterosexual now, for example, and you wake up gay or lesbian, your sexual feelings about women and men would be different. But what about how people perceive and treat you in ways

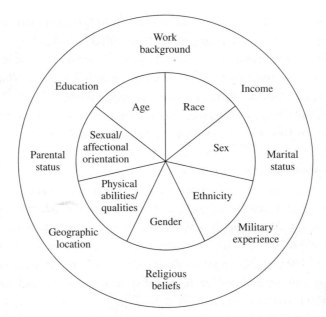

FIGURE 1. The Diversity Wheel. Adapted Loden, Marilyn; Rosener, Judy B. *Workforce America: Managing Employee Diversity as a Vital Resource.* New York, NY: McGraw-Hill Education, 1991, p. 20. Copyright © 1991 by McGraw-Hill Education. All rights reserved. Used with permission.

unrelated to sex? Would they treat you differently at school or work? Would friends treat you differently, or parents and siblings? What opportunities would open or close? What rewards would or would not come your way?

For most people, shifting only a few parts of the wheel would be enough to change their lives dramatically. Even though these specific characteristics may not tell us who we are as individuals in the privacy of our hearts and souls, they locate us in relation to other people and society in ways that have huge consequences.

The trouble surrounding diversity, then, isn't just that people differ from one another. The trouble is produced by a world organized in ways that encourage people to *use* difference in order to include or exclude, accept or reject, reward or punish, credit or discredit, elevate or oppress, value or devalue, leave alone or harass.

This is especially true of characteristics in the center of the wheel, which are difficult to change (except disability, which can happen to anyone at any time). It is true that medical assistance is available for transgender people who decide that they want to transition from one sex to the other (transsexual), and that it's possible for some people to "pass" for a race or gender or sexual orientation that is other than what they and others believe themselves to be. But this is quite different from being married one day and divorced the next, or getting a new job that suddenly elevates your class position. Unlike the outer portion of the wheel, the inner portion consists of characteristics that, in one way or another, we must learn to live with, regardless of how we choose to reveal ourselves to others.

Perceptions are difficult to control, however, because we tend to rely on quick and often unconscious impressions of race, sex, gender, age, sexual orientation, and disability status. Some are based on blanket assumptions—that everyone, for example, is heterosexual until proven otherwise. Or if they *look* "white," they *are* white. We may not realize how routinely we do this until we run into someone who doesn't fit neatly into an established category, especially sex and gender. It can be startling and can hold our attention until we think we've figured it out.

Our culture allows for only two genders, and anyone who doesn't fit one or the other is perceived as an outsider. This is why intersex babies are routinely altered surgically in order to fit the categories of female and male. In contrast, in traditional Native American Diné (Navajo) culture, a person born with physical characteristics that are not clearly male or female is placed in a third category—called *nadle*—which is considered to be as legitimate as female and male. In some Native American plains tribes, people were allowed to choose their gender regardless of their physical characteristics, as when men might respond to a spiritual vision by taking on the dress of women.[5]

Most of our ways of thinking about sexuality are also based on culture. The idea of using "heterosexual" and "homosexual" to describe kinds of people living particular kinds of lives, for example, has been around for little more than a hundred years.[6] And while differences in sexual behavior have long been recognized, whether gay or lesbian or heterosexual behavior is regarded as normal or deviant varies from one culture and historical period to another.

Characteristics at the center of the wheel, then, are hard to change and are very often the object of quick and firm impressions that can profoundly affect our lives. Clearly, diversity is not just about the variety the word suggests. It could just be that; but only in some other world.[7]

The Social Construction of Difference

The African American author James Baldwin once offered the provocative idea that there is no such thing as whiteness or, for that matter, blackness or, more generally, race. "No one was white before he/she came to America," he wrote. "It took generations, and a vast amount of coercion, before this became a white country."[8]

What did Baldwin mean? In the simplest sense, he was pointing to a basic aspect of social reality—that most of what we experience is filtered through a cultural lens. In other words, it is to some degree made up, even though it doesn't seem that way. There are all kinds of variations in physical appearance, including skin color, but unless a culture defines such differences as significant, they are socially irrelevant and therefore, in that sense, do not exist. A dark-skinned woman in Africa, whose culture does not include the concept of race, has no reason to think of herself as "black" or experience herself as black, nor do the people around her. African, yes, a woman, yes, but not a *black* woman.

When she comes to the United States, however, where privilege is organized around the idea of race, suddenly she becomes black, because people identify her as such and treat her differently as a result. In similar ways, as Baldwin argues, a 19th-century Norwegian farmer had no reason to think of himself as white so long as he stayed in Norway. But when he came to the United States, he quickly discovered the significance of being seen as white and the privilege that comes with it, making him eager to adopt "white" as part of his identity.[9]

Baldwin is telling us that the idea of race has no significance beyond the systems of privilege and oppression in which they are created, through what is known as the "social construction of reality."[10] The construction of race is especially visible in how its definition has changed, by including groups at one time that were excluded in another. The Irish, for example, were long considered by the dominant Anglo-Saxons of England and the United States to be members of a "nonwhite" race, as were Italians, Jews, Greeks, and people from a number of Eastern European countries. As such, immigrants from these groups to England and the United States were excluded, subordinated, and exploited. This was especially true of the Irish in Ireland in relation to the British, who for centuries treated them as an inferior race.[11] It may occur to you that skin color among the Irish was perhaps indistinguishable from that of the "white" English, which raises the point that the objective facts of physical difference have never been the determinants of race. More important is the dominant group's power to define racial categories in any way that serves its interests by including some and excluding others.

The social construction of reality also applies to what is considered "normal." While it may come as a surprise to many who think of themselves as nondisabled, for example, disability and nondisability are cultural creations. This doesn't mean that the difference between, say, having or not having full use of your eyes or memory, is somehow made up with no objective reality. It does mean, however, that how people notice and think about such differences, and how they treat people as a result, are a matter of culture.

Human beings, for example, come in a variety of heights, and many of those considered normal are unable to reach high places such as kitchen shelves without the assistance of physical aids such as chairs and stools. In spite of their limited ability, they are not defined as disabled. Nor are the roughly 100 million people in the United States who cannot see properly without the aid of eyeglasses. Why? Because the dominant group has the authority to define what is normal. In contrast, people who use wheelchairs, for example, to get from one place to another—to "reach" places they cannot otherwise go—do not have the cultural authority to include their condition in what is considered to be normal, that is, as one more instance of the fact that in the course of life, people come in many shapes and sizes and physical and mental conditions.

Disability and nondisability are also constructed through the use of language. When someone who cannot see is labeled a "blind person," for example, it creates the impression that an inability to see can be used to sum up an entire person. In other words, "blind" becomes what they *are*. The same thing happens when people are described as "autistic" or "crippled" or "deaf"—the person becomes the disability and nothing more. Reducing people to a single dimension of who they are separates and excludes them by marking them as "other," as people outside the boundaries of normality, and therefore inferior. The effect is compounded by portraying people with disabilities as helpless victims who are "confined" or "stricken" or "suffering from" some "affliction" and then lumping them into an undifferentiated class—*the* blind, *the* crippled, *the* deaf, *the* mentally ill, *the* disabled.

Of course, using a wheelchair or being unable to see both affect people's lives; pointing out that the concepts of disability and nondisability are socially constructed is not intended to suggest otherwise. But there is a world of difference between being treated as a normal human being who happens to have a disability, or being treated as invisible, inferior, unintelligent, asexual, frightening, passive, dependent, and nothing more than your disability. And that difference is not a matter of the disability itself but of how it is constructed in society, how that shapes how we think about ourselves and other people, and how we treat them as a result.[12]

What makes socially constructed reality so powerful is that we rarely recognize and experience it as that. We are encouraged to think that the way our culture defines something such as sexuality or race or gender is simply the way things *are*, that the words we use are naming an objective reality that exists independently of how we think about it. The truth, however, is that once human beings give something a name, it acquires a significance it otherwise does not have. More important, the name quickly takes on a life of its own as we forget the social process that created it and start treating it as real in and of itself.

This process is what allows us to believe that something like "race" actually points to a set of clear and unambiguous categories into which people fall, ignoring the fact that the definition of various races changes all the time and is riddled with inconsistencies and overlapping boundaries. In the 19th century, for example, U.S. law identified those having *any* African ancestry as black, a standard known as the "one-drop rule," which defined "white" as a state of purity in relation to "black." Native American status, in contrast, required at *least* one-eighth Native American ancestry in order to qualify. Why the different standards? Adrian Piper argues that it was mostly a matter of economics. Native Americans could claim financial benefits from the federal government, making it to whites' advantage to limit the number of people considered Native American. Designating someone as black, however, took *away* power and *denied* the right to make claims against whites. In both cases, racial classification has had little to do with objective characteristics and everything to do with preserving white privilege and power.[13]

Race has been used to mark a variety of groups in this way. When Chinese were imported as a source of cheap labor during the 19th century, for example, the California Supreme Court declared them not to be white. Mexicans, however, many of whom owned large amounts of land and did business with Anglo "whites," were also considered white. When the stakes are privilege and power, dominant groups often ignore such inconsistencies when it serves their interests.

What Is Privilege?

No matter what privileged group you belong to, if you want to understand the problem, the first stumbling block is usually the idea of privilege itself. When people hear that they benefit from some form of privilege, it's not uncommon for them to get angry and defensive or claim it does not exist, or that it has nothing to do with them. "Privilege" has become one of those loaded words that names an important aspect of reality, making denial of its existence a serious barrier to change (so serious that it has a chapter of its own). It is important, then, to have a clear idea of what it means before going any further.

As Peggy McIntosh describes it, privilege exists when one group has something of value that is denied to others simply because of the social category they belong to, rather than anything they have done or failed to do.[14] If people take me more seriously when I give a speech than they would a woman saying the same things in the same way, I am benefiting from male privilege. A heterosexual black woman's freedom to reveal the fact that she is married to a man is a form of privilege because lesbians and gay men often find themselves in situations where revealing their sexual orientation would put them at risk.

Note that privilege is not the same as simply having something good that others do not. Having loyal friends, for example, is both lucky and good. But it is not a form of privilege unless it is systematically allowed for some and denied to others based on membership in social categories, *which must be socially recognized and conferred.* In other words, having or not having access to privilege depends on how other people see us in relation to categories such as male or female.

Note also in these examples how easy it is for people to be unaware of how privilege affects them. When someone says good things about one of my presentations, for example, it might not occur to me that they would be more critical and less positive if I were Latino or female or gay. I might not *feel* privileged in that moment, just that I did a good job and should enjoy the rewards that go with it.

The existence of privilege does not mean I *didn't* do a good job or that I don't deserve to be rewarded for what I do. What it does mean is that I am *also* receiving an advantage that other people are denied, people who are like me in every way except for being assigned to different categories. In this sense, my access to privilege does not determine or guarantee my outcomes, but is an *asset* that loads the odds in ways that make it more likely that whatever talent, ability, and aspirations I have will result in something good for me.[15] In the same way, although being female or of color does not determine people's outcomes, they count as *liabilities* that make it less likely that talent, ability, and aspirations will be recognized and rewarded.

This is also true of people with disabilities. Nondisabled people often assume that people with disabilities lack intelligence, for example, or are needy, helpless victims who cannot take care of themselves—people whose achievements and situation in life depend solely on their physical or mental condition and not on how they are treated or the obstacles placed in their way by a society designed to suit people without disabilities.[16]

The ease of not being aware of privilege is an aspect of privilege itself, what has been called "the luxury of obliviousness" (known in philosophy as "epistemic privilege"). Awareness requires effort and commitment, which makes it a form of privilege, having the attention of lower-status individuals without the need to give it in return. African Americans, for example, have to pay close attention to whites and white culture and get to know them well enough to avoid displeasing them, since whites control jobs, schools, government, the police, and other sources of power. Privilege, however, gives whites much less reason to pay attention to African Americans or how racial oppression affects their lives.[17]

In other words, as James Baldwin put it, "To be white in America means not having to think about it."[18] We could say the same about being a man or any other form of privilege. So strong is the sense of entitlement behind this luxury that men, whites, and others can feel put upon in the face of even the mildest invitation to pay attention to what is going on. "We shouldn't *have* to look at this stuff," they seem to say. "It isn't *fair.*"

Two Types of Privilege

According to McIntosh, the first type of privilege is based on "unearned entitlements," which are things of value that all people *should* have, such as feeling safe or working in a place where they are valued and accepted for what they have to offer. When an unearned entitlement is restricted to certain groups, however, it becomes an "unearned *advantage*," a form of privilege.

Sometimes it's possible to do away with unearned advantages without anyone losing out. When a workplace changes so that everyone is valued, for example, the unearned entitlement is available to all and, as such, is no longer a form of privilege. In other cases, however, unearned advantage gives dominant groups a competitive edge they are reluctant to acknowledge, much less give up. This can be especially true of men and whites who lack the advantages of social class and know all too well how hard it is to improve their lives and hang on to what they've managed to achieve. This can blind them, however, to the fact that the cultural valuing of whiteness and maleness over color and femaleness loads the odds in their favor in most situations that involve evaluations of credibility or competence. To lose that advantage would greatly increase the amount of competition for white men, who are a shrinking minority of the U.S. population.

The second form of privilege, "conferred dominance," goes a step further by giving one group power over another. The common pattern of men controlling conversations with women, for example, is grounded in a cultural assumption that men are superior and supposed to dominate women. An adolescent boy who appears too willing to defer to his mother risks being called a "mama's boy," in the same way that a husband who appears in any way controlled by his wife can be labeled "henpecked" (or worse). The counterpart for girls carries no such stigma: "Daddy's girl" is not considered an insult in this culture, and there are no insulting terms for a wife who is under the control of her husband.

Conferred dominance also manifests itself in white privilege. In his book *The Rage of a Privileged Class,* for example, Ellis Cose tells the story of an African American lawyer, a partner in a large firm, who goes to the office one Saturday morning and is confronted by a recently hired young white attorney, who has never met the partner.

"Can I help you?" says the white man pointedly.

The partner shakes his head and tries to pass, but the white man steps in his way and repeats what is now a challenge to the man's presence in the building: "Can I *help* you?" Only then does the partner reveal his identity to the young man, who in turn steps aside to let him pass. The white man has no reason to assume the right to control the older man standing before him, except the reason provided by the cultural assumption of white dominance, which can override any class advantage a person of color might have.[19]

The milder forms of unearned advantage are usually the first to change because they are the easiest for privileged groups to give up. In the decades leading up to the election of Barack Obama as president, for example, national surveys showed a steady decline in the percentage of whites holding racist attitudes toward blacks. This trend is reflected in diversity programs that focus on appreciating or tolerating differences—in other words, extending unearned entitlements to everyone instead of the dominant group alone.

It is much harder, however, to do something about power and the unequal distribution of wealth, income, and other resources and rewards. This is why issues of conferred dominance and the stronger forms of unearned advantage get much less attention, and why, when these issues are raised, they can provoke hostile defensiveness and denial. Perhaps more than any other factor, the reluctance to recognize the more serious and entrenched forms of privilege is why most diversity programs serve as little more than a distraction and produce limited and short-lived results.[20]

Privilege As Paradox

A paradox of privilege is that even though it is received by and benefits individuals, access to it has nothing to do with who they are as people. Male privilege, for example, is more about *male* people than it is about male *people,* making me eligible when people assign me to that category, which they can do without knowing a single other thing about me.

This means that actually *being* male is not required in order to receive male privilege. The film, *Shakespeare in Love,* for example, is set in Elizabethan England, where acting on the stage was reserved for men. The character of Viola wants to act more than anything, and finally realizes her dream, not by changing her sex and becoming male but by masquerading as a man, which is all it takes. In similar ways, gays and lesbians can have access to heterosexual privilege if they don't reveal their sexual orientation. And people with hidden disabilities such as epilepsy or learning disabilities can receive nondisabled privilege so long as they do not disclose their status.

You can also *lose* privilege if people think you *don't* belong to a particular category. If I told everyone that I'm gay, for example, I would lose my access to heterosexual privilege (unless people refused to believe me), even though I would still be, in fact, heterosexual. As Charlotte Bunch put it, "If you don't have a sense of what privilege is, I suggest that you go home and announce to everybody that you know—a roommate, your family, the people you work with—that you're a queer. Try being queer for a week."[21]

The paradoxical relationship between privilege and individuals has several consequences. First, doing something about issues of equity and justice takes more than changing people. As Harry Brod writes,

> We need to be clear that there is no such thing as giving up one's privilege to be "outside" the system. One is always *in* the system. The only question is whether one is part of the system in a way which challenges or strengthens the status quo. Privilege is not something I *take* and which I therefore have the option of *not* taking. It is something that society *gives* me, and unless I change the institutions which give it to me, they will continue to give it, and I will continue to *have* it, however noble and egalitarian my intentions.[22]

A second consequence is the paradoxical experience of *being* privileged without *feeling* privileged. This often results from how we use other people as standards of comparison—what sociologists call "reference groups"—to construct a sense of how good, bad, high, or low we are in the scheme of things. In doing this, we usually don't look downward in the social hierarchy, but to people we identify as being on the same level as or higher than our own. This is why pointing out to someone who lives in poverty in the United States that they're better off than many people in India doesn't make them feel better, because they don't use Indians as a reference group. Instead, they gauge how well they're doing by comparing themselves with those who seem like them in key respects.

Since, for example, being white is valued in this society, whites tend to compare themselves with other whites, not with people of color. In the same way, men tend to use other men as a reference group. This means, however, that whites tend not to feel privileged *by race* in comparison with their reference group, because that group is also white. In the same way, men won't feel privileged by gender in comparison with other men. A partial exception to this is the hierarchy between heterosexual and gay men, by which heterosexuals are more likely to consider themselves "real men" and therefore socially valued above gays. But even here, the mere fact of being identified as male is unlikely to be experienced as a form of privilege, because gay men are also male.

A common exception to these patterns occurs for those privileged by gender or race but ranked low in terms of social class. To protect themselves from feeling and being seen as on the bottom of the ladder, they may go out of their way to compare themselves to women or people of color by emphasizing their supposed gender or racial superiority. This can appear as an exaggerated sense of manliness, for example, or as overt attempts to put women or people of color "in their place" by harassment, violence, or behavior that is openly contemptuous or demeaning.

A corollary to being privileged without knowing it is to be on the *other* side of privilege without feeling *that.* I sometimes hear women say something like, "I've never been oppressed as a woman," as an assertion that male privilege does not exist. But this confuses the social position of woman and man as social categories with individual women's subjective experience of belonging to one of those categories. The two are not the same.

For various reasons—including social class or family experience or being young—she may have avoided exposure to many of the consequences of being a female in a society that privileges maleness and manhood. Or she may have managed to overcome them to such a degree that she does not feel hampered. Or she may be engaging in denial. Or she may be unaware of how she is discriminated against—unaware, perhaps, that being a woman is one of the reasons her science professors ignore her in class.[23] Or she may have so internalized her subordinate status that she doesn't see it as a problem, thinking, perhaps, that women are ignored because they are not smart enough to say anything worth listening to.

Regardless of what her experience is based on, it is just that—her experience—and it doesn't have to square with the larger social reality that everyone, including her, must deal with in one way or another. It is like living in a rainy climate and somehow avoiding being rained on yourself. It is still a rainy place to be, and the possibility of getting wet is something people have to deal with.

The Paradox That Privilege Doesn't Necessarily Make You Happy

I often hear men and whites deny the existence of privilege by saying they don't feel happy or fulfilled in their own lives, as if misery and privilege cannot go hand-in-hand. As we saw earlier, this rests in part on the failure to distinguish between social categories and individual people's lives. Being identified as male and white, for example, doesn't mean you'll get into the college of your choice or land the job you're qualified for or never be stopped (or shot) by police when you've done nothing wrong. But it does load the odds in your favor.

Another reason privilege and happiness don't always go together is that privilege can exact a cost from those who have it. To have privilege is to participate in a system that confers advantage and dominance on some at the expense of others, which can cause pain and distress to those who benefit. Although white privilege, for example, comes at a huge cost to people of color, on some level white people often struggle with this knowledge. This is where all the guilt comes from and the lengths to which white people often go to avoid feeling and looking at it. In similar ways, male privilege exacts a cost as men compete with other men and strive to prove their manhood, so they can be counted among "real men" who are worthy of being set apart from—and above—women, a standard of control and power that most men are unable to meet. It should therefore come as no surprise that men or whites may feel unhappy and associate their unhappiness with the fact of being white or male.[24]

What Privilege Looks Like in Everyday Life

As Peggy McIntosh showed in her unpacking of the "invisible knapsack of white privilege,"[25] privilege shows up in the details of everyday life in almost every social setting. Consider the examples below based on gender, race, sexual orientation, and disability status.[26] Most rely on quantitative data, such as income statistics or studies of bias in health care or housing or the criminal justice system. Some are based on qualitative data from the rich literature on privilege and oppression that records the experience of living in this society (see the "Resources" section at the end of the book).

As you read through the list, there are several things to keep in mind. Note that many of these examples of privilege—such as preferential treatment in the workplace—apply to multiple dominant groups, such as men, whites, and the nondisabled. This reflects the intersectional nature of privilege, by which each form has its own history and dynamics, and yet they are also connected to one another and have much in common. Also, consider how each example might vary depending on other characteristics a person has. How, for example, would preferential treatment for men in the workplace be affected by race or sexual orientation? Finally, remember that these examples describe how privilege loads the odds in favor of whole *categories* of people, which may not be true in every situation and for every individual, including you.

Here they are. Take your time.

- Whites who are unarmed and have committed no crime are far less likely than comparable people of color to be shot by police, to be challenged without cause and asked to explain what they are doing, or subjected to search. Whites are also less likely to be arrested, tried, convicted, or sent to prison, regardless of the crime or circumstances. As a result, for example, although whites constitute eighty-five percent of those who use illegal drugs, less than half of those in prison on drug-use charges are white.[27]

- Heterosexuals and whites can go out in public without having to worry about being attacked by hate groups. Men can assume they won't be sexually harassed or assaulted just because they are male, and if they are victimized, they won't be asked to explain their manner of dress or what they were doing there.

- Those who are heterosexual, male, white, cisgender, and without disabilities can usually be confident that whether they are seen as qualified to be hired or promoted, or deserving to be fired from a job, will not depend on their status,* an aspect of themselves they cannot change.[28] Nor do they run the risk of being reduced to a single aspect of their lives (as if being heterosexual, for example, sums up the kind of person they are). Instead, they can be viewed and treated as complex human beings. They also do not have to worry that their status will be used as a weapon against them, to undermine or discredit their achievements or power.

- Although many superstar professional athletes are black, black players are generally held to higher standards than whites. It is easier for a "good but not great" white player to make a professional team, for example, than it is for a comparable black.[29]

---

* A reminder that the word "status" is used here to refer to characteristics such as "male" or "female" that locate people in social systems.

Similarly, in most professions and upper-level occupations, men are held to lower standards than women. Male lawyers, for example, are more likely to make partner than are comparably qualified women.[30]

■ Men, people without disabilities, and whites are more likely to be given opportunities to show what they can do at work, to be identified as candidates for promotion, to be mentored, to be given a second chance when they fail, and to be allowed to treat failure as a learning experience rather than as an indication of who they are based on their status.[31]

■ The standards used to evaluate men *as men* are consistent with the standards used to evaluate them in other roles, such as their occupation. Standards used to evaluate women as women are often different from those used to evaluate them in other roles. For example, a man can qualify both as a "real man" and as a successful and aggressive lawyer, while an aggressive woman lawyer may succeed as a lawyer but be judged as falling short as a woman.

■ Nondisabled people can ask for help without having to worry that people will assume they need help with everything, and can assume that they will get what they deserve without having to overcome stereotypes about their ability. They are less likely to be shuttled into dead-end, menial jobs, given inadequate job training, be paid less than they are worth regardless of their ability, and be separated from workers who are unlike themselves.

■ Men and whites are less likely to find themselves slotted into occupations identified with their status, as blacks are often slotted into support positions (community relations, custodial) or Asians into technical jobs ("techno-coolies") or women into "caring" occupations such as daycare, nursing, secretarial, and social work.[32]

■ People who are heterosexual, male, white, cisgender, and without disabilities can assume that their status will not work against the likelihood that they'll fit in at work, and that teammates will feel comfortable working with them.

■ Men, whites, and people without disabilities can succeed without others being surprised at their success due to their status.

- People who are white, nondisabled, or male are more likely to be rewarded for working hard and "playing by the rules," and are more likely to feel justified in complaining if they are not.

- Whites are more likely than comparable blacks to have loan applications approved and less likely to be given the runaround during the application process, to be given poor information or have information withheld. During the economic collapse of 2008, they were also less likely to receive subprime mortgages than people of color and less likely to lose their homes through foreclosure.[33]

- Nondisabled people, men, and whites are charged lower prices for new and used cars, and residential segregation gives whites access to higher-quality goods of all kinds at cheaper prices.[34]

- When whites go shopping, they are more likely to be viewed as serious customers and not potential shoplifters or lacking the ability to make a purchase. When they try to cash a check or use a credit card, they are less likely to be hassled for additional identification and more likely to be given the benefit of the doubt.

- White people are more likely to receive the best medical treatment that they can afford.[35]

- People without disabilities and whites have greater access to quality education and health care. They are less likely to be singled out based on stereotypes that underestimate their abilities and to be put in special education classes that do not afford them the chance to develop to their full potential.[36]

- Representation in government and the ruling circles of corporations, universities, and other organizations is disproportionately high for white, male, heterosexual, and nondisabled people.

- Nondisabled people can go to polling places on election day knowing they will be able to exercise their rights as citizens with access to voting machines that allow them to vote in privacy and without the assistance of others. They can assume that when they need to travel, they will have access to buses, trains, airplanes, and other means of transportation and will be taken seriously and not treated as children.

- Most whites and people without disabilities are not segregated into communities that isolate them from the best job opportunities, schools, and community services. Nor are nondisabled people segregated into living situations such as nursing homes and special schools and sports programs that isolate them from the everyday activities of social life.

■ It is easier for heterosexuals, whites, and cisgender people to find a place to live where they don't have to worry about neighbors disapproving of them based on negative cultural stereotypes.

■ Toxic waste dumps, industrial pollution, and nuclear waste are less likely to be located near neighborhoods and communities inhabited primarily by whites, a phenomenon known as environmental racism.[37]

■ People who are male, white, heterosexual, cisgender, or without disabilities can usually assume that national heroes, success models, and other figures held up for public admiration will share their status.

■ Heterosexuals, people without disabilities, men, cisgender people, and whites can turn on the television or go to the movies and be assured of seeing characters, news reports, and stories that reflect the reality of their lives, and can assume that people who share their status will be placed at the center of attention.[38]

■ Those who are white, cisgender, or nondisabled can choose whether to be self-conscious about their status, or to ignore it and regard themselves simply as human beings.

■ Whites, people without disabilities, and those who are cisgender do not have to deal with an endless and exhausting stream of attention to their status, which they can view as unremarkable to such an extent that they experience themselves as not even having one. As a cisgender white person, for example, I don't have people coming up to me and treating me as if I were some exotic "other," gushing about how "cool" or different I am, wanting to know where I'm "from" and can they touch my hair, asking if the name I give is my real name or what do my genitals look like. In similar ways, men do not have to deal with excessive attention to their physical appearance.

■ If men, whites, cisgender people and people without disabilities do poorly at something or make a mistake or commit a crime, they can generally assume that people will not attribute the failure to their status. Mass murderers, for example, are almost always white and male, but rarely is this fact identified as an important issue.

- Men, whites, and people without disabilities are more likely to control conversations and be allowed to get away with it and to have their ideas and contributions taken seriously, including those previously voiced in the same conversation by a person of color, a woman, or a person with a disability, who are then ignored or dismissed.[39]

- Nondisabled people can assume they won't be looked upon as odd or out of place or as not belonging, and that most buildings and other structures will not be designed in ways that limit their access. Cisgender people have the ability to walk through the world and generally blend in, not being constantly stared or gawked at, whispered about, pointed at, or laughed at because of their gender expression.[40]

- Whites are not routinely confused with other whites, as if all whites look alike. They are more likely to be noticed for their individuality, and they may feel entitled to take offense whenever they are put in a category (such as "white") rather than being perceived and treated as individuals without a race.[41]

- Heterosexuals are free to reveal and live their intimate relationships openly—by referring to their partners by name, recounting experiences, going out in public together, displaying pictures on their desks at work—without being accused of flaunting their sexuality, or risking discrimination.

- Heterosexuals and cisgender people can live in the comfort of knowing that other people's assumptions about their sexual orientation are correct.

- Nondisabled people can live secure in other people's assumption that they are sexual beings capable of an active sex life, including the potential to have children and be parents.

Regardless of its form, privilege increases the odds of being accepted, included, and respected, of having things your own way, of being able to set the agenda in a social situation, and to determine rules and standards and how they are applied. Privilege grants the cultural authority to make judgments about others and to have those judgments stick. It allows people to define reality and to have prevailing mainstream views fit their own experience.

Privilege means being able to decide who gets taken seriously, who gets attention, who is accountable to whom and for what. And it grants a presumption of superiority and social permission to act on that presumption, without having to worry about being challenged or otherwise held to account.

Privilege bestows the freedom to move through your life without being marked in ways that decrease your life chances or detract from how you are seen and valued. As Paul Kivel writes, "In the United States, a person is considered a member of the lowest status group from which they have any heritage."[42] This means that if you can trace your lineage to several ethnic groups, the one that lowers your status is the one you're most likely to be tagged with, as in, "she's part Jewish" or "he's part Vietnamese," but rarely, "she's part white." In fact, as we saw earlier, having any black ancestry is still enough to be classified as *entirely* black in many people's eyes. People are tagged with other labels that point to the lowest-status group they belong to, as in "woman doctor" or "black writer" but never "white lawyer" or "male senator." Any category that lowers our status relative to other categories can be used in this way.[43]

It's important to note that privilege operates not only within societies, but between them as well. The sex trafficking of girls and women is global, for example, and disproportionately harms those in nonindustrial societies, whose people are overwhelmingly of color, a phenomenon that reflects both male and white privilege. The inhabitants of white-dominated industrial societies are also primarily responsible for producing the conditions that have led to climate change, and yet are also the most protected from its most immediate and devastating consequences, a global example of environmental racism.[44]

If you are male or heterosexual or white or nondisabled and you find yourself shaking your head at these descriptions of privilege—"This isn't true for *me*"—this might be a good time to revisit the paradoxes of privilege discussed earlier in this chapter.

Oppression: The Flip Side of Privilege

For every social category that is privileged, one or more others are oppressed in relation to it. As Marilyn Frye describes it, the concept of oppression points to social forces that tend to "press" on people and hold them down, to hem them in and block them in their pursuit of a good life. Just as privilege tends to open doors of opportunity, oppression tends to hold them shut.[45]

Like privilege, oppression results from the relationship between social categories, which makes it possible for individuals to vary in their personal experience of being oppressed. This also means, however, that in order to have the experience of being oppressed, it is necessary to belong to an oppressed category. In other words, men cannot be oppressed *as men,* just as whites cannot be oppressed as whites or heterosexuals as heterosexuals, because a group can be oppressed only if there exists another group with the power to oppress them. The negative side effects of privilege may *feel* oppressive, but to call this oppression distorts the nature of what is happening and why.

It ignores the fact that the costs of male privilege, for example, are far outweighed by the benefits, while the oppressive costs of being female are not outweighed by corresponding benefits. Misapplying the label of "oppression" also tempts us into making the false argument that if men and women are *both* oppressed because of gender, then one oppression cancels out the other and no privilege can be said to exist. So, when we try to label the pain that men feel because of gender (or that whites feel because of racism) whether we call it "oppression" or "pain" makes a huge difference in how we perceive the world and how it works.

The complexity of systems of privilege makes it possible, of course, for men to experience oppression if they also happen to be of color or gay or disabled or in a lower social class, but not simply because they are men. In the same way, whites can experience oppression for many reasons, but in a system of white privilege, it isn't because they're identified as white.

Note also that because oppression results from relations between categories, it is not possible to be oppressed by society itself. Living in a particular society can make people feel miserable, but that doesn't qualify as oppression unless it arises from being on the losing end in a system of privilege. That cannot happen in relation to society as a whole, because a society isn't something that can have privilege. Only people can belong to privileged categories in relation to people in categories that are not.

Finally, being in a privileged category that has an oppressive relationship with another category is not the same as being an oppressive *person* who behaves in oppressive ways. That the relationship between the social categories of male and female is one of privilege and oppression, for example, is a social fact. That does not, however, tell us how a particular man thinks or feels about particular women or behaves toward them. This can be a subtle distinction to hang on to, but hang on to it we must if we are going to maintain a clear idea of what oppression is and how it works in defense of privilege.

As we become more aware of how pervasive is the damage of privilege and oppression in people's lives, it is easy to start feeling helpless and to wonder, "What can anyone do?" If you find yourself feeling that way now or later on, turn to Chapter 9, which is devoted to that question.

CHAPTER 3

Capitalism, Class, and the
Matrix of Domination

There are few areas of social life as important as economics, because this is how a society is organized to provide what people need for their material existence. Economic systems are the basis for every social institution—whether family and tribe or the state—which cannot survive and function without an economic base. It takes a great deal of material and labor to build a university, for example, or to pay for political campaigns or maintain a police force or an army. This means that the central role of economics in social life gives individuals and systems powerful reasons to go along with the dominant system. Industrial capitalism has been that system for several hundred years, and since the demise of the Soviet Union, it is virtually the only game in town.

Every form of privilege has an economic dimension, which means that the nature of capitalism as a system profoundly affects how privilege and oppression work. The most powerful example of this is race, not only as it operates today, but, even more significantly, where it came from in the first place. Whenever I teach about race, there comes a point when students start saying things like, "We don't get it. If race is socially constructed and doesn't exist otherwise, and if human beings don't have to be afraid of one another, then where does racism come from? Why all the oppression and hostility and violence over something that's made up? And why would people make it up this way?"

Finding the answer leads us into the history of race, where we learn two things that usually startle students as much as they did me when I first learned of them.[1] First, racism in its modern form hasn't been around very long—hardly more than several centuries and certainly not as long as people have been aware of the physical differences now used to define race.

Second, racism came into being in Europe and the Americas at the same time as the growth and expansion of capitalism as an economic system, which relied on both the aggressive colonizing of non-European peoples and the institution of slavery. Capitalism thus played a critical role in the development of white privilege and still plays a critical role in its perpetuation. As such, the capitalist economics behind race and racism have much to teach us about how privilege works, in all its forms.

Before going any further, however, it's important to be clear about what I mean by race and racism.

Europeans were certainly not the first to think themselves superior to other peoples and cultures. But what they added to this was a belief in the idea that race provides a *biological* basis for superiority and inferiority, transmitted from one generation to the next through reproduction. This kind of thinking emerged with the African slave trade as a way to justify the wholesale enslavement of not only those kidnapped into slavery, but the perpetual enslavement of their descendants. Racism, in turn, developed as a set of practices that enact and perpetuate privilege and oppression based on race.[2]

An understanding of how capitalism figures in all this begins with understanding capitalism itself.[3]

How Capitalism Works

In describing capitalism, it's important to distinguish its modern form from the ideal envisioned by Adam Smith in his 1776 book, *The Wealth of Nations*. Smith saw capitalism as a collection of small, independent producers and entrepreneurs competing with one another to provide what people need at a price they are willing to pay. This early version all but disappeared well over a century ago as it was replaced by a form of monopoly capitalism dominated by large corporations that are, in turn, owned and controlled by a wealthy elite.[4]

Modern capitalism also developed a close relationship to government authority, legitimacy, and power. More than simply an economic system, what we have is a form of political economy—through which the power and resources of the state are used to protect and promote the capitalist system and those who benefit most from it. This aspect of modern capitalism has progressed to the point where democracy is giving way to an oligarchic form of government in which power is held by a few. In the 2016 presidential election, for example, just 158 wealthy families (from a population of more than 300 million people) donated more than half of all the money used in the early stages of the campaign through which candidates are nominated.[5] Presidential and Congressional elections require enormous amounts of money, and would-be candidates must secure the support of the wealthy, giving elites a great deal of power in deciding who become the final candidates.

The political consequences of concentrated economic power can also be seen by studying how federal legislation gets passed: Economic elites have a substantial impact on law and policy, while the vast majority of the population has little or none.[6] In a typical scenario, legislation is passed or policies are enacted that are opposed by a clear majority of the citizenry but are supported by, and serve the interests of, the wealthy. Corporations also routinely receive what critics have called "corporate welfare" (or "crony capitalism") in the form of government subsidies, grants, tax breaks and loopholes, cheap credit, and, most famously, bailouts, such as the multi-billion dollar Wall Street bailout of 2008.[7]

The goal of modern capitalism is to turn money into more money. Capitalists invest in what it takes to produce goods and services—raw materials, machinery, electricity, buildings, and, of course, human labor. It does not matter what is produced so long as capitalists can find a market in which to sell it at a profit—for more than it cost to have it produced—and end up with more money than they started with. Whether the results enhance human life (providing food, affordable housing, health care, and the like) or do harm (tobacco, alcohol, drugs, weapons, slavery, pollution) may be an issue for the conscience of the individual capitalist. But the system itself does not depend on such moral or ethical considerations, because profit is profit and there is no way to tell "good" money from "bad." Even the damage done by one enterprise can serve as a source of profit for another, such as when industrial pollution creates opportunities for companies that specialize in cleaning it up.

Capitalists employ workers to produce goods and services, paying them wages in exchange for their time. Capitalists then sell what workers produce.

For capitalists to make a living (unless they produce something themselves), they have to get workers to produce goods and services that are worth more than the wages capitalists pay them. The difference between the two is profit for capitalists and investors.

Why, however, would workers accept wages worth less than the value of what they produce? The general answer is that they don't have much choice, because, under capitalism, the tools and factories and other means for producing goods and services are not owned by the people who actually do the work. Instead, they are owned by capitalists and individual and organizational stockholders. For most people to earn a living, they must work for one capitalist employer or another, which means choosing—unless the workplace is unionized, which most are not—between working on the capitalist's terms or not working at all. As corporate capitalism has extended its reach into every area of social life, even professionals have to confront this choice. Physicians, for example, who were once regarded as the model of independent professionals, are increasingly compelled to become highly paid employees of health maintenance organizations. As a result, some have lobbied Congress for the right to engage in collective bargaining with HMOs (health maintenance organizations)—in other words, to form a labor union for physicians. Similar things are happening in the legal profession.[8]

Since capitalists profit from the difference between the cost of producing goods and services and what they can sell them for, the cheaper the labor, the more money is left over for them. This is why capitalists are concerned about increasing "worker productivity"—finding ways for workers to produce more goods for the same or less pay. One way to accomplish this is through the use of technology, in particular, machines that can replace people altogether. Another is to threaten to close down or relocate businesses if workers won't make concessions on wages, health and retirement benefits, job security, and working conditions. A third and increasingly popular strategy in the global economy is to move production to countries where people are willing to work for less than they are in Europe or North America. Capitalists who rely on this strategy also benefit from authoritarian governments in these new locations, which may control workers and discourage the formation of unions and other sources of organized resistance, often with the direct support of government.[9]

Capitalism and Class

The dynamics of capitalism produce enormous amounts of wealth, but they also produce high levels of inequality, both within societies and globally. The richest ten percent of the U.S. population holds more than seventy-five percent of all the wealth, including seventy percent of cash, more than half the land, more than ninety percent of business assets, and ninety-two percent of stocks. The richest twenty percent of households receive fifty-nine percent of all income, leaving forty-one percent to be divided among the remaining eighty percent of households.[10]

Such patterns of inequality both result from and perpetuate a class system based on widening gaps in income, wealth, and power between those on top and everyone below.[11] It is a system that produces oppressive consequences. For those near the bottom, the costs are enormous, with living conditions among the rural poor, for example, including some Native American reservations, similar to if not worse than what is found in the most impoverished nonindustrial societies.[12] Even among the employed members of the working class, as well as many in the middle class, chronic insecurity takes a physical and emotional toll. A great many jobs are alienating, boring, mind-numbing, and have little use for the talents that people performing those jobs have to offer. And the vast majority of workers have little if any control over the work they do or whether they keep their jobs.

It also doesn't take much to see that with a large majority of the population having to divide up a small fraction of all income, there will not be enough to go around. While capitalism produces an overall abundance of goods and services, it distributes that wealth so unequally that it simultaneously creates conditions of scarcity for most of the population. This makes life for tens of millions of people an ongoing competition that is often full of anxiety and struggle. For most people, it would not take very much—a divorce or a serious illness or being laid off—to substantially lower their standard of living, even to the extent of putting them out of their homes.[13]

The "American Dream" aside, most people also have relatively little power to improve their class position.[14] Much of the increase in household wealth, for example, is built on a growing mountain of debt, people working two or more jobs, and families relying on multiple wage earners to provide the standard of living their parents managed with one. Even when unemployment is low, and during the "recovery" from the economic collapse of 2008, most new jobs that have been created over the last several decades have been low-paying and with little chance of advancement. In addition, studies of occupational mobility show that most people are as likely to move downward as they are upward in the class system. Because of this, and the widening gulf separating the upper class from everyone else, the middle class is shrinking.[15] Since 1964, the percentage of people who see themselves as middle class has fallen from sixty one to forty two, while the percentage seeing themselves as working class has risen from thirty five to forty six.[16]

In short, in an era of corporate downsizing, the flight of well-paying industrial jobs overseas, and the rapid growth of low level service occupations, the struggle to move up, for most people, rarely gets them anywhere but hanging on to what they have.[17] There is, of course, upward movement by some, but excluding jobs in high-technology and health-related fields that are currently in demand, this almost always comes at the expense of others who must move down to make room for them, creating what economist Lester Thurow calls a "zero-sum" society—in which gains for some are offset by losses for others.[18] This makes it inevitable that a substantial proportion of the population will live in poverty or close to it and that different groups will see one another as competitors and threats to their livelihood.

As we will see below, such dynamics play a key role in systems of privilege, especially in relation to gender and race.

Capitalism, Difference, and Privilege: Race and Gender

Given how capitalism works, its connections to race are both direct and indirect. The direct connection is most apparent in the enslavement of Africans on cotton and tobacco plantations, especially with the invention of the cotton gin in 1792 (just sixteen years after Adam Smith published *The Wealth of Nations*) that made it possible to process vastly more cotton than before.[19] The number of enslaved blacks in the U.S. jumped from one million in 1800 to almost four million in 1860, just before the start of the Civil War.[20] The primacy of profit was also apparent in the reactions of businesses that relied on paid white workers: they did not object to slavery on moral grounds, but complained that the cost of slave labor was so low that it amounted to unfair competition.[21]

Following the Civil War, the demand for cheap labor was no less than before, and freed blacks were now often held in a new form of bondage by an oppressive system of tenant farming that kept them perpetually in debt.[22] Beyond the South, the profitability of racism showed itself in the widespread use of Chinese immigrant labor to build the western railways under harsh and demeaning conditions. Even farther west, Japanese immigrants had similar experiences on sugar and pineapple plantations in Hawaii.[23]

Capitalism's direct connection to race also appears in the acquisition of land and raw materials, which, like cheap labor, play a key role in the rapid growth of industry and wealth. In the heyday of capitalist expansion during the 19th century, Europe and then the United States found an abundance of what they needed in Africa, Asia, and the Americas. To acquire it, they relied on varying combinations of military conquest, political domination, and economic exploitation.[24] They were spectacularly successful at it, especially Great Britain, a small island nation with few natural resources of its own, which nonetheless managed to become the world's first global industrial power. Unlike Britain, the United States was rich in natural resources, but whites could get at them only by taking them from Native American tribes who inhabited most of the land, as well as from Mexico, which encompassed most of what is now the far west and southwest United States. Whites took what they wanted through a combination of conquest, genocide, and a complex array of treaties that they routinely ignored.[25]

To justify such direct forms of empire building, whites developed the idea of whiteness to define a superior and privileged social category, elevated above everyone who was excluded from it.[26] This was a way to reconcile oppressive and often brutal methods with the nation's newly professed ideals of democracy, freedom, and human dignity. If whiteness defined what it meant to be human, then it was seen as less of an offense against the Constitution (not to mention God) to dominate and oppress everyone else as the United States progressed toward what was popularly perceived as a divinely ordained Manifest Destiny.[27]

Other capitalist connections to race have been less direct. Capitalists, for example, have often used racism as a strategy to control white workers and thereby keep wages low and productivity and profits high. This has been done in two ways. First, beginning early in the 19th century, there was a campaign to encourage white workers to adopt whiteness as a key part of their identity— something they had not done before—and to accept the supposed superiority of whiteness as compensation for their low class position. No matter how badly treated they were by their employers, they could always take comfort in being white and free and therefore elevated above people of color, even those who might have a class position higher than their own.[28]

With the emancipation of slaves following the Civil War, however, lower- and working-class whites could no longer point to their freedom as a mark of superiority. The response to this loss was a period of violence and intimidation directed at blacks, much of which was perpetrated by the newly formed Ku Klux Klan, with no serious opposition from the federal government or whites in the North or South.

Another way for capitalists to control workers is to keep them worried over the possibility of losing their jobs if they demand higher wages or better working conditions. Racism has a long history of being used in this way. The oppressed condition of people of color encourages them to work for wages that are lower than what most whites will accept. Employers have used this to pose an ongoing threat to white workers, who have known employers could use racial minorities as an inexpensive replacement. This has worked most effectively in breaking strikes and unions. As labor became more powerful at the turn of the 20th century, for example, employers often brought in black workers as strikebreakers. This strategy worked to draw the attention of white workers away from issues of capitalism and class and toward issues of race. It focused their fear and anger on the supposed threat from black workers, which made them less likely to see their common condition as workers and instead join together against the capitalists. In this way, racial division and conflict became an effective strategy for dividing different segments of the working class against one another.[29]

Similar dynamics operate today. The controversy over affirmative action programs, for example, as well as the influx of immigrant workers from South and Central America and the "outsourcing" of jobs to other countries, all reflect an underlying belief that the greatest challenge facing white workers is unfair competition from people of color both here and abroad. This ignores how the capitalist system is organized to increase the wealth of capitalists and investors by controlling workers in order to keep wages as low as possible. The result is that a small elite is able to control the vast majority of wealth and income, leaving a small share to be divided among everyone else. Such dynamics encourage competition not only in the working and lower classes but, increasingly, in the middle class.

Given the historical legacy that cultivates among whites a sense of superiority and entitlement in relation to people of color, such competition is bound to provoke anger and resentment directed at people of color rather than at those whose wealth and power lie at the heart of the problem of inequality. In this way, dynamics of class fuel racial conflict, which, in turn, draws attention away from capitalism and the class oppression it produces. The result, as Michael Reich shows, is that white racism actually hurts white workers by strengthening the position of capitalists at the expense of the working class.[30]

Beyond race, capitalism also exploits people with disabilities through "sheltered workshops" in nonprofit organizations that secured for themselves an exception to the 1938 minimum wage law, enabling them to hire people with disabilities at less than minimum wages. Working conditions often separate workers with disabilities from nondisabled workers, place them under the supervision of nondisabled people, and provide little opportunity for challenge or advancement.[31]

Capitalism also makes use of gender inequality.[32] The cultural devaluing of women, for example, has long been used as an excuse to pay them less and exploit them as a source of cheap labor, whether in the corporate secretarial pool or garment sweatshops or electronics assembly plants.[33] Women's supposed inferiority has also been a basis for the belief that much of the work that women do is not work at all and therefore isn't worthy of anything more than emotional compensation.[34] Capitalism could not function without the army of women who do the shopping for households (which is how most goods are purchased) and do the labor through which those goods are consumed, such as cooking meals. On a deeper level, women are still primarily the ones who nurture and raise each new generation of workers on which capitalism depends, and this vital service is provided without anyone having to pay them wages or provide health and retirement benefits.[35] Women do it for free—even when they also work outside the home—to the benefit of the capitalist system and those who control and profit from it. Capitalism, then, provides both the economic context for the trouble that pervades privilege and one of the engines that makes it happen. And the class dynamics that arise from capitalism interact with privilege and oppression in ways that both protect capitalism and class privilege and perpetuate privilege and oppression based on difference.

The Matrix of Domination and the Paradox of Being Privileged and Oppressed At the Same Time

As the dynamics of capitalism and class suggest, systems of privilege are complicated. This is one reason why people can belong to a privileged category such as male or white and yet not experience themselves as privileged, because they also feel the limitations of being working class or gay or having a disability. So a middle-class white lesbian's race privilege and class make her less sensitive to issues of race and class, or her experience of gender inequality and heterosexism foster the illusion that she is informed about other forms of privilege and oppression. Or a working-class white man feels so pushed around and looked down on that the idea that whiteness and maleness give him access to privilege seems ridiculous.

Part of such feelings comes from seeing privilege as something that is just about individuals. From that perspective, either he is privileged or he's not, and if he can show that he's oppressed in one way, then that would seem to cancel out any claim that he is privileged in another.

But the truth is more complicated than whether *he* is privileged, because, as we saw earlier, privilege is not really about him, even though he is certainly involved in and affected by it. He stands to benefit from being identified as white and male, for example, but being working class can set up barriers that make it harder for him to access those benefits. If he cannot earn a good living, for example, he may have a hard time feeling like a man bonded to other men in their superiority to women. The social privileging of manhood still exists, but his class position gets in the way of the advantages that go with it.

Another complication is that categories that define privilege exist all at once and in relation to one another. People never see me solely in terms of my race, for example, or gender, but always as part of a package deal. Whether, for example, readers of my books perceive me as intelligent, credible, and competent is affected by more than the fact that I'm a published author, for they also perceive a person of a certain gender, race, and, from various cues, disability status and class, including my PhD. Even if they first meet me on the internet, they will form impressions of me if only by assuming I am white and male unless I indicate otherwise.

Given that reality, it makes no sense to talk about the effect of being in one of these categories—say, white—without also looking at the others and how they relate to whiteness. My experience of being identified as white is affected by my being seen as male, heterosexual, nondisabled, and of a certain class. If I apply for a job, white privilege will load the odds in my favor over a similarly qualified Latino. But if the people doing the hiring think I'm gay, my white privilege might lose out to his heterosexual privilege, and he might get the job instead of me.

It is tempting to use such comparisons to calculate a net cost or benefit associated with each status. In other words, you get a point for being white, male, heterosexual, or nondisabled, and you lose a point if you are of color, female, gay or lesbian, or have a disability. Add up the points and you have your score on the privilege scale. That would put nondisabled white male heterosexuals on top (+4) and lesbians of color with disabilities in "quadruple jeopardy" at the bottom (–4). White nondisabled lesbians (0) and nondisabled gay men of color (0) would fall in between and on the same "level." Life and privilege are not that simple, however, with being male giving you a certain amount of privilege and being white giving you more of the same, and being gay taking half of that away. Privilege takes different forms that are connected to one another in ways that are far from obvious. For example, historically, one way for white men to justify domination over black men has been to portray them as sexual predators targeting white women. At the same time, they've portrayed white women as pure and helpless and therefore needing white men's protection, a dependent position that puts them under white men's control. Note, then, how dynamics of gender and race are so bound up with each other that it is all but impossible to tell where one ends and the other begins. How much race or gender "counts" all by itself cannot be determined.

This is why such systems have been described as a "matrix of domination" or "matrix of privilege," and not merely a collection of different kinds of inequality that don't have much to do with one another. As Patricia Hill Collins, Estelle Disch, and others argue, each form of privilege is part of a much larger and interconnected system.[36]

Looking at privilege in this way makes it clear that each form exists in relation to all the rest, so that we can stop trying to figure out which is the worst or most oppressive. It also frees us from the trap of thinking that everything is a matter of either/or—either you're oppressed or you're not, privileged or not—because in reality most people belong to both privileged and oppressed categories at the same time.

There are several ways in which dimensions of privilege are connected to one another. One form of privilege, for example, can defend or reinforce another, as when women who challenge male privilege are called lesbians as a way to discredit them, encouraging other women to remain silent regardless of their sexual orientation. In this way, the prejudice of heterosexism is used to support male privilege by silencing women.

Access to one form of privilege can affect access to others. Because the advantages of race, for example, generally give white men greater access to class privilege compared with men of color, white men also have fuller access to male privilege. This happens in part because male privilege is increased by men earning more than their female partners, an advantage that is more difficult for men of color to achieve, given their oppression because of race. Note, however, that this works only for heterosexual white men, since being gay can limit a man's access to male privilege.

Access to one form of privilege can also serve as compensation for not having access to another. Men of color, for example, can make use of male privilege to compensate for the effects of racial oppression, just as white women can use race privilege to compensate for the effects of gender. Finally, as we saw earlier, subordinate groups are often pitted against one another in ways that draw attention away from the system of privilege that hurts them all. Asian Americans, for example, are often held up as a good example—a "model minority"—which makes other peoples of color look bad by comparison and encourages them to blame Asian Americans for their own disadvantaged status.[37] In this way, Asian Americans serve as a distraction and a buffer between whites and other peoples of color, as Korean Americans did in Los Angeles after the police who assaulted Rodney King were acquitted and the rage of black people spread to Korean neighborhoods, where stores were burned to the ground. Only when the rioting reached the edges of white neighborhoods did police finally respond to pleas for help.[38]

The complexity of the matrix makes it clear that work for change needs to focus on privilege itself, in all its forms that condition how we think of ourselves in relation to inequalities of power. We will not get rid of racism, in other words, without doing something about sexism and class, because the system that produces the one also produces the others and connects them to one another in powerful ways.

CHAPTER 4

Making Privilege and Oppression Happen

Although privilege is attached to social categories and not to individuals, people are the ones who make it happen through what they do and don't do in relation to others. This almost always involves some form of discrimination by treating people unequally because they belong to different categories.[1] Whether done consciously or not, discrimination helps maintain systems of privilege by enacting unearned advantage. When musicians audition for orchestras, for example, women are more likely to be hired—and men less likely—if candidates perform behind a screen so that judges cannot identify the musician's gender.[2]

Like all behavior, discrimination is connected to how we think and feel about people, and prejudice plays a powerful role in this, both fueling discriminatory behavior and providing a rationale to justify it.[3] Prejudice is complicated because it involves both ideas and feelings. Cultural ideas about race, for example, include values that elevate whiteness above color and the belief that whites are smarter, more honest, law-abiding, and hardworking. They also include negative feelings toward people of color—contempt, hostility, fear, disgust, and the like—along with positive (or at least neutral) feelings toward whites.

Privilege and oppression happen in many ways, from the overt and violent hate crime to the subtlety of all the ways there are to dismiss or devalue, make visible or invisible, include or exclude.[4] It works at every level, from the spirit and the body to having a decent place to live and enough food to eat to getting home alive. As sociologists Joe Feagin and Melvin Sikes point out, the oppressive consequences of privilege must be understood as lived experience that both damages people in the moment and accumulates over time to affect not only their behavior but also their understanding of themselves and life itself.[5] And no matter what form privilege takes, it involves everyone in one way or another.

It's important to stress that discrimination does not have to be conscious or intentional in order to have an effect. In orchestra auditions, for example, the judges' bias may be unconscious, what Harvard psychologist Mahzarin Banaji calls "implicit bias," with the judges being oblivious to the distinctions they are making based on gender, until they become aware of the effect of "blind" auditions.[6] As far as they're concerned, they're doing nothing more than picking the best musician for the job.

Note also that implicit bias can take the form of preferential treatment or favoritism that, on the surface, may appear unremarkable and unmotivated by prejudice *against* anyone. An Australian study, for example, finds that when passengers get on a bus and say they don't have enough money for the fare but really need to get to the next stop, they are twice as likely to be given a free ride if they are white. People of color are less likely than whites to get free rides even when they wear business suits or military uniforms.[7] Drivers are not supposed to give free rides to anyone, so that denying them to people of color doesn't require conscious prejudice or hostile acts against them. The drivers are just doing their jobs. On the other hand, when they give a rider in distress a helping hand, they can see it as an act of compassion and generosity without being aware of the implicit racial bias that operates in deciding whom to help and whom to refuse.

Implicit bias can also appear in acts of microaggression that may seem insubstantial, even trivial, to dominant groups while having real and negative consequences for others.[8] When a white person, for example, asks a person of color, "What are you?" it may appear to the speaker as mere curiosity, while having the effect of marginalizing the person of color by turning them into an object, a strange and exotic "other" in relation to the white standard and point of view. Or when a man expresses admiration for a female coworker's body or puts up photographs of nude women in the workplace, what he may think is a harmless gesture enacts male privilege by sexually objectifying women and underscoring men's authority to judge women on the basis of their bodies. Because a microaggressive act can be defended as "small" and ambiguous ("I was only kidding"), it can have an outsized effect by encouraging members of subordinate groups to doubt themselves—"Am I being too sensitive?"—as they try to figure out what to make of it and its significance. Such moments can accumulate into an exhausting source of distraction, frustration, and anger in the midst of everything else people have to do in their lives.

In all its forms, implicit bias may account for a wide range of discrimination—from hiring to health care to police deciding who to stop and frisk, or even to shoot[9]—with men, whites, and other privileged groups incorrectly perceiving themselves to be free of bias and therefore not part of the problem. The consequences, however, are the same.

Avoidance, Exclusion, Rejection, and Worse

Of all human needs, few are as powerful as the need to be seen, included, and accepted by other people, which is why shunning and banishment are among the most painful punishments to endure, a kind of social death. It is not surprising, then, that inclusion, acceptance, and being seen are key aspects of privilege. To see how, consider all the ways we affect whether other people feel welcome and valued, or like outsiders who don't belong:

- Whether we look at people when we talk with them, including whether we make—or, in some cultures, avoid—eye contact as a way to indicate interest and/or respect

- Whether we smile at people when they come into the room, or stare as if to say, "What are you and what are you doing here?" or whether we stop the conversation with a hush they have to wade through to be included in the smallest way

- Whether we listen and respond to what people say, or drift away to someone or something else; whether we talk about things they know about, or stick to what's familiar to us

- Whether we acknowledge that diversity exists and make room for it, or act as though everyone is either like us or that somehow, by default, they ought to be

- Whether we accept people as they are or ask them to explain themselves—who are you, what are you, where are you from

- Whether we acknowledge people's presence, or make them wait as if they weren't there; whether we avoid touching their skin when giving or taking something; how closely we watch them to see what they're up to
- Whether we share with newcomers the informal rules they need to know in order to belong, succeed, and get along
- Whether we invite people over to our home or out to socialize
- Whether we say hello to people when they move into the neighborhood
- Whether we avoid someone going down the sidewalk, giving them a wide berth when we pass or even crossing to the other side

Avoidance, exclusion, rejection, and devaluing often happen in ways noticed only by the person experiencing them, and they can happen without anyone intending harm. It can be as subtle as shifting your gaze, leaning away, or editing your speech. It can be faint praise ("Uh-huh, okay"), or praise that's so effusive ("You speak English really well!"), that it signals surprise at someone exceeding low expectations. It can be repeatedly asking someone if they understand what you've said. It can be using images of darkness and blackness as negative, and light and whiteness as positive, or using "queer" or "gay" as insults, or "having balls" (but not ovaries) as a metaphor for courage. It can be paying more attention to a woman's looks than to her ability or character, implicitly encouraging her to do the same. It can be as unmindful as assuming that all people are Christian ("Merry Christmas!") or able to climb a flight of stairs. It can be as simple as not paying attention, as when elegantly dressed black presidential candidate Jesse Jackson was tipped by a white woman who confused him with a bell-man who had just helped her in a New York hotel.[10] It can be telling what seems to be a joke but in fact signals the low esteem in which people are held simply because they are female or of color or with a disability or gay.

To look at racism in particular, it also happens openly and on purpose. It appears in swastikas and anti-black, anti-Muslim epithets scrawled on dormitory walls, in Asian American students receiving hate mail or being spat on as they walk across campus, in sometimes fatal acts of violence directed at those identified as Latino, Asian, black, or Arab. It appears in crosses burned on front lawns of African Americans who have just moved into a neighborhood, and in churches, synagogues, and mosques set on fire and graveyards strewn with toppled tombstones.

It happens when real estate agents steer people of color away from white neighborhoods and lenders deny them mortgages and business loans that are readily granted to whites who are no more qualified, making blacks the most residentially segregated group in the United States. The consequences of this inequity are almost incalculable, for study after study shows that where people live makes a huge difference in the quality of life, from job opportunities and community services (schools, health care, street maintenance, trash disposal), to public safety and access to political power.[11]

Racism comes out in police harassment, brutality, and neglect in moments of crisis or in being pulled over and having your car searched for a "DWB" ("Driving While Black") violation.[12] It comes out in black parents having to train teenage sons to avoid the police, to never run away if they encounter them, to keep their hands out in the open, to never give cause for suspicion—in other words, to never act like a child moving through the world freely and without fear. It comes out in unarmed black men being shot dead by police. It comes out in Harvard Professor Henry Louis Gates being arrested in broad daylight on the front porch of his own home when he becomes indignant at police demands that he prove who he is.[13] It comes out in "nigger" or "towelhead" muttered in passing on a crowded sidewalk or scrawled on public bathroom walls, and in billboard advertising campaigns for cigarettes and alcohol that target lower- and working-class African American neighborhoods. It comes out in vacant apartments that suddenly become unavailable, in hotel reservations mysteriously "lost" when a person of color arrives to register.

For African Americans in particular, the result is a constant, daily grind of feeling vulnerable to judgments based solely on their race, because mistakes and failures are never just that but always carry the potential to "confirm the broader, racial inferiority they are suspected of."[14] Racism means living in a society that predisposes whites to see the worst in people of color and ignore the best, a society in which acceptance must be won anew every day. It means having to carry a continuing "minority sense," a "race watch" for the possibility of hostility, and a "second eye" to decide whether to give whites the benefit of the doubt.[15] This has continued in spite of the historic election of Barack Obama. In fact, in the four years after he first took office, with high personal approval ratings from whites, negative views of blacks actually increased in the white population.[16]

"It is utterly exhausting being Black in America," writes children's advocate Marian Wright Edelman. "Physically, mentally, and emotionally . . . There is no respite from your badge of color."[17]

It is, as a black college professor put it, to lead "lives of quiet desperation generated by a litany of daily large and small events that, whether or not by design, remind us of our 'place' in American society."[18] It is to experience a precarious balance between paranoia and the desire to live life simply as it comes, an endless struggle against humiliation, depression, and rage.

Racism, of course, is not the only form of exclusion and oppression. An ongoing epidemic of violence threatens women and people who are LGBT, for example, at home, at work, on university campuses, and on the street. A majority of girls and women in U.S. schools and workplaces report being sexually harassed, domestic violence is a leading cause of injury to women, and almost half of all females born in the United States can expect to experience an attempted or completed rape sometime during their lives.[19] The result is patterns of women and girls learning to circumscribe their lives in order to reduce the odds of being singled out for harassment or attack.

When subordinate groups get fed up and express rage, frustration, and resentment, there is always the danger that powerful others—men, whites, Anglos, the nondisabled, heterosexuals, the middle and upper classes—will not like it and will retaliate with accusations of being "unprofessional" or "malcontents," "maladjusted whiners," "troublemakers," "overly emotional," "bitches," "out of control," "male-bashers."[20] Given the cultural authority and the power to harm that such retaliation carries, it can be hard to defend against, further adding to the burden of oppression and increasing the unearned advantage of privilege.

The problems that privilege engenders infect both our outer and inner lives and flow between the two in ways that intensify and perpetuate the consequences to both. It appears in unequal distributions of income and wealth that grow worse as competition intensifies for jobs that pay a living wage. It appears in unequal treatment, access, and opportunities, in glass ceilings and occupational ghettos. While education helps, in many ways it doesn't help much. African Americans and Latinas/Latinos with four or more years of college are, respectively, sixty-seven and fifty-four percent more likely to be unemployed than comparable whites.[21] African American and Latina/Latino families with college-educated householders are two to three times more likely than similar white families to live below the poverty line.[22] Similar dynamics are at work in regard to gender inequality. Although the gender gap in income has shrunk somewhat over the long haul, the pace of that change is extremely slow and over the last few decades has been essentially flat. In 1982, women college graduates who worked full time and year round earned an average of $17,000 compared with $28,000 for men, a ratio of sixty-two cents to the dollar. By 2014, thirty-two years later, the comparable averages had risen to $60,057 for women and $86,050 for men, a ratio of just seventy cents to the dollar.[23]

Among people with disabilities, the unemployment rate is twelve times higher than it is for people without disabilities, in spite of the fact that the vast majority of unemployed people with disabilities want to work. People with disabilities are also three times more likely to live in households with incomes of $15,000 or less, in part because many of those who work must accept jobs that pay less than the minimum wage.[24] Many of these jobs lack benefits such as health insurance, and, as a result, people with disabilities are more than twice as likely to postpone needed health care because they cannot afford it.[25]

In all its forms, the problem of privilege and oppression stands between us and the kind of world in which all people have the best chance to thrive. To do something about it, we first have to see how it affects us, because only then are we likely to feel compelled to do something about it.

A Problem for Whom?

No matter where we look—and for all the controversy over affirmative action—the evidence is clear that the position of dominant groups shows little sign of weakening. This does not mean, however, that men, whites, and others escape the negative consequences of living in a system of privilege. Consider, for example, the impoverishment of men's lives caused by the culturally encouraged emotional gulfs between them and their fathers, sons, and male friends. Consider the damage men often do to themselves and one another in trying to measure up as "real men," how they limit their humanity, deny their needs, don't ask for help, and often live with chronic fear, anxiety, isolation, and loneliness. Consider men's fear of other men's violence and aggression, and boys who feel driven to shoot down classmates and teachers. Consider the difficulty of friendship across genders and of men's predictable defensiveness around women, feeling vulnerable to accusations of sexism or harassment in a world organized to elevate them at women's expense. Consider the range of reactions to the most subtle mention of male privilege—hypersensitive, huffy, hurt, worried, hostile, confused, shut down, tuned out, unable to "get it," rushing to backpedal, dismiss, counter, refute, condescend, patronize, trivialize, ridicule, or walk away.

The disadvantages of male privilege are similar to those of heterosexual privilege. By definition, gay men and lesbians bear the brunt of heterosexism and homophobia.[26] But the dynamic that harms them also has destructive effects on heterosexuals. In the simplest sense, weapons used against gays and lesbians are also used among heterosexuals, especially as men jockey for status and try to measure up to the dominant standards of manhood. As part of this dynamic, the same insults and intimidation that heterosexual men use against gay men—"fag," "queer," "fairy," "cocksucker"—they also routinely use against other heterosexual men to enhance their status. Sometimes such tags are used openly, but the message is often coded in words such as "wimp," "wuss," "pussy," or "whipped." In either case, whenever a man's manhood is challenged, his vulnerability to being tarred with cultural references to being gay is never far off, regardless of whether his sexual orientation is truly in doubt. As we saw earlier, similar dynamics operate to intimidate women into silence on the subject of male privilege for fear of being tagged as lesbians.[27]

This particular dynamic among men gives only a hint of the trouble heterosexuals are in. Consider the enormous amount of male aggression and violence directed at girls and women, from child sexual abuse to battering, rape, stalking, and sexual harassment.[28] Studies of male violence show that control is the core issue, especially through the cultural connection between power ("potency") and heterosexual relationships. Manhood is defined in terms of always being in control, and sexuality is identified as a primary way for men to prove it. Since violence is a means of exerting control and asserting superiority, the cultural association between heterosexuality and power promotes male violence against women in heterosexual relationships.

Because heterosexuality plays such a large part in defining gender inequality—"real" men and women are always defined in heterosexual terms—gender violence commonly has a sexual aspect to it. Understanding this makes clear the roots of and relationship between violence inflicted on lesbians and gay men by heterosexual men and the violence between heterosexual couples.[29] Many heterosexual men who attack lesbians and gay men do so not because of moral or religious conviction, but because they feel threatened by the mere existence of people whose sexual orientation and relation to women raise questions about their own. Since lesbians and gay men do not follow heterosexual models, the example they set challenges heterosexual men's claim to a monopoly on manhood, especially as measured by power over women. The example set by gay men also deeply challenges the one set by the dominant masculine model, by gays not relating to women as objects of sexual control. Lesbians further challenge the model by not choosing or submitting to men as sexual partners. This makes it hard to separate the dynamics of gender inequality in heterosexual relationships from the trouble heterosexuals make for lesbians and gays.

Just as there is gender trouble for men and heterosexist trouble for heterosexuals, there is race trouble for whites. It shows up in all the things white people do to get around the fact that the injustice and suffering caused by racism have something to do with the idea of race in general and whiteness in particular. This applies no matter how whites may see themselves as individuals.[30] It is reflected in discomfort around and fear of people of color, in hypersensitive defensiveness around issues of race.[31] You can see the race trouble for whites in the uneasy feeling they often get when they realize they are not trusted and are being told what they want to hear rather than the truth. You can see it in how white people may deaden themselves against the pain they would feel if they realized how deeply racism touches their own lives, how much it deadens the spirit and flattens the emotional landscape, how it sets whites up to look at the "rhythm" and "life" in non-European cultures with the feeling that something is lacking in their own.

You can see the race trouble for whites in the toll it takes on their moral integrity, because racism requires hypocrisy toward deeply held cultural values of fairness, decency, and justice. You can see it in the lengths to which white people will go to distort current and historical reality in order to maintain the illusion of being the chosen and superior race, the standard against which others are to be measured. You can see it in how poorly prepared white people are to be effective on a global scale, where whites, for all their current power in the world, are a small and ever-shrinking minority. You can see it in the angry, wishful, persistent naïveté of "I don't see color. I don't see race." You can see it in the pointed ignoring of the "deceptively comfortable prison" of racism that white people live in and the chronic fear that "the murky waters of despair and dread that now flood the streets of black America" will at any moment touch them, too, if not sweep them and everything they cherish away.[32]

But the trouble of race already touches white people along with everyone else. We are all of us in it up to our necks just by being here.

What we don't realize most of the time is that the "isms"—sexism, heterosexism, ableism, racism—affect more than just those who are women, LGBT, with disabilities, or of color. It is impossible to live in a world that generates so much injustice and suffering without being involved in one way or another. Everyone has a race, a sex, a gender identity, a sexual orientation, a disability status. Whether we like it or not, we all figure in and embody the differences on which privilege and oppression are built. The bad news is that no matter who we are, the trouble belongs to us. But that is also the good news, because it gives us both a reason and the power to do something about it.

And That's Not All

The trouble around privilege also affects not only individuals, but organizations, communities, and society as a whole. From corporations to the military to hospitals and neighborhood schools, the prevalence of privilege and oppression is among our worst kept secrets. Much of the time, people manage to act as though nothing is wrong—and then another scandal explodes on to the front pages: hate crimes against those who are LGBT; racist talk and behavior at the highest levels of responsibility and power; sexual violence and harassment in colleges, universities, the military, and corporations. In 2013, for example, a number of prominent universities— including Dartmouth, Swarthmore, and the University of California at Berkeley—were the focus of a federal investigation into allegations of mishandling sexual assault cases and failure to protect their students.[33] In 2015, a wave of anti-racism protests swept college campuses across the country. And in 2016, many Americans were shocked by the hostility toward people of color, Muslims, and others that emerged from the presidential campaign rhetoric of Donald Trump, prompting massive protests in cities across the country following his election.

Most organizations either deny the trouble or are somehow oblivious to it. When a crisis breaks through the routine of business as usual, the typical reaction is a panicked effort of damage control to minimize legal exposure and bad publicity. Invariably, the attention is directed to a few misbehaving individuals, in the belief that getting rid of or fixing them or learning how to spot them before they do something wrong is enough to take care of the problem.

Between crises and scandals, privilege and oppression continue the insidious work of making organizations increasingly dysfunctional and vulnerable. The position of white people and men in the world leaves them ill equipped to know what their female and minority subordinates, coworkers, and colleagues are up against as they try to make their way in organizations. The path of least resistance is, for those in a privileged position, to see little or no reason to examine themselves in relation to the oppression that damages so many people's lives, to come to terms with how living in a world organized around privilege has shaped them, and how they see other people and themselves. They might try to be fair, which is to say, to treat women as they would men, or people of color as they would whites. But this approach pretends that racism and sexism do not exist beyond conscious awareness and personal intentions, and makes it easier for them to feel unconnected to the trouble. It makes even the possibility of diminishing that dysfunction and vulnerability—for, say, a white male to mentor white women and people of color—everything *but* a path of least resistance. It also does not serve the needs of people on the outside looking in.

If the teacher or the boss or the superior officer does not talk about or acknowledge privilege and oppression, the subordinate trying to learn the ropes and get along is unlikely to risk making powerful people uncomfortable by bringing it up. With so much of importance left unsaid, it is hard to trust those in power. As a result, people do not learn what they need to know. They wind up stuck in place, or in some backwater position within the organization, their talents and abilities unrealized and of no particular use to anyone, including themselves. Or they strike out on their own, dropping out of school or transferring to another university or leaving a job to start their own business or to work for a company that understands the importance of meeting the issues head on.

For the organizations that these individuals leave behind, the investment made in training and development is lost, and the word begins to get out that if you are not male, are not white, are not heterosexual, have a disability, and are not desperate, you'll do better someplace else, someplace where you can look at those with power and influence and see more people like yourself. And as competition intensifies and the population of students and workers diversifies, those "someplace elses" wind up with the advantage, doing better because they attract and keep talent that comes in all kinds of people.

Most organizational failures in the area of diversity result not from being run by mean-spirited bigots—they're not—but from poorly dealing with issues of privilege or, more likely, not dealing with them at all unless a crisis forces the issue. Even then, the response rarely goes beyond making the issue *seem* to go away without confronting the deeper reality of privilege and oppression.

The failure doesn't happen all at once in some dramatic moment of truth. The splashy scandals—the inflammatory incident, the executive or politician or university president forced to resign—are not the problem. The problem is the same culture of denial and neglect that permeates society as a whole. Little by little, day by day, people are worn down by the struggle to earn a living or a degree while maintaining a sense of dignity and self worth in the face of one sign after another that they don't really matter or belong.

The oppressive effect of privilege is often so insidious that dominant groups complain whenever it's brought up for discussion. They feel impatient, threatened, and imposed upon. "Come on," they say, "stop whining. Things aren't so bad. Maybe they used to be, but not anymore. It's time to move on. Get over it." But people on the receiving end of privilege have to ask themselves how they would know how bad it really is to be a person of color or a lesbian or a woman or gay or disabled or working- or lower-class. What life experience, for example, would qualify a white person to know the day-to-day reality of racism? Unlike people of color, white people do not live with the oppressive consequences of racism twenty-four hours a day. They may know what it's like to get bad service in a restaurant, for example, or feel like an outsider, but they have no idea what it's like for such things to happen so often—and to have it happen to all of their friends and family—that they cannot escape the reality that their experience is tied to how other people see them as human beings simply because of their race.[34]

None of this means that everything said by people in subordinate groups is true. But it does mean there is every reason for dominant groups to give them the benefit of the doubt long enough to take in and take seriously what they're talking *about*.

We Cannot Heal Until the Wounding Stops

There is much talk these days about "racial healing," healing "gender wounds," and "reconciliation" of various kinds, inspiring images of finally and collectively turning ourselves to the difficult but (ultimately) triumphant work of undoing the damage and healing the wounds. If true, it would be a blessing, but in fact it is wishful thinking, because the problem is far from over. Every day, privilege and oppression cause damage to tens of millions of people. The patterns of history continue into the present and show every sign of going on into the future unless people do something to change them. And the only way to do that is to change how these patterns make privilege possible.

Images of healing are also problematic because they imply that the damage being done is primarily emotional. The goal becomes one of getting along better by being nicer and more tolerant, forgiving and forgetting, living in more authentic ways. As reasonable as it sounds, it ignores the fact that a lot of the trouble does not begin and end with interpersonal relations and emotional wounds. Much of it is embedded in structures of power and inequality that shape almost every aspect of life in this society, from segregation to economics, politics, religion, schools, and the family. The idea that we are going to get out of this by somehow getting to a place where we are kinder and more sensitive to one another ignores most of what we have to overcome—which is all that has kept us from it for so long. It sets us up to walk right past the trouble toward an alternative that does not, and cannot, exist until we do something about what creates and drives privilege and oppression in the first place. And that is something that needs to be changed, not healed.

In some ways, appeals to healing turn out to be—in effect if not intent—another way to deny the depth of the trouble we are in. They feed on the desperate illusion that if we ignore it long enough or try to replace it with good intentions, it will go away. But the hope for something better depends on the ability to work together to face that illusion and go through it to the truth on the other side. To do that, we first have to understand how the trouble that surrounds privilege is made worse by how we think about it—the trouble we have with the trouble.

CHAPTER 5

The Trouble with the Trouble

I am in a three-day meeting of human resource managers. It's one of the most diverse groups I've ever worked with—women and men, whites and people of color, from all over the United States and a dozen European countries. They share a deep and in many cases lifelong commitment to ending privilege and oppression and account for some of the best success stories organizations have to tell.

And yet, as I listen to them talk about their work, it is clear how frustrated they are in spite of all they have accomplished. Progress is painfully slow and easily undone, but the malaise goes deeper, to the horns of a dilemma that emerges as the day wears on. They know that the only way to deal effectively with these issues is to engage those with the power to shape organizational culture, who set the norms and examples that bring others along. The group is also acutely aware of the fact that most powerful people are white heterosexual nondisabled males, and that the key to change is to engage those people with the problem of privilege as an ongoing, permanent part of their lives, in which privilege is as much an issue for them as it is for those who bear the brunt of oppression.

In other words, men must see sexism as *their* problem, white people must see race as *their* issue, nondisabled people must see ableism as a problem for *them*. But they rarely do, and, even then, it's not for long or with much effect.

"Why not?" I ask, and the responses pour out of them. Dominant groups don't see privilege as a problem, for many reasons:

- *Because they don't know that it exists in the first place.* They're oblivious. The reality of privilege doesn't occur to them because they don't go out of their way to see or ask about it, or because no one dares bring it up for fear of being tagged a troublemaker or making things worse. They have no idea of how privilege oppresses others, an obliviousness that allows them to attend to their own lives with only an occasional sense of trouble somewhere "out there" beyond the fringe of their awareness. And they have a low tolerance for anyone who would make them aware, consciously or unconsciously seeing themselves as entitled not to have to know, with silence the default and any mention of the trouble perceived as an imposition on their lives.[1]

- *Because they don't have to.* Even if they acknowledge that the trouble exists, they don't have to pay attention, because privilege insulates them from the worst consequences of that trouble. There is nothing to compel anything more from them, except, perhaps, a lawsuit or a strike or a demonstration that disrupts the status quo.

- *Because they think it's a personal problem.* They think people get what they deserve, which makes the trouble just a sum of individual failure and success. If males or whites get more than others, it's because they work harder, they're smarter, more honest and law-abiding, more capable. If others get less, it's up to them to improve themselves.

- *Because they want to hang on to their privilege.* They know that they benefit from the way things are and don't want it to change. Some have mixed feelings, such as a white man who said in a workshop that he felt "torn between wanting to make things right and not wanting to lose what I have." Many others, however, feel a sense of entitlement, that they deserve everything they've got, including whatever advantages they have over others. As a young man at a university in Colorado said to me, "Why should men's athletic programs have to give up any funding to women? If they want more money, let them go find it." Such feelings can be especially powerful among those who lack class privilege and struggle to succeed in a system based on competition and scarcity, making them reluctant to lose anything that might give them an edge. But similar dynamics also appear among those privileged by class position, as with a group of highly successful white professional women I once worked with, who were happy to talk about how male privilege frustrated their upward mobility, but became furious when pressed on issues of race and the possibility that white privilege was something they might need to look at.

■ *Because they're consciously prejudiced.* They are aware of their hostility toward blacks or women or lesbians and gay men, but see themselves not as prejudiced, but as reasonable people responding to the world as it is. They believe in their own superiority, and the belief is like a wall. The more you try to get through or over it, the higher and thicker it gets.

■ *Because they're afraid.* They may be sympathetic to doing something about privilege and oppression, but they're afraid of being criticized for acknowledging that it even exists. They're afraid of not knowing what to do, of being seen as incompetent, of making mistakes, of looking like fools. They're afraid of being saddled with guilt just for being male or white, of being attacked with no place to hide. They're afraid that other men or other whites will see them as disloyal for calling attention to issues of equity and making them feel uncomfortable or threatened. And they are already worried or frightened about other things in their lives—at work, at home, at school—and see this as one more thing to add to the list of reasons for feeling overwhelmed.

The above do not apply to everyone in the same way or to the same degree, in part because "they" are not a homogeneous group. But regardless of variations and exceptions, if members of dominant groups pay attention to privilege and oppression, it is always in spite of all the reasons not to, which bring us to the core of the problem.

If the roomful of managers were responsible for so many success stories, why, I asked, were they so frustrated? Because, they said, their progress depended on two strategies that are effective only to a limited degree and not for very long.

The first strategy, the "tin cup" approach, appeals to a sense of decency, fairness, and good will toward those less fortunate. It is to lend a helping hand as a good and noble thing to do, which can move some people to action. But as a strategy for long-term and fundamental change, it fails for several reasons. For one, it depends on moments of generosity, which may come and go as people feel more or less secure in their own situations. This do-a-good-deed approach also rests on a sense of "us" and "them"—the "us" who help the less fortunate and "them" who are helped. The problem is that the former feel little reason to identify with the latter, as when "we" who are not poor or don't have disabilities, for example, help "those people" who are poor or have disabilities, creating a separation and distance even at the moment of reaching out to help. The act of helping—of being able to help—affirms the social distance between the two groups and heightens everyone's awareness of it. Every such act of giving is a statement, intended or not, of one group's ability to give and the other's inability to get along without it. And in a society that counts independence, autonomy, and self-sufficiency among its highest cultural values, it is hard to avoid the negative judgments attached to those on the receiving end and the status-enhancing credit conferred on those who give.

Although doing the right thing can be morally compelling, it usually rests on a sense of obligation to principle more than to actual people, which can result in a sense of disconnection rather than connection. We take care of family members, for example, not only because it's the right thing to do or the neighbors would disapprove if we didn't, but because we feel a connection to them that carries a responsibility for their welfare. It isn't that we *owe* them something as a debtor owes a creditor. It's that our lives are bound up in their lives and theirs in ours, which makes us aware that what happens to them also happens to us. We do not experience them as "others" who we decide to help because we feel charitable in the moment. The family is something larger that we participate in, and we cannot be part of that without paying attention to what goes on within that family of which we are a part.

Another problem with acting from a sense of principle or virtue is that part of its appeal is the good feeling it gives people when they do it, which usually works only as long as the feeling lasts. Confronting issues such as sexism and racism is hard and sometimes painful and risky work, and feeling good about ourselves is unlikely to be enough to sustain us over the rugged course of it.

What is sustaining is a sense of ownership, that the trouble is truly our own and not someone else's, because this means our responsibility to do something no longer feels like an option. It isn't something we get to choose if we're in a generous mood or can "afford" it at the moment, but is instead one of the terms of our participation in the world, however large or small we define it to be. Without that sense of ownership, serious work on issues of privilege will always be what Roosevelt Thomas calls a "fair weather" item on the agenda.[2]

As an alternative to the tin cup approach, Thomas urges us to act not simply because it's the right thing to do, but because it makes organizations more effective. It helps businesses compete for customers and talented employees, and universities attract the best students, faculty, and staff. It raises morale and productivity and lowers costly turnovers. It protects against lawsuits and bad publicity and the energy that goes into worrying about them.

In an important sense, of course, he's right that the "business case" for dealing with issues of privilege can be compelling. When women and racial minorities leave unsupportive workplaces and take their training and talent with them, the annual loss to organizations can run into the millions of dollars, far more than the cost of programs to improve the conditions that prompt people to leave. When you factor in the other costs and liabilities that result from an unsupportive or hostile environment, you would think organizations would fall over themselves to do something about it.

But most of the time they don't,[3] and when they do, it often amounts to little more than a halfhearted, short-lived, "flavor-of-the-month" program that leaves people feeling cynical and, having had their expectations raised and dashed, even worse than before. ("It pisses me off," said a line supervisor at one of the largest manufacturers in the United States, "that they're doing this just to make a buck."). Or the program is serious and intense but lacks follow up, or fades away when key people leave or budgets are cut or companies merge. The problem with relying on the business case is that it sees ending the trouble as a means to an end, a practical, rational, profitable strategy. This approach is only as good as the results it produces in comparison with alternatives, which may include doing nothing about privilege at all, or, for that matter, exploiting it as a source of competitive advantage.

This is why the business case, for all its appeal, cannot be the *only* reason to act. At the right moment, the business case can appeal to fear or greed or both, but as anyone knows who watches the ups and downs of the stock market, fear is something that comes and goes, and greed easily gets attached to whatever looks good at the moment. This is especially true from the short-run perspective that dominates today's competitive and insecure global capitalist economy.

Certainly life would be better in a world without privilege and oppression. Surely removing the resentment, fear, injustice, and suffering that go with them would dramatically improve life in schools, workplaces, neighborhoods, and communities. Short-run competitive thinking, however, makes that goal all but impossible to achieve, because that kind of change is a long-term project, rooted in a sense of community and common purpose. Even when people can see the potential benefits somewhere in the future, they still need something to hold them to the vision and see them through the long journey from here to there. What is needed is a binding sense of ownership in relation to the problem as well as to the paths that lead toward its solution. What is needed is a reason to feel committed to change in ways powerful enough to overcome all the reasons that dominant groups have to leave the problem to someone else—anger, fear, resentment, entitlement, detachment, inattention, and ignorance, all wrapped up in the luxury of obliviousness. Our personal stake in issues of privilege has to run deeper than that, to the realization that we are all connected to a great deal of suffering and injustice in the world, and when we allow ourselves to be aware of that, we are bound to feel obliged to do something about it.

We need a third choice to take us beyond appeals to goodness or boosting the bottom line. We need a way to remove barriers that prevent well intentioned people from seeing themselves as part of both the problem and the solution. We need ways not only to have serious conversations across difference, but to *act* decisively to end the most destructive source of unnecessary suffering in the human experience.

This third choice, this opening for meaningful action, begins with what most of us do not want to face: what privilege, power, and difference have to do with us.

CHAPTER 6

What It Has to Do with Us

In order to do something about privilege and oppression, we have to talk about it, which can be hard to do, especially for dominant groups. As Paul Kivel writes, for example, "Rarely do we whites sit back and listen to people of color without interrupting, without being defensive, without trying to regain attention to ourselves, without criticizing or judging."[1]

Discomfort, defensiveness, and fear come, in part, from trying to avoid guilt and blame, which will hold us back from ever starting the discussion until we find a way to reduce the risk. The key to that is to understand what makes talking about privilege *seem* so risky, by which I don't mean that the risk isn't real, but that there is no way to engage these issues without ever feeling uncomfortable or frightened or threatened. The risk, however, is not as big as it seems, because, like the supposed human fear of the strange and unfamiliar, the problem begins with how we think about it and who we are in relation to it.

Individualism: Or, the Myth That Everything Bad is Somebody's Fault

We live in a culture that encourages us to think that the social world consists of nothing more than individuals, as if an organization or community or even a society is just a collection of people, and everything that happens begins and ends with what each of us thinks, feels, and intends.

If we understand individuals, the reasoning goes, then we also understand social life, which is an appealing way to think—being grounded in what we know best—which is our experience as individuals. But it also gets us into trouble by boxing us in to a narrow and distorted view of reality.

Which is to say, it isn't true.

If we use individualism to explain sexism, for example, it's hard to avoid the idea that sexism exists simply because men *are* sexist, that sexist feelings, beliefs, needs, and motivations are aspects of who men are and make them behave in sexist ways. If sexism produces bad consequences, it's because men *are* bad, consciously hostile and malevolent toward women.

In short, every bad consequence is always somebody's fault, which is why talk about privilege and oppression so often turns into a game of hot potato that encourages women, for example, to blame men, and sets men up to feel attacked if anyone mentions gender issues—including men's violence against women—and to define those issues as a women's problem. It also encourages men who do not think or behave in overtly sexist ways—the ones most likely to become part of the solution—to conclude that sexism has nothing to do with them, that it's just a problem for a few bad men. And if well-intentioned men don't include themselves in the problem, they're unlikely to go out of their way to make themselves part of the solution.

Individualistic thinking also makes us blind to the very existence of privilege, which, by definition, is not about who we are as individuals, but the social categories people put us in. Individualistic thinking, however, assumes that everything has *only* to do with individuals and *nothing* to do with social systems and their categories, leaving no room to see, much less consider, the role of privilege and oppression in social life.

Breaking the paralysis begins with realizing that the social world consists of far more than individuals. We are always participating in something larger than ourselves—social systems—and systems are not collections of people. A university, for example, is a system in which people participate, but people are not the university, and the university is not a collection of people. This means that to understand what happens—from classroom dynamics, faculty and staff diversity and graduation rates to football games and Saturday night parties—we have to look at both the university and how individual people participate in it. In the same way, patterns of privilege and oppression are never just a matter of people's personalities, feelings, or intentions. Those things certainly matter; but we also have to understand how they result from our participation in particular kinds of systems, which shapes both our behavior and its consequences.

Individuals, Systems, and Paths of Least Resistance

To understand how patterns of privilege and oppression happen, we must first understand the dynamic between people and systems of privilege. As the figure below shows, this has two parts. The arrow on the right represents the idea that as we participate in systems, we are shaped as individual people in two ways. Through the process of socialization we learn to participate in social life. From families, schools, religion, and the mass media, through the examples set by parents, peers, coaches, teachers, and public figures, we are exposed to ideas and images of the world and who we are in relation to them and other people. We learn to name things and people, to value one thing or kind of person over another, to distinguish what's considered "normal" and acceptable from what is not.

We also develop a sense of personal identity—including gender, sex, race, ethnicity, class, religion, disability status, and sexual orientation—and how that positions us in relation to other people and social systems, especially in terms of inequalities of power. As I grew up watching movies and television, for example, one message that came through loud and clear was that heterosexual white men are the most important people on the planet, because they are the ones routinely shown doing the most important things. They are the strong ones who build; the heroes who fight the good fight; the geniuses, writers, and artists who create; the decisive leaders who govern; and even the evil—but always interesting—villains. Even God is gendered male and racialized as white.

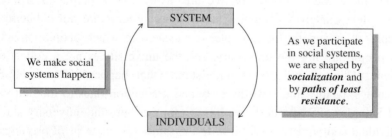

Figure 2. Individuals and Systems.

Among the many consequences of such messages is to encourage dominant groups to feel a sense of entitlement in relation to everyone else. Men are encouraged to expect women to take care of them, to defer to and support them no matter how badly they behave. In a typical episode of the television sitcom *Everybody Loves Raymond,* for example, Ray Barone routinely behaves toward his wife, Debra, in ways that are insensitive, sexist, adolescent, and downright stupid, but by the end of each half hour we see (yet again) that she puts up with it, year after year, because, for reasons that are never made clear, she just loves the guy. This sends the message that it is reasonable for a heterosexual man to expect to "have" an intelligent and beautiful woman who will love him and stay with him regardless of how he behaves.

Invariably, some of what we learn through socialization turns out not to be true, and then we may have to deal with that. I say "may" because powerful forces encourage us to remain in a state of ignorance and denial. We do this when we adopt the dominant version of reality as if it were the only version available. We rationalize what we've learned in order to keep it safe from scrutiny and to protect our sense of who we are, all in the hope of being accepted by other people, including family, peers, teachers, and employers.

In addition to socialization, we are shaped by a system's paths of least resistance, which present us with the easiest course to follow in any given situation. There are an almost limitless number of things a human being could do at any moment. Sitting in a movie theater, for example, we could go to sleep, sing, eat dinner, undress, dance, surf the Internet, carry on loud cell phone conversations, or dribble a basketball up and down the aisles—to name just a few. All of these paths vary in how much social resistance we'd run into if we followed them, with the odds loaded toward those paths with the *least.* We often choose a path of least resistance because it's the only one we see, as when we get on an elevator and turn and face front along with everyone else. It rarely occurs to us to do it any other way, such as facing the rear, and if we did, we'd soon be reminded how some paths bring on more resistance than others.

I once tested this idea by walking to the rear of an elevator and standing with my back toward the door. As the seconds went by, I could feel people looking at me, wondering what I was up to and wanting me to turn around. You could say that I was just standing there minding my own business, but I was also violating a social norm that makes facing the door a path of least resistance. The path is there all the time—it's built into riding the elevator as a social situation—but the path wasn't clear until I stepped onto a different one and felt the resistance rise up against it.

Similar dynamics operate around issues of privilege. In many workplaces, for example, the only way to get promoted is to have a mentor or sponsor see you as someone with potential and bring you along, teaching you what you need to know and acting as your advocate who opens doors and creates opportunities. In a society that separates and privileges groups in various ways, there are few opportunities to get comfortable with people across lines of difference, setting up a path of least resistance that leads managers to feel drawn to employees who resemble them, who are most often white, heterosexual, nondisabled, and male.

Managers who fit this profile probably won't even realize they are following a path of least resistance, one that is always shaping their choices, until they're asked to mentor someone they don't resemble. The greater resistance to the path of mentoring across difference may result from something as subtle as feeling uncomfortable in the other person's presence, but that is all it takes to make the relationship ineffective—or to ensure that it never happens in the first place.[2] And as each manager follows the path to mentor and support those most like themselves, systemic patterns of privilege and oppression are perpetuated, regardless of what people consciously feel or intend.

In other cases, people may know alternative paths exist, but they stay on the path of least resistance for fear of what will happen if they don't. When managers are told to lay off large numbers of workers, for example, they may hate the assignment and feel a great deal of distress and not want to do it, but the path of *least* resistance is to do as they are told, rather than to put themselves at risk. To make it less unpleasant, they may use euphemisms like "downsizing" and "outplacement" and "letting people go" to soften the painful reality of taking away people's means of making a living. (Note in this example how the path of least resistance is not necessarily an easy one to follow.)

In similar ways, a man may feel uncomfortable when he hears a friend tell a sexist joke or sees that same friend taking advantage of a woman too drunk to say no to sex she doesn't want. He may feel compelled to object in some way, but the path of least resistance may be to leave it be and avoid the risk of being ostracized or ridiculed for siding with a woman against a man, especially one who is his friend, and making *him* feel uncomfortable.

The other half of the relationship between individuals and systems (the left arrow in the figure) represents the idea that as we participate in a social system, we make it happen. A college, for example, is a system that does not "happen" until students and staff and faculty come together and perform their roles in relation to one another. Since people make a system happen, they can also make it happen differently, changing the consequences as well.

In 1960, for example, four African American students in Greensboro, North Carolina, entered a Woolworth's lunch counter that, like most such stores across the South, had a policy of not serving people of color. Having previously been denied service, the students had decided to come in one day and sit down on stools and ask to see menus, stepping off the path of least resistance as a way to challenge this aspect of the system of white privilege. In the days that followed, they were threatened and abused both physically and verbally, but they held their ground and were eventually joined by others until the sit-in occupied the entire restaurant. Soon, similar actions began in communities across the South, and within six months, lunch counters in twenty six cities had been successfully desegregated and segregation was being challenged in public facilities such as swimming pools, libraries, and theaters.[3]

Social life, then, works through the dynamic relationship between individuals and systems and cannot be understood by looking at either one alone. To see what I mean, consider the game of Monopoly, in which a player wins by taking everything from the other players—all their money and property—and forcing them out of the game, at which point the winner is supposed to feel good for having won, that being the point of the game and the only reason to play it. Why, after all, land on a property and not buy it, or own a property and not improve it, or have other players land on your property and not collect the rent?

How do we understand such patterns of greedy behavior? Do we behave in greedy ways simply because we *are* greedy? In a sense, the answer is yes, in that greed is part of the human repertoire of possible motivations, just like compassion, altruism, and fear. But how, then, do we explain the fact that people often do not behave in such ruthless and greedy ways when they're not playing Monopoly? To understand such differences in behavior, it's not enough to focus only on our thoughts and feelings, intentions and personalities, because we are the same people from one situation to another. Clearly, the answer has to include *both* ourselves as individuals capable of making all kinds of choices *and* something about the situation in which we make them. It is not one or the other. It is *both* in *relation* to each other.

If we think of Monopoly as a social system—something larger than ourselves in which we participate—then we can see how people and systems come together in a dynamic relationship that produces patterns of social life, including privilege and oppression. People make social systems happen. If no one plays Monopoly, it's just a box full of stuff with writing inside the cover. When we open it up and identify ourselves as players, however, Monopoly begins to *happen*. People are essential to that, but we should not confuse them with Monopoly itself. We are not the game and game isn't us.

But *how* do we make it happen? How do we know what to do? How do we choose from the millions of things that, as human beings, we could do? The answer is the other half of the dynamic relationship between individuals and systems, through which we make the game happen from one minute to the next, at the same time that our participation shapes how *we* happen as people—the experience of what we think and feel and do. This doesn't mean that systems control us in a rigid and predictable way, like robots, but that they are organized in ways that load the odds in certain directions through paths of least resistance.

This is how social life happens through a complex dynamic between systems—families, schools, workplaces, communities, entire societies—and the choices people make as they participate and make them happen. How we experience the world and ourselves, our sense of other people, and the ongoing reality of the systems themselves, all arise, take shape, and happen through this dynamic.

And, of course, social life produces all kinds of consequences, including privilege and oppression.

What It Means to Be Involved in Privilege and Oppression

If we use the relationship between individuals and systems as a model for understanding ourselves and the world, it's easier to bring problems into the open where we can see both of them in relation to us and ourselves in relation to them.

A white woman, for example, who uses an individualistic model of the world, and is told that she is "involved" in racism, is likely to hear that as an accusation of being a racist person who harbors ill will toward people of color. From an individualistic perspective, "racist" is a word that points to a moral failure or personality flaw and is even a matter of conscious intent, because individualism divides the world into different kinds of people— good and bad. It encourages us to think of the isms as a kind of disease that infects people and makes them sick. And so we look for a cure that will turn diseased, flawed individuals into healthy, good ones, or at least isolate them so they cannot infect anyone else. And if we cannot cure them, then we can at least try to control their behavior through rules and laws.

But what about everyone else? Who are they in relation to privilege and oppression? What about the white people, for example, who tell survey interviewers that they are not racist and have nothing against people of color, who even voted for Barack Obama not once, but twice? Or what about the majority of men who say they would never rape anyone and support an Equal Rights Amendment to the U.S. Constitution? From an individualistic perspective, if you are not consciously or overtly prejudiced or hurtful, then you are not part of the problem. You might show disapproval of those people who are, and even try to help those who are hurt as a result. Beyond that, however, the trouble doesn't have anything to do with you.

But there is more, because patterns of oppression and privilege are rooted in systems that we all participate in and make happen every day, consciously or not. When science professors take more seriously students who are male, for example, they don't have to be self-consciously sexist in order to help perpetuate patterns of male privilege.[4] They don't have to be bad people in order to play a "game" that produces bad consequences. As with Monopoly, the consequences are predictable so long as most people follow the paths of least resistance most of the time, *because that is how the system is organized to work.* The only way to change the outcome is to change how we see and play the game and, eventually, change the game itself and its paths of least resistance.

Of course there are people in the world who have hatred in their hearts, who go out of their way to harass, beat, rape, or kill, and it is important not to minimize how dangerous they are. Paradoxically, however, they are not the key to understanding privilege or doing something about it. They are participating in something larger than themselves that, among other things, steers them toward certain targets for their rage. It is no accident that they rarely target privileged groups, but instead single out those who are culturally devalued and excluded. Hate crime perpetrators may have personality disorders that bend them toward victimizing *someone,* but their choice of whom to victimize is not part of any mental illness. That is something they have to learn, and culture is everyone's most powerful teacher. In choosing targets, they follow paths of least resistance built into a society that everyone participates in, that everyone makes happen, regardless of how we feel or what we intend.

So, if we notice that someone plays Monopoly in a particularly ruthless way, we have to ask how a system like Monopoly rewards such ruthless behavior more than do other games. We have to ask how it loads the odds in favor of such behavior by creating conditions that make it a path of least resistance, normal and unremarkable, even to be admired. And since we are playing the game, too, we are among those who make it happen as a system, and its paths must affect us, too.

Our first reaction might be to deny that we follow those paths. We're not ruthless, greedy people. But this misses the key difference between systems and those who participate in them: we don't have to be ruthless people in order to support or follow paths of least resistance that lead to behavior with ruthless consequences. After all, we are all trying to win only because that is the point of the game. However gentle and kind we are as we take their money when they land on our Boardwalk with its hotel, take it we will and gladly, too. "Thank you," we say in our most sincerely unruthless tone, or even "Sorry," as we drive them out of the game by taking their last dollar and their mortgaged properties. Us, ruthless? Not at all. We're just playing the game the way it's supposed to be played. And even if we don't try that hard to win, the mere fact that we play at all supports and legitimates the game and its paths of least resistance, making it seem normal and acceptable, especially if we are silent about the consequences.

This is how most systems work and how most people participate, including systems of privilege. Good people with good intentions make systems happen in ways that produce all kinds of injustice, inequity, and suffering. Reminders of this are everywhere. I see it, for example, every time I look at the label in a piece of clothing. I just went upstairs to my closet and noted where each of my shirts was made. Although each carries a U.S. brand name, only three were actually made here. The rest were made in the Philippines, Thailand, Mexico, Taiwan, Macao, Singapore, or Hong Kong. And, of the amounts I paid, it's a good bet that the people who made them—primarily women and children—received pennies for their labor performed under terrible conditions that resemble slavery. The same can be said for many electronic devices, as was revealed about Apple's production of iPads and iPhones in China under conditions harsh enough to drive some workers to suicide.[5]

The only reason to exploit workers in such horrible ways is to maximize profit in a capitalist system, and to judge from the iPad on my desk, that clearly includes money that came from me. I do not intend by my purchase that people should suffer for it, but I do not have to have that intention in order to participate in a system that nonetheless results in that suffering.

But isn't our participation a mere drop in the bucket? Does it matter?

The question makes me think of the devastating floods of 1993 along the Mississippi and Missouri rivers. The news was full of images of people from all walks of life working feverishly side by side to build dikes to hold back the raging waters that threatened their communities. Together, they filled and placed tens of thousands of sandbags, and when the waters finally receded, much had been lost, but a great deal had been saved. I think about how it must have felt to be one of those people, how proud they must have been, the satisfying sense of solidarity with the people with whom they had labored. The sandbags that each individual contributed were the tiniest fraction of the whole—drops in the bucket—and yet they were part of a collective effort that made an extraordinary difference.

It works that way with good things that come out of people pulling together to participate in the systems that make up our social lives. It also works that way with the bad things, with each "sandbag" adding to the problem instead of the solution.

To perpetuate privilege and oppression, we don't have to consciously support it. Even by our silence, we provide something essential for its future, for no system of privilege can continue to exist without most people's consent. If most men spoke out against other men's violence, for example, or if most whites stood openly against racism, it would be a critical first step toward revolutionary change. But the vast majority of us are silent, and the path of least resistance is to read that silence as consent and even support.

As long as we participate in social systems, we do not get to choose whether to be involved in the consequences that result. We are involved because we are here. As such, we can only choose *how* to be involved, whether to simply be a part of the problem or to *also* to be part of the solution. That is where our power lies, and our responsibility.

CHAPTER 7

How Systems of Privilege Work

What kind of social system would lay down paths of least resistance such that, if most people follow them most of the time, the result will be the patterns of privilege and oppression described in previous chapters? How would it be organized and what would distinguish it from other systems? And what do the characteristics of such a system tell us about the individuals who participate in it and make it happen? The answer to this last question is, very little, for if we look at the game of Monopoly, for example, we can describe it without ever talking about the characteristics of people who might play it. We can do the same with any system, whether it's a family, a community, a society, or global capitalism.

Systems organized around privilege have three key features: they are *dominated by* privileged groups, *identified with* privileged groups, and *centered on* privileged groups. All three characteristics support the idea that members of privileged groups are superior to those below them and, therefore, deserve the advantages that come with it. A patriarchy, for example, is male dominated, male identified, and male centered,[1] just as ableism works through systems that are dominated by, identified with, and centered on nondisabled people.

Dominance and Control

In systems of privilege, the default is for power to be held by members of dominant groups, and to be identified with them in ways that make it seem appropriate for them to have it.

In a patriarchy, for example, power is gendered through its cultural association with men and manhood. This makes power look natural on a man but unusual and even problematic on a woman, marking her as an exception to be scrutinized and explained. When Margaret Thatcher was prime minister of Great Britain, for example, she was often referred to as "the Iron Lady," drawing attention to both her strength as a leader and the need to mark it as an exception. There would be no such need to mark a strong male prime minister ("Iron Man," for example), because his power would be assumed. In similar ways, for someone like Hillary Clinton to become president of the United States, she would have to prove that she could satisfy the requirements of manhood even though she was not male, a burden of proof that did not apply to her husband when he became president.

This kind of thinking supports a structure that routinely allocates power to men. In almost every organization, the farther down you look in the power structure, the more numerous women are. The higher up you go, the fewer women you will find. This is what a male-dominated system looks like.

Just because a system is male-dominated doesn't mean all men are powerful. Most men are not, spending their days doing what others tell them to do whether they want to or not. Male dominance does mean, however, that every man can *identify* with power as a cultural value associated with manhood, and this makes it easier for any man to assume and use power in relation to others. It also encourages a sense of entitlement in expecting women to meet men's personal needs, whether listening or getting coffee or providing sex.

Since women are culturally *dis*identified with power, it's harder for them to make use of it without being challenged. Female professors, for example, often tell stories of having their authority, expertise, and professional commitment routinely questioned not only by colleagues, but by students, men in particular, who may argue or question every point and feel free to interrupt.[2] They may go so far as to comment on her physical appearance or turn away, roll their eyes, go to sleep, or hold side conversations.

"I'm still routinely asked if I've ever taught the course before," says one seasoned female professor. "They look utterly shocked when I say I've taught most of my courses 15–18 years—sometimes longer than they've been alive."[3]

Powerful women—whether news anchors or presidential candidates—are routinely made the object of sexist humor and judgments of their physical appearance. They are open to being called bitches or lesbians as a way to discredit and negate their power.[4] When women gather together, even just for lunch, men may suspect them of "being up to something"—planning a subversive use of power that needs to be monitored and contained. Men's anxiety over this may come out as humor ("What little plot are you hatching?"), but the gender dynamic underlying male dominance and women's potential to subvert it is clearly there. In the home—the one place where women can somewhat consistently manage to carve out some power for themselves— even here, their power is routinely seen as problematic in ways that men's power in relation to women is not. The abundance of insulting terms for men who are dominated by women, for example, and the absence of such terms for comparable women show clearly how patriarchal culture legitimizes male dominance.

The fact that patriarchy is male-dominated also doesn't mean that most men have domineering personalities and need or want to control others. In other words, "male dominance" is not a term used to describe men, but rather the patriarchal system in which both men and women participate, including the gendered patterns of unequal power and the paths of least resistance that support them.

For men, such paths include trying to appear in control of themselves, others, and events. I am aware of this path, for example, in how I feel drawn to respond to questions whether I know the answer or not, to interrupt in conversations, to avoid admitting that I'm wrong, to take up room in public spaces. One day some years ago, my spouse, Nora, and I were having a conversation about something that began when she raised a question. I responded right away and went on until she interrupted to ask, "Do you actually know that, or are you just saying it?" I was startled to realize how easily I could say whatever was coming into my mind and without hesitation, as if I knew exactly what I was talking about.

But my answer to her question was no, I did not know that what I was saying was true, at least no more than what anyone else might say, provided, of course, I gave them the chance. This included her, who'd been sitting there listening to me as she followed a corresponding path for women: silent attentiveness, hesitation, self-doubt, humility, deference, supporting what men say and do, and taking up as little space as possible. When she stepped off that path, she shook an entire structure by revealing its existence and how both of us were participating in it. She also raised the possibility of alternative paths—of men learning about silence and listening, doubt and uncertainty, supporting others and sharing space.

Why call such patterns of control and deference "paths of least resist-ance"? Why not say that men have controlling personalities or that women naturally tend to be unassertive? The answer is that we all swim in a dominant culture that is full of images of men seeking control, taking up time and space, competing with other men, and living with a sense of entitlement in relation to women. And each of those is matched by images of women letting men do all of that, if not encouraging them or even insisting on it. The images permeate popular culture—from film and television to advertising and literature—and shape the news, from politics to sports.

What these images do is place a value on male power and control that serves as a standard for evaluating men in almost every aspect of their lives. Men who live up to it are routinely rewarded with approval, while men who seem insufficiently manly are vulnerable to ridicule and scorn, primarily from other men.[5] And so if I feel drawn to control a conversation or to always have an answer, it isn't simply because I am a controlling *person,* no more than greedy behavior happens in a Monopoly game just because people are greedy.

This is what Deborah Tannen misses in her widely read books that describe how gender differences in talking styles enable men to control conversations.[6] In Tannen's explanation of why this is so, she ignores how those differences promote male privilege at women's expense. Instead, she argues that women and men talk differently because as children they played in same-sex groups and learned from their peers distinctively male or female ways of speaking. What she does not tell us is how those peers happened to acquire their gendered styles of talking. The answer is that they learned them from adults in families, the mass media, and in school. In other words, they learned by participating in a society where conversation is one of the arenas in which male privilege is enacted.

Patterns of dominance and control and the paths of least resistance that sustain them show up in every system of privilege. White dominance, for example, is reflected in an unequal racial balance of power in society and its organizations and institutions. The same is true of heterosexuality, although so many lesbians and gay men may still be in the closet that it's hard to be sure about the sexual orientation of people in power.

The result of such patterns of dominance and control is that if you are female, of color, or in some other way on the outside of privilege, when you look upward in most power structures you rarely see people like you. Your interests are not represented where power is wielded and rewards are distributed, and you get no encouragement to imagine yourself as one of those with access to power and its influence and rewards. Those who do not look like people in power will often feel invisible—and in fact *be* invisible— because they are routinely overlooked. This was true for people of color even with the election of Barack Obama as president of the United States. Not only did negative perceptions of blacks increase among whites, but as president of a white-dominated society, it was politically impossible for him to advocate on behalf of people of color. This illustrates how even the most exalted success of individuals in subordinate groups is not enough to change the oppressed status of the groups themselves, which is a major way in which systems of privilege continue.

Identified with Privilege

"It's a man's world" is an expression that points in part to the male-dominated character of society that puts power in the hands of men, just as one could say that it's a white world or a straight world or a nondisabled world. But there is more than power at work here, because privileged groups are also considered to be the standard of what is considered normal and socially valued. This is what it means to say that a system is male- or white-identified.

On most college campuses, for example, students of color feel pressured to talk, dress, and act like middle-class whites in order to fit in and be accepted.[7] In similar ways, most workplaces define appropriate appearance and ways of speaking in terms culturally associated with being white, from clothing and hairstyles to diction and slang. People of color often experience being marked as outsiders, to the extent that many navigate the social world by consciously changing how they talk from one situation to another, a phenomenon known as code switching.[8] In shopping for an apartment over the telephone, for example, many African Americans know they have to "talk white" in order to be accepted (which may come to nothing once they show up in person and are told the apartment has been rented).[9]

Because privileged groups are assumed to represent humanity and society as a whole, "American" is culturally defined as white, in spite of the diversity of the population. You can see this in a statement like "Americans must learn to be more tolerant of other races." I doubt that most people would see this as saying that we need Asians to be more tolerant of whites or blacks to be more tolerant of Native Americans. The "Americans" are assumed to be white, and the "other races" are assumed to be races *other* than white. "Other" is the key word in understanding how systems are identified with privileged groups, the assumed "we" in relation to "them." The "other" is the "you people" whom the "we" regard as problematic, unacceptable, unlikable, or beneath "our" standards.

Note also how such assumptions operate on a larger scale in my use of "American" in the preceding paragraph. People in the United States routinely refer to themselves as Americans, as if "America" and "United States" mean the same thing. But they do not. "America" refers to the entire western hemisphere—South, Central, and North America—and "American" includes many societies in addition to our own. (In fact, Amerigo Vespucci, the Italian on whose name "America" is based, never even saw North America, not getting farther north than Brazil.) The implication that only citizens of the United States are Americans encourages the perception of everyone else as "other" and reflects dynamics of privilege and oppression among nations.

In a white-identified system, white is the assumed race unless something other than white is marked—hence the common use of "nonwhite" to lump together various peoples of color into a single category in relation to a white standard. (To get a sense of the effect of this practice, imagine a society in which whites are referred to routinely as "noncoloreds.")

White identification means that whether one is arrested for a crime or wins a Nobel Prize, whites are rarely if ever identified *as* white, because it is assumed. For everyone else, however, racial tags are common, from "black president" and "black physician" to "Latina writer" and "Asian actor." If a group of white citizens marched on Washington to protest a policy that had nothing to do with race, news reports would not mention their race, nor try to figure out the significance of their all being white. The protesters would simply be described as citizens or protesters or members of an organization. If a group of Chicanas/os did the same thing, however, they would be identified as such and asked why there were no whites among them. And this isn't because Chicanas/os stand out as a numerical minority, since the same pattern would hold for women, who would be tagged as women even though they outnumber men in the population.

Such patterns of identification are especially powerful in relation to gender. It is still common to use masculine pronouns to refer to people in general, or to use "guys" to refer to women and men alike, or "man" to refer both to males and to the entire species (as in "mankind"). In a similar way, men and manhood are held up as the standards for humanity. The idea of brotherhood, for example, is clearly gendered, since women cannot be brothers (or guys) by any stretch of the imagination, yet it also carries powerful cultural meaning about *human* connection, as in "America the Beautiful," "And crown thy good with brotherhood from sea to shining sea."[10] Brotherhood is defined as a quality of human relation (see the table, opposite) that embodies warmth and good feeling, especially across social differences. It is linked to the idea of fellowship—the general human capacity for companionship, common interest or feeling, friendliness, and communion—which is based on being a fellow, which is also clearly defined as male. By comparison, although African American women have made powerful use of the idea of sisterhood, in a patriarchal culture it amounts to little more than the biological fact of being someone's sister, which is to say, being female and sharing the same set of parents. Its other meanings are narrowly confined to groups of women—such as nuns and feminists— even when it refers to the quality of relationships.

In short, in a patriarchal culture, to be male is to be human, while women are merely women. So, when she is celebrated at the office and everyone joins in a round of "For She's a Jolly Good Fellow," no one laughs or objects to the oxymoron, because in a male-identified society, it's an honor to be considered "one of the guys," to be associated with men and the standards by which men are measured. Nor are many people disturbed by the fact that there are no words that associate women with a quality of human relation in the way that "fellow" and "fellowship" do for men. Consider in contrast the reaction we might expect if we changed the words of "America the Beautiful" to "crown thy good with sisterhood."[11]

Male identification is woven into every aspect of social life. Most high-status occupations, for example, are organized around qualities associ- ated with masculinity and manhood, such as aggression, competitiveness, emotional detachment, and control. This is what it takes to succeed in law, medicine, science, academia, politics, sports, or business. No woman (or man) is likely to become a corporate manager, get tenure at a university, or be elected to public office by emphasizing their capacity for cooperation,

The Word "Brotherhood" as an Instance of Male-Identified Language

Sisterhood	Brotherhood
1. The state of being a sister.	1. The condition or quality of being a brother.
2. A group of sisters, especially of nuns or of female members of a church.	2. The quality of being brotherly, **fellow**ship.
3. An organization of women with a common interest.	3. A fraternal or trade organization.
4. Congenial relationship or companionship among women.	4. All those engaged in a particular trade or profession or sharing a common interest or quality.
5. Community or network of women who participate in support of feminism.	5. The belief that all people should act with warmth and equality toward one another regardless of differences in race, creed, nationality, etc.

Fellow	Fellowship
A man or boy.	1. The condition or relation of being a fellow; the fellowship of humankind.
	2. Friendly relationship.

sharing, emotional sensitivity, and nurturing. This also applies to the most highly rewarded blue-collar jobs, such as policing, firefighting, and skilled construction trades.

This puts women in a bind. If they pattern themselves on ideals that are culturally defined as feminine, they are likely to be seen as not having what it takes to get ahead in a male-identified world. But if they pursue a more masculine path toward success, they open themselves to being judged as not feminine enough—uncaring, cold, a bitch. Students usually hold their female college professors, for example, to a higher standard of caring and emotional availability than they do male teachers. But if a woman professional comes across as *too* warm and caring, her credibility, competence, and authority are invariably at risk of being undermined and challenged. In a male-identified system, she cannot fit the model of a successful professional or manager and at the same time measure up as a real woman. It is the kind of classic double bind that is one of the hallmarks of social oppression—she runs a risk of being devalued no matter what she does.[12]

The world of work is also male-identified in the definition of a career and the timing of key stages in the route to success. In most organizations, for example, the idea of a career assumes an almost complete commitment to work, making it impossible to have both a career and a family without someone to take care of children and other domestic responsibilities. Despite all the talk about "the new fatherhood," this almost always means a woman. Furthermore, the key years for establishing a career overlap with a woman's best years for starting a family. In this way, "serious" work is structured to fit the demands of most men's lives far more easily and with far less conflict than most women's lives.[13] So "profession" and "career" are words that on the surface don't appear to be gendered, but are in fact male-identified.

Male identification shows up in more subtle ways as well, from popular culture to the comings and goings of everyday life. In Ken Burns's PBS documentary on baseball, for example, he tells us that "Baseball defines who we are," apparently not giving much thought to who "we" includes. I doubt he meant that baseball defines who women are or how they see their society. But if the statement is likely to ring true for men, then, in a male-identified world, it is assumed that it rings true for everyone who matters.

In this way, male identification can make women invisible, just as white and nondisabled identification tend to make people of color or with disabilities invisible. The other day I made an airline reservation and the clerk gave me a confirmation code. "PWCEO," she said, and then, to make sure I had gotten it right, added, "That's Peter, William, Charles, Edward, Oscar."

The Center of Attention

Because systems are identified with privileged groups, the path of least resistance is to focus attention on them—who they are, what they do and say, and how they do it. In the news you will find that the vast majority of people pictured, quoted, and discussed are men who also happen to be heterosexual, white, and middle or upper class. If Latinos/as, white women, or African Americans are there, it is usually because of something that's been done to them (murdered, for example) or something they've done wrong (rioted, murdered, stolen, cheated, and so on). There are exceptions, of course—a Barack Obama as president or Hillary Clinton as candidate, or a Sonia Sotomayor on the U.S. Supreme Court or black athletes—the latter being one of the few areas where people of color are allowed to excel. But exceptions are what they are.

To judge from television and film, most of what happens of significance in the world happens to heterosexual, white, nondisabled men.[14] It is rare to see a film or television show in which the most powerful character is identified as female, gay, lesbian, transgender, with a disability, working class, or African American, Latino/a, or Asian, or if they are, to have them still be alive when the credits roll. Working-class characters are rarely the focus, and when they do appear they are typically portrayed as criminals or as ignorant, crude, bigoted, shallow, and immoral.[15] People of color are rarely cast in prominent roles, while a powerful gay man is seen as a contradiction in terms and powerful lesbians are routinely dismissed as not being real women at all.

As an experiment, make a list of what you regard as the ten most important movies ever made, movies that reflect something powerful about the human experience, about courage and personal transformation, the journey of the soul, the testing of character, finding out who we really are and what life is all about. Once you have your list, identify the key character in each, the one whose courage, transformation, journey, testing, and revelations are the point of the story. Chances are that at least nine out of ten will be white, Anglo, nondisabled, heterosexual males, even though they are less than twenty percent of the population.

My version of this experiment was to list the films that have won the Oscar for best picture over the last fifty years (see the following table). Of these, all of which were judged better and more important than all the rest, not one set in the United States places people of color at the center of the story without their having to share it with white characters of equal importance (*Driving Miss Daisy* and *In the Heat of the Night*). The one film that focuses on Native Americans (*Dances with Wolves*) is told from a white man's point of view with Native Americans clearly identified as "other." Only three focus on non-European cultures (*The Last Emperor, Slum Dog Millionaire*, and *Gandhi*). Although *Out of Africa* is set in Africa, the story focuses exclusively on whites

Academy Award Winning Films in the Category "Best Picture," 1965–2015

2015	*Spotlight*	1989	*Driving Miss Daisy*
2014	*Birdman*	1988	*Rain Man*
2013	*Twelve Years a Slave*	1987	*The Last Emperor*
2012	*Argo*	1986	*Platoon*
2011	*The Artist*	1985	*Out of Africa*
2010	*The King's Speech*	1984	*Amadeus*
2009	*The Hurt Locker*	1983	*Terms of Endearment*
2008	*Slumdog Millionaire*	1982	*Gandhi*
2007	*No Country for Old Men*	1981	*Chariots of Fire*
2006	*The Departed*	1980	*Ordinary People*
2005	*Crash*	1979	*Kramer vs. Kramer*
2004	*Million Dollar Baby*	1978	*The Deer Hunter*
2003	*Lord of the Rings*	1977	*Annie Hall*
2002	*Chicago*	1976	*Rocky*
2001	*A Beautiful Mind*	1975	*One Flew Over the Cuckoo's Nest*
2000	*Gladiator*		
1999	*American Beauty*	1974	*The Godfather, Part II*
1998	*Shakespeare in Love*	1973	*The Sting*
1997	*Titanic*	1972	*The Godfather, Part I*
1996	*The English Patient*	1971	*The French Connection*
1995	*Braveheart*	1970	*Patton*
1994	*Forrest Gump*	1969	*Midnight Cowboy*
1993	*Schindler's List*	1968	*Oliver!*
1992	*Unforgiven*	1967	*In the Heat of the Night*
1991	*The Silence of the Lambs*	1966	*A Man for All Seasons*
1990	*Dances with Wolves*	1965	*The Sound of Music*

and, without any critical comment, their exploitation of the African continent. This same list of films also contains only five that are female-centered (*Million-Dollar Baby, Chicago, Out of Africa, Terms of Endearment,* and *The Sound of Music*) and none with any major characters who are gay or lesbian.

When a film does focus on someone in a subordinate group, such as *Selma* and *The Color Purple*, it has little chance of drawing serious attention, much less winning the Academy Award. *Selma*, for example, won only the Oscar for best song, and, even though *The Color Purple* was nominated for eleven Academy Awards, it did not win a single one, losing to *Out of Africa*.

The handful of films that do focus on people in subordinate groups are likely to be tagged (and devalued) as "women's films" ("chick flicks") or "black films" or "gay films" or "lesbian films," even though all the rest are never called "men's films" or "white films" or "heterosexual films." In a society identified with dominant groups, such films are supposedly about everyone, or at least everyone who counts.

Films that focus on people with disabilities—*The King's Speech, Rain Man, Forrest Gump, A Beautiful Mind*—reflect an important aspect of this phenomenon. While the main character in each film has a disability, in every case the story is *about* the disability, rather than being a human story told through the life of a character who happens to have a disability. Similar things happen with films that focus on people of color—*Twelve Years a Slave, Crash, In the Heat of the Night* and *Driving Miss Daisy*—all have race as the central focus of the story. And if there is ever an Academy Award winning film whose main character is gay, lesbian, or transgender, we can be sure that sexual orientation and/or gender identity will be its major theme. Not so, however, with films that focus on members of dominant groups, whose stories are presented as those of the human being.

Because systems of privilege center on dominant groups, those who are excluded have reason to feel invisible, as if their lives are being erased from mainstream culture, because in an important social sense, they are.[16] Black, Latino/a, and white female students routinely report that instructors don't call on them in class, don't listen to what they say, or don't let them finish without interruption. Research shows that men receive the overwhelming majority of attention in classrooms at every level of education,[17] a pattern that repeats itself in the workplace and everywhere that women and men meet.

This happens in part because in a world that centers attention on men and what they do and say, the path of least resistance for men is to claim attention by, for example, calling out answers in class without being recognized, even thinking them up as they go along. When men don't jump in, teachers tend to gravitate toward them anyway, standing closer to them in the room, looking to them for the most interesting or productive answers, challenging and coaching them more than women, all the while assuming that women won't say something worth hearing.[18] None of this has to be done consciously in order to center attention on dominant groups at the expense of everyone else.

It simply follows a well-traveled path of least resistance that puts visibility and invisibility at the heart of privilege and oppression.

Often the only way marginalized groups can get attention is to make an issue of how social life is centered on dominant groups. Women form their own support groups at work or attend women's colleges where they do not have to overcome the cultural weight of male centeredness. Blacks form their own dorms or clubs or "safe spaces" on campus and sit at their own tables in the dining hall.[19] Schools create special programs that focus on women or people of color. Women participate in a "Take Our Daughters to Work" day, or people who are LGBT organize pride marches to draw attention to the simple fact that they exist ("We are everywhere").

Drawing attention away from dominant groups—even the slightest deviation—can be seen as unfair, a loss of something to which they are entitled, provoking a demand to return the focus to themselves. As long as men overwhelmingly dominate conversations, for example, the participation of women and men is perceived as roughly equal. But if women's talk rises to as little as a quarter or a third of the total interaction, men tend to perceive the women as taking over. Such perceived shifts can result in howls of protest over the unfairness of giving subordinate groups "special" attention—"Why not a 'Take Our Sons to Work Day'?" "Why do gays and lesbians have to call attention to themselves?" "When do we get to have a White History Month?"

As so often happens, subordinate groups are in a double bind. If they do not call attention to themselves, the paths of least resistance make them invisible and devalued. If they do call attention to themselves, if they dare to put themselves at the center, they risk being accused of being pushy or seeking special treatment. This is why white women and people of color, for example, are often labeled "special-interest groups" with biased agendas, whereas men and whites are not.

The Isms

Most of the time, words like "racism," "sexism," "ableism," "transphobia," and "heterosexism" are used to describe how people feel and behave. Racism, for example, is seen as a flawed part of people's personalities, an attitude, a collection of stereotypes, a bad intention, a desire or need to discriminate or do harm, a form of hatred. From that perspective, doing something about racism means changing how individuals feel, think, and, as a result, behave.

But racism is also built into the systems in which people live and work. Given this reality, it doesn't make sense to ignore everything but personality and behavior, as if we live in a social vacuum. For this reason, sociologist David Wellman argues for a broader definition of racism that includes but also goes beyond the personal. Racism refers to the patterns of privilege and oppression themselves and *any*thing—intentional or not—that helps to create, enact, or perpetuate those patterns. If we extend this to other forms of privilege, then the isms point to more than personal hostility or prejudice and in fact include everything that people do or do not do that promotes privilege.[20]

To see what Wellman means, consider not only what people do or say, but also what they don't. Consider, for example, the power of silence to support and perpetuate privilege and oppression. Human beings depend on one another for standards of who is regarded as okay and who is not. Although there will always be those who don't care what other people think, most will avoid doing something that others would criticize. But if others are silent, then perpetrators are free to interpret that as support for what they do.

From the late 1800s through the mid-1940s, for example, white Southerners lynched more than three thousand African Americans.[21] The actual violence was done by a relatively small number of individuals, but they acted from the assumption that most people in their communities and states either approved of their actions or would not do anything to stop them even if they disapproved. Many lynchings were advertised in advance in newspapers and drew huge crowds, including families, people coming from a wide area, with pictures taken of the atrocities and later sold as postcards.[22]

Since the lynchers could not possibly know everyone in their community or state personally, in order for them to so confidently assume they would get away with it was to see themselves as living in a particular kind of society—white-dominated, white-identified, and white-centered—that placed such a low value on black people's lives that publicly torturing and killing them was unlikely to be made an issue, much less treated as a crime. The real power lay not with lynchers as individuals but with society and the great collective silence in the face of a racist horror, a silence that included the federal government, a silence that spoke as loudly as the violence itself, regardless of how people felt about it as individuals.[23]

Just as most whites, both North and South, were silent about lynching, the vast majority of men are silent on the issue of sexual harassment and violence and do nothing more than privately disapprove or assure themselves that they would never do such a thing. In the same way, most whites do nothing to raise consciousness about how racism works in their communities or workplaces. They may acknowledge overt behavior that perpetuates privilege and oppression. "Yes," they'll say when asked about discrimination, "it's a terrible thing." And they will mean it. But what they do not see most of the time is how silence and not looking and not asking are *in effect* just as racist as overt behaviors, because oppression depends on this collective silence in order to continue. White professors or managers who do not go out of their way to ask about race in classrooms or workplaces may be good people who would never act from ill will toward people of color. But how good or bad they are is beside the point, for what counts is not just what they do, but even more what they do not.[24]

When I think about this, I imagine a scene in which a gang of white men are beating a person of color in broad daylight on a city street. I am standing in a crowd of white people who are watching. We are not hurting anyone. We feel no ill will toward the man being beaten and may even feel sorry for him. We do not cheer the attackers or show any outward signs of approval. We just stand there in silence, minding what we think is our own business. And then one of the men stops, looks up, and says to us, "We want you to know that we appreciate your support. We couldn't do this without you."

This is an essential part of how racism and other forms of privilege persist day after day, the result of a kind of passive oppression that works by simply doing nothing to stop it. Most white people in the United States engage in racism not by acting from feelings or thoughts of racial hostility or ill will but "because they acquiesce in the large cultural order that continues the work of racism."[25] That is all that's required of most members of dominant groups for privilege and oppression in all their forms to continue—that they not notice, that they do nothing, that they remain silent.

The Isms and Us

It is tempting for members of dominant groups to suppose they could be raised in a society organized around privilege, and participate in it day after day, without being affected. But this is a dream that, for everyone else, is a nightmare of denial. There is no way to escape that kind of immersion unscathed, to be an exception who miraculously does not internalize any of the ideas, attitudes, or images that pour in a steady stream from the dominant culture and make privilege and oppression normal and regular features of everyday life.

In other words, on some level, *of course* I've internalized aspects of racism, sexism, ableism, and heterosexism in myself in the same way that I automatically dream in English and prefer certain foods. I wish it wasn't so, but it is. The assumption, for example, that some tendency toward racism resides in every white person, is a reasonable one in this society,[26] just as I would assume that everyone I meet speaks English until I was shown otherwise, and I make that assumption not based on what I know of them as individuals, but what I know about the culture of this society. In the same way, I would assume that racism touches and shapes everyone in one way or another and leaves a mark that cannot be erased. To assume otherwise is to engage in wishful thinking and live in a world that does not exist.

Although benefiting from privilege doesn't make someone a bad person, it does mean that no member of a dominant group escapes having issues of privilege to deal with both internally and in relation to the world around them. The system of privilege was handed to us when we were children with no sense of what was wise and good to take into ourselves and what was not. And so we accepted it, uncritically, unknowingly, even innocently, but accept it we did. It was not our fault. We have no reason to feel guilty about it, because we did not *do* anything. But now it is there for us to deal with, just as it is there for women, people of color, people with disabilities, people who are LGBT, who *also* did nothing to deserve the oppression that so profoundly shapes their lives.

CHAPTER 8

Getting Off the Hook: Denial and Resistance

No one likes to see themselves connected to injustice or someone else's suffering, no matter how remote the link, prompting us to look for ways to get ourselves off the hook. The fact is, however, that we are all of us on the hook every day, because there is no way to avoid being part of the problem, in spite of the paths of least resistance that may allow us to imagine we are not. The more aware we are, however, of all the ways there are to distract and fool ourselves, the more likely we are to wake up and work instead to become part of the solution.[1]

Deny and Minimize

Perhaps the simplest way to get off the hook is to deny it even exists.

"Racism and sexism aren't problems anymore. Younger generations don't have these issues."

"There is no such thing as privilege."

"The American Dream is available to anyone willing to work for it."

"There are no people with disabilities where I work, so it's not an issue."

"Affirmative action has turned the tables—if anyone's in trouble now, it's whites and men." Or, as a cover of the *Atlantic Monthly* proclaimed, "Girls Rule!"[2]

Shoulder to shoulder with denial is the tendency to minimize—by acknowledging that the trouble exists but then claiming that it doesn't amount to much. When women and people of color are accused of whining, for example, they are being told that whatever they have to deal with is not so bad, and they should just get over it. Denying the reality of oppression also denies the privilege that drives it, which is exactly what it takes to convince yourself that you're off the hook.

When dominant groups practice this kind of denial, it rarely seems to occur to them how poorly positioned they are to know what they're talking about when it comes to other people's lives. Adults do this all the time with children, as when a child falls down or wakes up from a nightmare and is told to stop crying, that it doesn't hurt that much or there's nothing to be afraid of, none of which may be true for the child. In similar ways, dominant groups are culturally authorized to impose their reality by interpreting other people's experience and denying the validity of their own accounts.

Denial also takes the form of seeing subordinate groups as the ones who are better off. I once knew a woman, for example, who would remark with a sense of envy on the qualities that black people have had to develop to survive in the face of centuries of racism. She sees in them a strength and depth of soul that she'd like to have herself. Whenever the subject of racism comes up, she will counter with a list of black advantages, as if weighing them against the privilege that comes with being white. Her tone mixes longing and resentment, as if she feels put upon to consider white privilege for even a moment when she feels such a lack in her own life. The paradoxical idea that envy and privilege can exist side by side does not occur to her, as she defends herself against seeing what she would rather not.

When denying the message doesn't work, a fallback position is to make it go away by attacking and discrediting the messenger. Over the years, for example, I have been accused of hating men, of hating white people and/or suffering from white guilt, of hating myself (being white and male), of being gay, a communist, a traitor to my sex, divisive, a racist, in league with the devil, and both an idiot and a moron. Such attacks are based on a profound difference in worldviews and the assumption that there can be only one such view; so how could someone express a view the opposite of my own and not have something wrong with them? This is paramount among the reasons the United States has become polarized and paralyzed by shouting matches in which opposing sides accuse each other not only of being wrong, but of acting from the worst of motives.[3]

When attacking the messenger doesn't work, more subtle forms of denial come into play—not feeling anything about the injustice and suffering, or feeling something but not seeing it as a moral issue or, failing that, denying there is anything we can do.[4]

Blame the Victim

We can acknowledge that terrible things happen to people and still get ourselves off the hook by blaming it all on them.[5] A man, for example, can tell himself that a woman who says she is sexually harassed is hypersensitive, or had no business being where she was, or was sending mixed signals, or that she "asked for it" in one way or another. If she fails to break through the glass ceiling, he can say she doesn't have the right stuff. If she allows herself to be openly emotional, he can point to that as a reason she hasn't reached the heights of her potential. And if she's *not* emotional, he can criticize her for not being "womanly" enough, too hard, too much like a man. If she is friendly, he can say she wants to have sex, and if she's not, then she's stuck up, cold, a bitch, and deserves whatever she gets.[6]

Blaming the victim is one of the most common and effective defenses of privilege. It is people of color being told that if only they were more like whites supposedly are, they would not have so much trouble, that their problem is being lazy and not minding poverty and living in high crime neighborhoods, or that if Latinos were smarter or worked harder or got an education, they'd be fine. It is people who are LGBT being told their problem is their choice of how to be who they are—not the response of everyone else to who they are. It is people with disabilities being told that what they can and cannot do is determined by the condition of their bodies and minds and not, also, by the narrow assumptions made by nondisabled people as they construct the social and physical world that everyone must navigate.

In a society organized around individualistic thinking, where everything bad must be somebody's fault, it is inevitable that dominant groups will use their authority to settle the blame on those least able to defend against it, who will then be the ones most likely to suffer as a result.

Call It Something Else

A more subtle way to deny an unpleasant reality is to call it something else, creating the appearance of being aware, but avoiding the obligation to do something about it. This occurs with all kinds of privilege—that segregated schools are about neighborhoods and not race, for example, or that people living in poverty are merely "less fortunate" or "underprivileged"—but the approach is especially powerful around issues of gender. Male privilege, for example, is often reduced to a charming battle of the sexes or biology or an anthropological curiosity, based on the idea that males and females come from different cultures, if not different planets. Or rape is portrayed as no more than a case of "bad sex" or a misunderstanding or boys being boys.

One reason for resorting to this subterfuge is that women and men depend on one another in ways that other groups do not. Most whites have no personal need for people of color, for example, but relationships across gender are the backbone of most people's lives. This is especially true for heterosexuals, but everyone has parents and most have siblings. How, then, do we live in such close quarters without confronting the painful reality of male privilege? In a patriarchal culture, the answer is that we see the world through a thick ideology of images and ideas that mask the reality of privilege and oppression by turning it into something else.

Men can find ways to make jokes, for example, about everything from violence against women to sex to who gets stuck with cleaning the house or changing the diapers. They can laugh about it in ways that would be unthinkable if the subject were race. This is not because gender oppression is less serious than other forms, but because it runs so deep in our lives that we must go to great lengths to make it appear normal, and so avoid seeing it for what it is.

It's Better This Way

The combination of denial and calling it something else often results in the claim that everyone actually prefers things the way they are. The thick ideology around male privilege, for example, is full of messages that women prefer strong men who dominate and make the "big" decisions; that when a woman says no to sex, she at least means maybe and probably yes; that women have only themselves to blame for being raped, harassed, or beaten; that male superiority is a natural arrangement dictated by biology, if not by God, and that men are meant to be the family breadwinners while women stay at home tending to children and keeping house.

It doesn't matter how much evidence is weighed against such beliefs, or how often women complain about male control or insist that no means no. It doesn't matter that women have been major breadwinners for virtually all of human history and that staying home and being supported by men is a historical anomaly that does not apply to the vast majority of people in the world, and never has.[7]

Rationalizing the status quo as something desirable for all also works around race, as when whites claim that people of color prefer to live in segregated neighborhoods, reflecting a supposedly natural tendency to choose the company of "your own kind." Segregation is also portrayed as a matter of economics in which people of color don't share neighborhoods with whites because they can't afford it. But the evidence is clear that most blacks would prefer to live in integrated neighborhoods, and it is the refusal of whites—not income, occupation, or education—that stands in the way of integrated communities and schools.[8]

But facts don't matter when it comes to ideology, its purpose being to support and perpetuate the status quo by making it appear normal, legitimate, and inevitable. And to get dominant groups off the hook.

It Doesn't Count If You Don't Mean It

In a culture that promotes an individual guilt and blame model to explain just about everything that goes wrong, it is difficult to avoid confusing intentions and consequences. If something bad happens, the cause must be bad intentions, and good intentions cannot produce bad results. In other words, if I can say I didn't mean it, then it didn't really happen, as if my conscious intent is the only thing that connects me to the consequences of what I do.

"I didn't mean it" can stop a conversation before it ever gets close to the reality that as far as consequences are concerned, it doesn't matter whether it was meant or not. This is the professor who has no conscious animosity or prejudice on race and yet calls only on whites in class, oblivious to the harm that results. It is the man who makes repeated sexual comments to a female colleague, and when she gets angry and tells him to stop, gets defensive and says it was only a joke, or that he just finds her attractive and meant no harm. What he does not do is acknowledge that regardless of his intent, he *has* done her harm, and she is likely to be left to deal with it on her own in an environment that now feels less safe than before. He acts as though a lack of intent means a lack of effect, as if *saying* it was only a joke or only being *aware* of it as a joke is enough to *make* it so.

Sometimes this insight can take us into unexpected places. A while ago, for example, a middle-aged man at a talk I gave expressed frustration and concern about whether to open doors for women. "The rules are changing," he said. "I always thought it was the polite thing to do, but now sometimes women get mad at me."

His dilemma reminds me of an online discussion that began with a woman pointing out that she doesn't like it when a man rushes ahead to open a door for her, or how stupid she feels sitting in a car while he scurries around to let her out. She objects to the "door-opening ceremony" because it seems to do more for him than for her, putting him in a position of control and independence (men can open doors for themselves) while she waits helplessly for him to do what she can do herself. She went on to point out that, like all rituals, opening doors conveys a cultural message, that men are active, capable, and independent, whereas women are passive, incapable, and dependent—yet another way to keep men in control.

The men roared back that they weren't *trying* to dominate anyone, they were just being *polite*.

She objected that there was more going on than the men would admit. She pointed out that if this were done only out of politeness, women would also feel obliged to open doors for men, since being polite runs both ways, although, yes, there are times when it goes in one direction, as when subordinates defer to superiors.

The men shot back that maybe that's what door opening is, a way for them to be servants waiting on women.

But, if that were so, came the reply, why is it so hard to get men to help us when we really need it? Why are we stuck with the scut work at home and at work?

It went on this way for quite a while, women objecting to *consequences* they didn't like and men defending against conscious *intentions* they didn't have. But consequences matter, regardless of what we intend. After all, the road to hell, as the saying goes, is paved with good intentions. More than that, the meaning of what we do and say is not up to us, because meaning is not a private matter: it depends on context and the culture in which we live. Men can *think* they are just being nice, but that doesn't mean that rushing ahead to open that door has no meaning or consequence beyond what they think or intend. In a patriarchal society, there is a good chance that the forms people follow—including being polite—are also patriarchal, which means both sides of the argument can be true—that men may not *intend* to put women down in elevating themselves, but that what men do often *does*.

In light of this, it's useful to consider what the common defense, "I didn't mean it," is really about. At a retirement party for a black manager, for example, a white colleague arranges a slide show that includes pictures of black people happily eating watermelon, an image with a long history of stereotyping blacks as lazy and not smart enough to care about anything more complex than having something sweet to eat. Blacks in the audience are shocked and angered, and when someone confronts the man later on, his reaction is, "I'm not racist. I didn't mean anything by it."

In effect, "I didn't mean it" comes close to "I didn't do or say it," which, of course, isn't true. What, then, is being said? Most of the time, the message is not that I didn't do or say it, but that I didn't *think* about it, a defense that assumes I am not *obliged* to think about it, or be held accountable when I don't. Contrast this with situations in which we are expected to think about it, as when I might decide, on a whim, to take someone's car and when I'm caught and brought before the judge I say I didn't mean anything by it, that I just wanted the car and didn't think much about it at the time. Or that I didn't consider whether the owner would mind or that getting arrested never crossed my mind. Undoubtedly, the judge would have none of that, reminding me that not thinking about it is a luxury I am not entitled to under the law, holding me responsible to act with awareness of the consequences of what I do.

But privilege works against such awareness and accountability. The manager should have been mindful of racial patterns in hiring, mentoring, and promotion. The white colleague should have thought about the cultural message behind demeaning stereotypes. The man should have been aware of what it's like to be a woman on the receiving end of harassment. But they were not, and such patterns are the norm, not the exception. Why?

An individualistic model tells us it's because people are callous or uncaring or prejudiced or too busy to bother with paying attention, especially those who live their lives in dominant groups. Sometimes, of course, this is true, but the luxury of obliviousness also makes a lack of conscious intent a path of least resistance that is, by its very nature, easy to follow without knowing it. The sense of entitlement and superiority that underlies most forms of privilege runs so deep, and is so entrenched, that people don't have to think about it in order to act upon it. They can always say they didn't mean it and, in a real sense, they are telling the truth. That is why "I didn't mean it" can be so disarming and such an effective defense of privilege— they *weren't* thinking, they *weren't* mindful, they *weren't* aware—all the things that go into meaning it. But this is precisely the problem with privilege and the damage that it does.

I'm One of the Good Ones

If bad things happen because of bad people, and I can make a case that I'm not one of those, then I have one more way to claim that the trouble has nothing to do with me. I can say, isn't it terrible that there are still bigots around, and isn't it too bad that some men don't know how to treat a woman, and that people can be so intolerant of those they don't understand. Unlike me, who does not belong to the KKK, whose family never owned slaves, who doesn't see color, who likes women and has no problem with people who are LGBT, and who wouldn't even think of parking in a handicapped space.

Having set myself up as a good person, I can feel disapproval or even compassion for all those bad, flawed, sick people who supposedly make trouble all by themselves in spite of decent, moral, well-intentioned people like me. And I can sympathize with those who suffer as a result. But the issue of just where *I* am in all of this drops out of sight. Apparently I'm on the outside looking in as a concerned observer. I might even have moments when I count myself as a victim, since I feel so bad whenever I think about it.

But the truth is that my silence, my inaction, and especially my passive acceptance of the everyday reality of privilege and oppression are all that it takes to make me just as much a part of the problem as any rapist or member of the Klan.

It is a point that is easy to miss, because we want people to see and judge us as individuals, and not as members of a category.[9] But to insist on that is to be naïve and even false, for the fact is that we *do* want people to treat us as members of categories when it gets us what we want.

When I go into a store, for example, I want to be waited on right away and treated with respect, even though the clerks don't know a thing about me as an individual. I want them to accept my check or credit card and not treat me with suspicion and distrust. But all they know about me is the categories to which they think I belong—a customer of a certain race, age, gender, disability status, and class—and all the things they think they know about people who fit those categories. I want that to be enough. I don't want to prove over and over again that I'm someone who deserves to be taken seriously. I want them to *assume* all of that, and the only way they can do that is to place me in the "right" categories.

This is how everyday social life works, and, by itself, it's not a problem. What many people resist, however, is seeing the other side of that process, where people are put into the "wrong" categories and treated badly, regardless of who they are as individuals.

We cannot have it both ways. If we are going to welcome the way social categories work to our advantage, whether we deserve it or not, we also have to consider that when that same process is used against others, through no fault of their own, it becomes our business, because we are being advantaged at their expense.

Some years ago, ABC News aired as a segment of *Prime Time* a documentary called *True Colors,* which still powerfully illustrates this dynamic. It focuses on two men who are quite similar in every observable way except that one is black and the other white. The crew uses hidden cameras and microphones to record what happens in various situations— applying for a job, accidentally locking oneself out of the car, trying to rent an apartment, shopping for shoes, buying a car, and so on. Again and again the two men are treated differently. In one instance, for example, the white man wanders into a shoe store in a shopping mall, and is barely across the threshold when the white clerk approaches him with a smile and an outstretched hand. He looks at some shoes and then goes on his way. Minutes later his black partner enters the store and from the outset is completely ignored by the clerk standing only a few feet away. Nothing the black man does makes a difference. He picks up and looks at shoes, walks up and down the aisles, gazes thoughtfully at a particular style, and after what seems an eternity, he finally leaves.

When I show *True Colors* to audiences and ask whites if they identify with anyone in the video, they almost invariably say no, seeing themselves neither in the black man's predicament nor in the behavior of the whites responding independently to both men. But crucially, they also do not identify with the white man receiving preferential treatment, which has the effect of making them and other whites invisible *as white people* in everyday life. It makes them unaware of how privilege happens to them, especially in relation to other whites, and oblivious to their own involvement in situations in which privilege plays a part. They do not see that simply being white locates them socially in relation to someone like the white store clerk (whose behavior they readily identify as racist) or that this affects both how people of color are treated and how they themselves are treated as whites.

The invisibility of whiteness illustrates how privilege can blind those who receive it to what is going on. As Ruth Frankenberg writes about a white woman she interviewed, "Beth was much more sharply aware of racial *oppression* shaping Black experience than of race *privilege* shaping her own life. Thus, Beth could be alert to the realities of economic discrimination against Black communities while still conceptualizing her own life as racially neutral—nonracialized, nonpolitical."[10]

Another way of looking at this is that white women and people of color are often described as being treated unequally, while men and whites are not. This, however, is logically impossible. *Unequal* means "not equal," which describes both those who receive less than their fair share *and* those who receive more. There cannot be a short end of the stick without a long end, because it is the longness of the long end that makes the short end short. To pretend otherwise is one more way to make privilege, and those who benefit from it, invisible.

So long as we participate in a society that transforms difference into privilege, there is no neutral ground on which to stand. If I'm in a meeting in which more attention is paid to what I and other men say than to women, for example, I am on the receiving end of privilege. My mere acceptance of it—whether conscious or not—is all that other men need from me. They need my consent in order for male privilege to work, which I know because if I resist that path by calling attention to it, I will feel the defensive resistance rise up to meet me. I don't have to be personally hostile to women in order to help maintain male privilege—and its attendant hostility to women—as a pervasive social fact. If anything, my lack of visible intent makes it all the more difficult to detect and challenge how privilege works.

As with gender, so with race. Whites need the consent of other whites, if only their silence, to affirm the perception that there *is* no issue to which they are accountable. The shoe clerk's racist behavior depends on his being able to assume that other whites won't have a problem with preferential treatment for whites, making it a path of least resistance. And every white person either supports or challenges that assumption when they choose, consciously or not, which path to follow.

As we look to one another to confirm or deny what we experience as reality, the odds are that the people around us will interpret our going down any given path as our acceptance of it, which means, no matter what I may intend, when someone treats me better because I'm white or male or heterosexual or nondisabled, my consent puts us on the path of privilege *together.* There is no such thing as doing nothing or being neutral or uninvolved. At every moment, social life is about all of us, and calls upon us to be aware of how we participate in it, and all of the consequences that result.

Not My Job

In corporations, universities, and other organizations, one of the most popular ways to get off the hook is to compartmentalize and isolate the problem, by assigning responsibility to someone with enough visibility and stature to satisfy the need for good public relations, but without the authority or the resources to effectively challenge the status quo. "Diversity" is the word most often used to title such positions—as in "Vice President for Diversity"—which serves the dual purpose of putting a systemic problem in the lap of a single individual while at the same time defining it in a vague and generalized way that obscures the reality of privilege and oppression.

It is a common practice that gives cover to both individuals and organizations, by providing a focal point for discontent, frustration, and responsibility. Presidents and CEOs can boast of their organization's commitment to change in glossy brochures, while administrators can send the problem cases down the hall to the typically underfunded, overworked, and understaffed Office of Diversity, most likely never to be seen or heard of again. And in universities, professors in most disciplines can avoid issues of privilege in their courses by referring students to departments designated for such things—Race and Ethnic Studies, for example, or Women's Studies. "It's not my job" turns a problem that belongs to everyone into the province of a few, freeing most people of responsibility, including science professors, for example, who may ignore the pervasive sexism in the teaching and practice of science, or issues of colonialism and race in the way the history of science is presented to their students.

"Not my job" is a subtle form of denial with far from subtle consequences. It puts the burden of change onto subordinate groups (people of color being those most often appointed to the variously-named role of diversity officer) while allowing both institutions and individuals in dominant groups to avoid responsibility for serious change, and providing a public appearance of commitment and good intent.

Sick and Tired

When all else fails, it is not unusual for dominant groups to comment on how sick and tired they are of hearing about privilege and oppression, most especially when the discussion lands on the subject of race. "It's always in your face," they say. When I ask how often is "always," and what does "it" consist of, they usually become a little vague. "It's in the news" and "all the time."

"Every day?"

"Sure seems like it."

"Every hour, every minute?"

"Of course not," they say, and I can tell they're starting to get a little annoyed, because they're not trying to describe an objective reality, but the feeling of being imposed upon. When you're annoyed or challenged by something, it can seem as though it's everywhere, with no escape. When it comes to privilege and oppression, dominant groups don't want to hear about it at *all* because it disturbs the luxury of obliviousness. This means it doesn't take much, that is, you don't have to bring it up very often for someone in a dominant group to feel put upon. "All the time" turns out to be enough to make them look at what they don't want to look at, enough to make them uncomfortable, which often isn't much.[11]

A similar dynamic operates with most forms of privilege. The middle and upper classes say they're sick and tired of hearing about welfare, poverty, and class. Nondisabled people are sick and tired of hearing about disability rights. And it takes almost no criticism at all for men to feel "bashed," as if there is some kind of open season on men. In fact, just saying something like "male privilege" or "patriarchy" or "men's violence," can start eyes rolling and evoke that exasperated look of *here we go again.*

In fact, however, among dominant groups, silence is the default on the subject of privilege, to never say or do anything that might make them feel challenged or in the spotlight. It is expected, of course, to draw attention to *people* who are male or white or nondisabled or heterosexual, since our society is centered on and identified with those groups. But this differs from drawing attention to "man," "heterosexual," "nondisabled," or "white," as categories to be examined and scrutinized.

Another reason for the "sick and tired" complaint is that life *is* hard for everyone, as in, "Don't bring me your troubles. I've got troubles of my own." Many men and white people, for example, spend a lot of time worrying about losing their jobs. Why, then, should they listen to white women or people of color talking about problems with work, or, even worse, that whites and men should be doing something about it? When Marian Wright Edelman says that it is "utterly exhausting being Black in America," many white people barely miss a beat in responding that they are tired, too.[12]

And, of course, they are. They're exhausted by the chronic insecurity, uncertainty, and pace of life in a competitive capitalist society, which can make it hard to hear about privilege and oppression. But it is one thing to have to hear about such things and another to have to live the reality and consequences of them every day. The quick, weary defensiveness of whites runs right past the fact that whatever it is that exhausts white people—being a parent or a worker or a spouse or a student who works all day and must study at night—their exhaustion is not endemic to, or inherent in, the fact of being white in our society.

By comparison, people in subordinate groups have to do each and every one of the things that the exhausted members of dominant groups must do, but in addition to struggling with the accumulation of the fine, grinding grit that oppression loads onto people's lives, simply because they happen to be in the "wrong" category.

The "sick and tired" defense allows dominant groups to claim the protected status of victims, which reminds me of those times when someone injures you in some way and you confront them about it, and they get angry because you've made them feel bad about what they did. And now, you are made to feel that you should apologize for bringing it to their attention. Children often use this defense, sulking, acting hurt and put upon, as if you had just laid an undeserved weight on their shoulders.

By encouraging dominant groups to be self centered and unaccountable, privilege also encourages them to behave as less than adult. And yet, at the same time, these are the groups in charge of organizations and institutions, who occupy the positions of responsible, adult authority. It is a combination guaranteed to perpetuate the system, unless the cycle of denial and defense is broken. The challenge for those in dominant groups is to see how they are kept from growing up, and how it diminishes everyone—including themselves.

Getting Off the Hook by Getting On

If being on the hook for privilege and oppression means being perpetually vulnerable to feeling guilty and, more generally, just bad, then we shouldn't be surprised that people do whatever they can to escape that feeling. But according to my dictionary, being on the hook calls for something larger and deeper—to be committed, obliged, and involved.

In this sense, "on the hook" is one way to distinguish adults from children, in that adults are on the hook and children are not. As an adult, I feel obliged to use my power and authority to take responsibility for what I can, to act, to make things happen. Being involved also makes me part of, and therefore responsible for, something larger, and I cannot stand alone as an isolated individual. Being obliged means more than carrying a burden, because it connects me to other people and makes me aware of how I affect them, and that we're all in this together, whether we like it or not. Being committed focuses my potential to make a difference and bonds me to those who feel the same way.

Off the hook, I am a piece of wood floating with the current. On the hook, I have forward motion and a rudder to steer by.

Off the hook, I live in illusion and denial, as if I have a choice in whether or not to be involved in the life of our society and the consequences it produces. On the hook, I am in my natural state as a human being, a social animal living in relation to others and to the world as it really is.

Keeping ourselves off the hook separates us from much of what it means to be alive. It makes us work to distance ourselves from most of humanity, because we can't get close to other people without touching the trouble that surrounds privilege and oppression. To live off the hook is to distance and isolate ourselves, and the more interconnected the world becomes, the harder it is to sustain the illusion and denial day after day, and the more it takes to maintain the distance and deny the connection. The result of illusion and denial is to become like a person who loses the ability to feel pain and risks bleeding to death from a thousand cuts that go unnoticed, untreated, and unhealed.

Sooner or later, dominant groups must embrace the hook we're on, not as some terrible affliction or occasion for guilt and shame, but as a challenge and an opportunity. It is where we have always been, where we are, and where we're going.

CHAPTER 9

What Can We Do?

I began this book by pointing out that we can't avoid being part of the problem, and now we've come to the question of how to make ourselves part of the solution.

"We," of course, are anything but a homogeneous group, coming from points of view defined by intersections of gender, race, sexual orientation, disability status, and social class, to name a few. Does a straight white woman, for example, hear the question as a woman struggling against male privilege, or as a white person or heterosexual or nondisabled in a system that advantages her at the expense of others? What difference does it make if she is a corporate manager or works nights at Walmart while putting herself through college? And how will her perspective and options differ from those of a gay black teenager or a Latino lawyer who uses a wheelchair or a Native-American woman teaching school on a reservation or a working-class white man who can't find a job or a Muslim woman running for a seat on the local school board?

We hear the question differently because our social characteristics locate us differently in relation to it, and differences in location bring with them differences in worldviews and resources, and in power, vulnerability, and risk. My choice to speak out on issues of privilege, for example, is not free of risk, but it is also aided by how I am identified in the world, including the enhanced credibility that comes with various forms of privilege. If I were differently located, I might still speak out, but the road by which I came to that would be very different.

There may be times, then, in the pages that follow, when you find yourself wondering, "Who is he talking about? Not me." Which may be true, although it would be worth considering what happens if you shift your point of view to some other aspect of your identity to see how it changes how you hear what I'm asking you to consider, how it might be about you after all.

Our different locations in the world can also affect our reasons for asking the question, or whether we ask at all. I sometimes find, for example, that people in dominant groups who are painfully aware of the oppressive effects of privilege, are looking for a way to escape feeling bad so they can get on with their lives. This is especially true of men and whites, who have the option of insulating themselves from many of the consequences of gender and race.

Regardless of who we are in relation to systems of privilege, working for change can be daunting when it comes to systems that have been around for hundreds or, in the case of gender, thousands of years. And so it's not uncommon to feel overwhelmed, as if changing the world is up to us as lone individuals, defeated before we start. We may feel afraid—of failing, of what people will think of us, of what we'll discover about ourselves, of losing a job, of being attacked or ostracized. Or we think it's all we can do to just keep up with everything else in our lives, whether it's school or work or taking care of kids or aging parents. Still, many feel compelled to find a way to do something that makes a difference, however small, and this chapter is written with them in mind.

Much of this book has been about understanding how the world works and how we participate to make it happen. Now it's time to look at how this positions us to be part of changing both systems and ourselves, a process that begins with some powerful myths about how change happens and what that has to do with us.

The Myth That It's Always Been This Way, and Always Will

If we don't make a point of studying history, it's easy to believe that things have always been the way we've known them to be. But when we look back, we find, for example, that white privilege has been a feature of human life for only a matter of centuries, and there is abundant evidence that male privilege has been around for only seven thousand years or so, which isn't very long when you consider that human beings have been on the earth for hundreds of thousands of years.[1] And history provides many examples of people coming together to make change happen. So, the smart money should be on *nothing* always being one way or any other—instead, we should bet on the fact that reality is always in flux and the only thing we can count on is change. Things only appear to stand still because we have such a short attention span, limited by the brevity of our lives. From the long view—the really long view—everything is in process all the time, including systems of privilege.

Some would argue that everything *is* process, the spaces between one point, one thing, and another. What we might see as permanent end points— global capitalism, western civilization, machine technology, patriarchy, white privilege, and so on—are the temporary states of an ever-changing reality on the way to becoming something else. Because systems happen only as people participate in them, they cannot help being a dynamic process of creation and re-creation. In something as simple as a man following the path of least resistance toward controlling women (and women letting him do it), the reality of male privilege is enacted. This is how it *happens* and comes into being, moment by moment. But this is also how we can make change by choosing paths of greater resistance, as when men choose not to seek control, or choose to intervene when other men do, or when women refuse their own subordination.

Since we can always choose paths of greater resistance, systems can only be as stable as the flow of human choice, consent, resistance, and creativity, all of which makes permanence impossible. Added to this are the dynamic interactions among systems—between capitalism and the state, for example, or between families and the economy, or societies and the earth (think climate change)—all of which produce the kind of tension, contra- diction, and conflict that make change inevitable.

An oppressive system often *seems* stable only because it limits our lives and imaginations so thoroughly that we can't see anything else. This is especially true when a system has existed for so long that its past extends beyond the collective memory of what came before, making it easy to confuse the terms and conditions of life within that system with a normal and inevitable human condition.

But the illusion of permanence masks a fundamental, long-term insta-
bility caused by the dynamics of oppression itself. Any system organized
around one group's efforts to subordinate and exploit another is ultimately a
losing proposition, because it contradicts the essentially uncontrollable nature
of reality, while also doing violence to basic human needs and values. Over
the last two centuries, feminist thought and action have challenged men's
dominance and violence, and patriarchy has become increasingly vulnerable
as a result. This is one reason that male resistance, backlash, and defensiveness are so intense, with so many men complaining about their lot, especially
their inability to meet the cultural standards for masculinity and manhood
that would have them controlling not only their own lives, but those of
women and other men.[2] Fear of and resentment toward women are pervasive—
from worrying about being accused of sexual harassment or rape, to railing
against affirmative action and custody decisions in divorce court.[3]

No system lasts forever. This is especially true of privilege. We cannot
know what will replace it, but we can be confident that it will go, that it *is*
going at every moment—it only being a matter of how quickly, by what
means, and what is coming next. And whether we do our part to make it
happen sooner rather than later, and with less, rather than more, destruction
and suffering in the process.

Gandhi's Paradox and the Myth of No Effect

The first thing in the way of acting for change is the belief that nothing
we do will make a difference, that the system is too big and powerful
for us to affect. The complaint is valid if we look at society as a whole and
in the short run, but if that is what it means to do something, then we've
set ourselves up to fail.

To shake off the paralyzing myth that we cannot make a difference, we
have to shift how we see ourselves in relation to a long term, complex
process of change. This begins with how we relate to time. Many changes
can come about quickly enough for us to see them happen, such as the
legalization of same-sex marriage or the election of a person of color or a
woman (or both) as president of the United States. But systems of privilege
are larger and more complicated than that, and take longer to change than
our short lives can encompass. For that kind of change, we cannot use the
human life span as a standard against which to measure effect.

What we need instead is what might be called "time constancy," analogous to object constancy. Very young children lack object constancy, which is to say, if you hold out a cookie or a toy and then put it behind your back, they will not go after it, because they're unable to hold on to the image of where it went. If they cannot see it, it might as well not exist. After a while, they develop the mental ability to know that things exist even when they're out of sight. In thinking about change, we need a similar ability in relation to time, so that we can hold on to the knowledge and the faith that systemic change can happen even if we're not around to see it.

We also need to be clear about how our choices matter and how they don't. Gandhi once said that nothing we do as individuals matters, but that it's vitally important that we do it anyway.[4] This touches on a powerful paradox in the relationship between society and individuals. Imagine, for example, that social systems are trees and we are the leaves. No individual leaf is essential to the life of the tree, but collectively the leaves are what allows the tree to survive.

Like the leaves, each of us matters, and we don't. What we do doesn't seem like much, because in important ways, it is not. But when people organize to work together, they can reach a critical mass that is anything but insignificant, especially in the long run. To be part of a larger movement for change, we have to learn to live with this paradox.

A related paradox is that we have to be willing to travel without knowing where we're going. We need faith to do what seems right without being sure of the effect that it will have. We have to think like pioneers, who may know the direction they want to move in or what they'd like to find, but without knowing where they will wind up. Because they are going where they've never been before, they cannot know whether they'll ever get anywhere they might consider a destination, much less the kind of place they had in mind when they started out. But if pioneers had to know their destination from the beginning, they might never go anywhere or discover anything.

In similar ways, in the search for alternatives to privilege and oppression, we have to move away from how social life is organized now and toward the certainty that alternatives are possible, even if we have no clear idea of what those are, or have never experienced them ourselves. It has to be enough to look at how the system works and how we participate, to question how we see ourselves as people at the intersection of all the varied aspects of our identity, to examine how we see capitalism and the scarcity, competition, and conflict it produces in relation to our personal striving to better our own lives. Then we can open ourselves to experience what happens next, and what is possible.

When we dare to question who we are and how the world works, things happen that we can't foresee. But they do not happen unless we *move,* if only in our minds. As pioneers, we discover what is possible only by putting ourselves in motion, because we have to move in order to change our position—and hence our perspective—on where we are, where we've been, and where we might go. This is how alternatives begin to appear.

The myth of no effect not only obscures the role we might play in the long-term transformation of society, but it also blinds us to our power in relation to other people. We may cling to the belief that there is nothing we can do, precisely because we know how much power we *do* have and are afraid to use because people may not like it. In other words, denying our power can be a way to let ourselves off the hook.

The reluctance to acknowledge and use our power comes up in all kinds of situations, such as when a committee is making hiring decisions and an applicant comes up for discussion and someone says "it's not a good fit" and everyone is silent or murmurs their assent. And then there is a critical moment when someone in the room—or several, but each imagining that they are the only one—cannot shake the feeling that something is wrong, that "not a good fit" is code for not-male, not-white, not-heterosexual, not-nondisabled—it being perfectly clear that the applicant is qualified. Do they say something, or do they not? It is just one moment among countless such moments woven into the fabric of everyday life, but it is a crucial moment, because the seamless response of the group to what is happening affirms the normalcy of that response and its unproblematic appearance in a system of privilege. It takes only one person to tear the fabric of collusion and apparent consensus. On some level, each of us knows that we have this potential, and this knowledge can either move us to speak or scare us into silence. We can change the course of that moment with something as simple as a question ("In what specific way is this not a good fit?"), and we know how uncomfortable this can make people feel and how they may ward off their discomfort by dismissing, excluding, or even attacking the bearer of bad news. We do not, then, choose silence because nothing we might say or do will matter. Our silence is our not daring to matter.

The power to affect other people is more than the ability to provoke discomfort. Just as paths of least resistance shape our choices, choosing a different path makes it possible for others to question their own.

In this way, we affect one another all the time without knowing it. When my family moved to our house in northwestern Connecticut, one of my pleasures was blazing walking trails through the woods. Some time later I noticed deer scat and hoofprints along the trails, and it pleased me to think they had adopted the path that I'd laid down. But then I wondered if I had followed a trail laid down by others when I cleared what I had thought was "my" trail, and I realized that there is no way to know whether anything begins or ends with me or the choices that I make. It is more likely that the paths others have chosen influence the paths I choose, just as my choices affect theirs.

The simplest way to help others make different choices is to make them ourselves, in the open, where everyone can see. As we shift the patterns of our own participation, we make it easier for others to do it too, and at the same time, we make it harder to stay on the old path. Instead of trying to change them, we create the possibility of their participating in change, in their own time, and in their own way. In this way we widen the circle of change without provoking the defensiveness that perpetuates paths of least resistance and the oppressive systems they enact.

It is important to see that to be effective, we are not required to change people's minds. In fact, changing minds may play a relatively small part in systemic change. We will not succeed in turning diehard misogynists into practicing feminists, for example, or overt racists into civil rights activists. But we can shift the odds in favor of new paths that contradict core values on which systems of privilege depend. We can introduce so many exceptions to the paths supporting privilege that the children or grandchildren of diehard racists and misogynists will start to change their perception of which paths offer the least resistance. Research on men's changing attitudes toward the male provider role, for example, shows that most of the shift occurs between generations, not within them.[5] This suggests that rather than trying to change individuals, the most important thing we can do is help shift entire cultures so that forms and values that support privilege begin to lose their obvious and taken-for-granted legitimacy and normalcy, and new forms emerge to challenge their privileged place in social life. And when this happens, the structures of privilege—segregation, violence, exploitation, and oppressively unequal distributions of wealth, power, resources, and opportunities—become harder to maintain.

This explains, in large part, how the acceptance of same sex marriage grew so rapidly in the United States. Gays and lesbians made their everyday lives so visible to heterosexuals that the simple fact that they are human beings like everyone else generated a dramatic shift away from cultural beliefs and values that had placed them outside the bounds of normality.[6]

In science, this is how one paradigm replaces another.[7] For hundreds of years, for example, Europeans believed that stars, planets, and the sun revolved around Earth. But Copernicus and Galileo found that too many of their astronomical observations were anomalies that did not fit the prevailing paradigm: if the sun and planets revolved around the Earth, then they would not move as they did. As such observations accumulated, they made it increasingly difficult to hang on to an Earth-centered paradigm. Eventually the anomalies became so numerous that Copernicus offered a new paradigm, which he declined to publish, for fear of persecution as a heretic, a fate that eventually befell Galileo when he took up the cause a century later. Eventually, however, the evidence was so overwhelming that a new paradigm replaced the old one.

In similar ways, we can see how systems of privilege are based on paradigms and worldviews that shape how we think about difference and how we organize social life in relation to it. We can openly challenge those paradigms with evidence that they do not work and never did, and that they produce unacceptable consequences for everyone. We can help weaken them by openly choosing alternative paths and thereby provide living anomalies that do not fit the prevailing paradigm. By our example, we can contradict both the assumptions and their legitimacy again and again. We can add our choices and our lives to tip the scales, toward new ways of organizing social life, ones that don't revolve around privilege and oppression. We cannot tip the scales overnight or by ourselves, and in that sense, we do not amount to much. But, as Gandhi noted, it is crucial where we choose to place what the poet Bonaro Overstreet called "the stubborn ounces of my weight."[8] It is in our small and humble choices that privilege, oppression, and the movement toward something better have happened many times in the past and will happen again.

Stubborn Ounces: What Can We Do?

There are no easy answers to the question of what can we do, no twelve-step program, no manual of instructions. Most important, there is no way around or over it: the only way out of it is through. We will not end oppression by pretending it isn't there or will somehow go away on its own.

Some will complain that those who work for change are being divisive when they draw attention to privilege and oppression. But when members of dominant groups mark differences by excluding or discriminating against subordinate groups and treating them as other, they are not accused of being divisive. Usually it's only when someone calls attention to how difference is used as a basis for privilege that accusations of divisiveness come up.

In a sense, it *is* divisive to say that privilege is real, but only insofar as it heightens our awareness of divisions that already exist, and challenges the perception that the status quo is normal and unremarkable. Privilege promotes the worst kind of divisiveness by cutting us off from one another and, by silencing the truth, cutting us off from ourselves and what we know.

What, then, does it mean to get out by going through? What can we do to make a difference?

Acknowledge That Privilege and Oppression Exist

A key to the continued existence of every system of privilege is for most people to act as if it isn't there, because it contradicts so many basic human values that awareness cannot help but arouse opposition. The Soviet Union and its East European satellites, for example, were riddled with contradictions so widely known among their people that the oppressive regimes fell apart with a speed that astonished the world. Similar things happened during the Arab Spring that sprouted revolutions across the Middle East.

It is one thing to become aware and another to stay that way, with so many paths of least resistance leading everywhere but toward a critical awareness of how the system works. Writing this in the fall of 2016, a presidential election year, it's hard to miss how rare it has been for debates and stump speeches to engage with issues of privilege and oppression, from men's violence against women to racial segregation, discrimination, and police misconduct. And, if the past is any guide, were it not for the candidacy of a self-identified democratic socialist, Bernie Sanders, there would have been no serious examination of the role of capitalism in creating and perpetuating patterns of inequality, scarcity, and exploitation.

By not examining the systems through which humans organize economic, political, and social life, we also engage in the fantasy that solving the problem of privilege is only a matter of changing how we think. I have, of course, spent most of this book talking about the importance of just that, and I haven't suddenly changed my mind. A commitment to understanding ourselves and how we participate is crucial, but, by itself, this is not enough, for, sooner or later, we have to apply an understanding of ourselves and how systems work to the job of changing systems themselves. Unlike the game of Monopoly, we cannot just stop participating in society if we don't like the consequences. The choice that is left is to change the system and how we participate in it.

Since there are many reasons we can come up with to avoid going down that road, the easiest thing to do after reading a book like this is to forget about it. Maintaining a critical consciousness takes commitment and work and the help and support of others. Awareness is something that we either maintain in the moment or we don't. And the only way to hang on to that awareness is to make it a part of our lives.

Pay Attention

Understanding how privilege and oppression operate and how you participate in it is where working for change begins. It is easy to have opinions, but it takes work to know what you're talking about. The simplest way to begin is to make reading about privilege a part of your life. Unless you have the luxury of a personal teacher, it is difficult to understand this issue without reading. Many people assume they already know what they need to know because it's part of their everyday lives, especially when it comes to the subordinate statuses they occupy. But they are usually wrong, because the *analysis* of our experience in relation to something larger than ourselves is not contained in the experience itself. Just as the last thing a fish would discover is water, the last thing people discover is the social systems in which our lives are embedded and how they work.

We also have to open ourselves to how deeply our minds have been shaped by our participation in a culture in which privilege and oppression are normalized and affirmed as natural and right. For a mind to reshape *itself* is serious and tricky work,[9] which is why activists talk with one another and spend time reading one another's writing, because seeing clearly is not an easy thing to do. There is also the danger that without other people around to challenge us, we can become smug or self righteous or fall into the arrogance of thinking we know the answer to everything. This is why people who are critical of the status quo are often self-critical as well—they know how complex and elusive truth can be and what a challenge it is to work toward it. People working for change are often accused of being ortho-dox and rigid—"politically correct"—but in practice they are often among the most self-critical people around.*

There is a huge literature on issues of privilege available through any library, although you would never know it to judge from its invisibility in the mass media and mainstream bookstores. This is not surprising, given that the media are corporations dominated by whites and men, with a vested interest in ignoring anything that questions the status quo in general and capitalism in particular. Instead, they routinely focus on issues that have the least to do with equity and justice, that follow the individualistic model of social life, and that set subordinate groups against one another. They will discuss whether women and men have different brains, for example, rather than critically examine the reality of manhood, men's violence, and male privilege. And they are quick to give front-page coverage to any woman willing to criticize feminism, or, for that matter, any person of color willing to attack affirmative action or blame other people of color for their disad-vantaged position in society. At the same time, the media ignore most of what is known about privilege, all but invisible to book reviewers, journal-ists, editorial writers, bloggers, columnists, and trade book publishers. So, if you want to know what's going on, you will have to make an effort to find it out.

As you educate yourself, avoid reinventing the wheel. Many people have already done a lot of work for you. There is no way to get through it all, but you don't have to in order to develop a clear enough sense of how to act in meaningful and thoughtful ways. A good place to start is with a basic text on race, class, and gender (see the Resources section of this book). Men who feel there is no place for them in women's studies might start with books about patriarchy and gender inequality that are written by men. In the same way, whites can begin with writings on race written by other whites. Sooner or later, however, dominant groups will need to turn to what people

---

* The term "political correctness" was first used by social activists as a way to monitor and evaluate their behavior and speech in order to make them consistent with their political principles. Talking about male privilege and the oppression of women, for example, in ways that focus entirely on the experience of white women would be consid-ered politically incorrect because while opposing one form of privilege, it tacitly supports another. Since then, the term has been appropriated, copied, and distorted by equity opponents who use it to refer to any infringement on any dominant groups' freedom to speak and behave without considering the consequences. As such, the term has been co-opted, losing its original meaning in ways that trivialize the reality of privilege and oppression.

in subordinate groups have written, because they are the ones who have done most of the work of figuring out how systems of privilege work.

Reading is only the beginning. At some point you will have to look at yourself and the world in which you live to identify how systems of privilege are organized and operate in the context of your own life, and how you participate in them. Once "path of least resistance" becomes part of your active vocabulary, for example, you will start seeing them everywhere you go. Although it can seem overwhelming at first, it is a good thing, because the more aware you are of how powerful those paths are, the better you are positioned to decide whether to go down them each time they present themselves.

It helps to live like anthropologists, participant-observers who watch and listen to other people and themselves, who notice patterns that come up again and again. You can pretend you are a stranger in a strange land who knows nothing about where you are and *knows* that you know nothing, what Buddhists call "beginner's mind." This opens you to recognize faulty assumptions and to the surprise of realizing that things are not what they seem. Following this path is especially challenging for people in dominant groups, whose privilege tells them they shouldn't have to work to figure out someone else, that it's up to others to figure *them* out. They fall into the trap of impatient, arrogant tourists who don't bother to educate themselves about where they are. But taking responsibility means not waiting for others to tell you what to do, to point out what's going on, to identify alternatives. If those in dominant groups are going to assume their share, it's up to them to listen, watch, ask, and listen again, to make it their business to find out for themselves. If they don't, they will slide down the comfortable, blindered path of privilege, and then they will be *just* part of the problem and they will be blamed and they will have it coming.

Learn to Listen[10]

Attentive listening is especially difficult for members of dominant groups because the path of least resistance is to put themselves at the center of attention, including their own. If someone confronts you with your behavior that supports privilege, de-center yourself and resist the pull to defend and deny. Don't tell them they're too sensitive or need a better sense of humor, and don't try to explain away what you did as something else than what they're telling you it was. Don't say you didn't mean it or that you were only kidding. Don't tell them what a champion of equity and justice you are or how hurt you feel by what they're telling you. Don't make jokes or try to be cute or charming, since only privilege can lead someone to believe these are acceptable responses to something as serious as this. Listen to what is being said. Take it seriously. Assume for the time being that it's true, because given the paths of least resistance, it probably is, at least enough to be heard. And then take responsibility to do something about it, beginning with understanding what it has to do with you.

For many years I taught courses on social inequality, seminars on gender, race, and class, small groups with lots of discussion. One day, a black student approached me to say that she had noticed, repeatedly, that I would interrupt her in ways that she never saw me do with whites. It made her feel invisible, dismissed, as if what she had to say didn't matter.

Not recognizing myself in what she said, the path of least resistance for me as a white person was to deny and defend by telling her that of course I value her as much as anyone else, that I wouldn't do such a thing, having spent my life working on issues of privilege and oppression, that she was being too sensitive, or even blaming her own lack of confidence on me. I might have given her advice about holding her own in a conversation, asserting herself more, perhaps.

I short, I would have made this about her and not me, by subordinating her experience to my own in refusing to see myself *as I was seen*; by dismissing anything I might do without conscious intent as if I had not done it at all; by presuming to know what I did not, about myself and about her. However gentle, however "reasonable" my tone, however "good" my intent, I would have put her in her place, so that I might stay comfortably in my own.

This is how ordinary racism happens much of the time, day after day, loading the odds in favor of whites in the shaping of a life, everything from getting a job or buying a house or excelling in school, to receiving healthcare or feeling accepted and safe. It is the kind of routine, mainstream racism that does not rely on acts that are outwardly vicious or mean. But in the cumulative weight of its effect, it may be worse than the sort of thing that makes the news.

But, you may wonder, was she right? Did I actually interrupt her more than whites?

I suppose it would matter if she was putting me on trial, if my "innocence" as a "good white person" was at stake. But it was clear as I listened to her that she was not calling on me to humble myself in guilt and shame, to admit to being one of those bad white people after all, to ask forgiveness and make amends. She was asking to be seen and heard, as one human being by another, that I consider her experience of me to be as real as my own, that I consider the consequence, that I pay attention, that I take responsibility for my part in what happens between us. And, in confronting her professor, she was taking a considerable risk to do it.

I told her that I had no awareness of the behavior she was talking about, but that I had to assume she was not imagining it or making it up, that I was sorry this had happened, it being the last thing I would want in my class. And I said I would do whatever I could to attend and notice so that it would not happen again, which was, after all, what both of us wanted.

I was not on trial that day, in part because I had no innocence to lose—the "good white person" being a fiction, a device to separate ourselves from the reality of race. Nor was I guilty of "being white," the fiction of white people born into an original sin for which we must spend our lives in guilt and shame. In a way, what happened was not about me at all. Or about her. It was the continuing legacy of race that she and I, in our own ways, were trying to see clearly and come to terms with, in the world and in ourselves. And, in that, I believe we found a common ground on which to stand, the ground of the human being.

Little Risks: Do Something

The more you pay attention to privilege and oppression, the more opportunities you'll see to do something about it. You don't have to mount an expedition to seek them out. They're everywhere, beginning with ourselves.

As I became aware of how male privilege encourages me to control conversations, for example, I also realized how easily men dominate meetings by controlling the agenda and interrupting, and without women objecting. This is especially striking in groups that are composed mostly of females but in which most of the talking nonetheless comes from men. I would find myself sitting in meetings and suddenly the preponderance of men's voices would jump out at me, male privilege in full bloom.

As I've become more aware, I've had to decide what to do, including trying out ways of listening more and talking less. At times it has felt contrived and artificial, such as counting slowly to ten (or more) to give others a chance to step in to the space afforded by my silence. With time and practice, new paths become easier to follow, and I now spend less time monitoring myself. But awareness is never automatic or permanent, because those paths will be there to choose or not as long as systems of privilege exist.

You might be thinking that everything comes down to changing individuals after all, since doing something is a matter of behavior. In a sense, of course, it's true that, for us, it comes down to what we do as people since that is what we are. But the key is to connect our choices to the systems in which we participate. When we *openly* change our behavior, we also change how the system happens, which changes the environment that shapes other people's behavior, which, in turn, further changes how the system happens. In doing that, we help change the consequences that come out of the dynamic between systems and individuals, including patterns of privilege and oppression. It doesn't get more powerful than that.

Sometimes stepping off the path is a matter of calling attention to how a system is organized. As you will see below, for example, it might involve pointing out the distribution of power and resources within an organization—loaded with white men at the top and with white women and people of color at the bottom. To call out such patterns means changing our own behavior, but it does more than that by revealing the system itself.

As you become more aware, questions will come up about what goes on at work, in the media, families, communities, religious institutions, government, on the street, at school—in short, just about everywhere. The questions don't come all at once, although it can feel that way. But if you remind yourself that it isn't up to you to do it all, you will see plenty of situations in which it's possible to make a difference, sometimes in surprisingly simple ways, as you'll see in the examples below.

As you consider the possibilities, keep in mind that the individualistic model encourages us to think of ourselves as isolated individuals acting without the support and company of others. To combat this tendency, the question to ask is not, "What can I do?" but "What can *we* do?" I'll have more to say about this later on, but for now, it's good to keep in mind the advice of the African American writer, orator, and abolitionist, Frederick Douglass: *organize, organize, organize.*

And then:

Dare to matter: Make noise, be seen. Stand up, volunteer, speak out, sit in, demonstrate, protest, write letters, sign petitions, march, show up.

If there's a rally, community forum, die-in, public testimony, teach-in—go and add your presence. Every oppressive system feeds on silence and people staying home as a form of consent[11] and, as Audre Lorde reminds us, our silence will not protect us.[12] Don't collude. Break the silence to undermine the assumption of solidarity and normality that every system depends on. If it feels too risky to do alone, invite someone to join you. And if you don't act this time, practice being aware of how silence reflects your consent, whether it's to protect yourself from retaliation and harm, or to show solidarity with a dominant group. Take it as an opportunity to be aware of how you participate in making privilege and oppression happen: "Today I colluded in silence, and this is the consequence. Next time will be different."

This is also an opportunity for dominant groups to discover the difference between being privately and personally non-racist or non-sexist or non-heterosexist or non-ableist, and being actively and publicly *anti*-racist, *anti*-sexist, *anti*-heterosexist, *anti*-ableist.

Seek out ways to withdraw consent and support from paths of least resistance and people's choices to follow them, starting with yourself. It can be as simple as not laughing at a racist or heterosexist joke or saying you don't think it's funny, or writing a letter to your senator or representative or the editor of your newspaper, objecting to sexism in the media. When my local newspaper ran an article whose headline referred to sexual harassment as "earthy behavior," for example, I wrote a letter pointing out that harassment is an assertion of male privilege and has nothing to do with being earthy.

The key to withdrawing consent is to interrupt the flow of business as usual. You can undermine the assumption that everyone is going along with the status quo by not going along yourself, giving other people the opportunity to notice, consider, and question. It's a perfect time to suggest alternatives, including ways to think about discrimination, harassment, and violence that do justice to the reality of what is happening and how it affects people's lives.

The human tendency to compare ourselves to other people to make sure we fit in gives each of us the power to disrupt the taken-for-granted assumptions that underlie social life. It might help to think of this process as inserting grains of sand in an oyster to irritate it into creating a pearl of insight, or as a way to make systems of privilege itch, stir, and scratch, and reveal themselves for all to see. Or as planting seeds of doubt about the desirability and inevitability of the way things are and, by example, planting seeds of what might be.

Dare to make people feel uncomfortable, beginning with yourself. At the next school board meeting, for example, you can ask why principals and other administrators are almost always white and male, while the teachers they supervise and the lower paid support staff are mostly white women and people of color. You can challenge the exploitation of Native American heritage and identity in the use of images and symbols as sports team mascots.[13] You can ask similar kinds of questions about privilege and difference in your place of worship, your workplace, and local government.

It may seem that such actions don't amount to much, until you stop long enough to feel your resistance to doing them—worrying, for example, about how easy it is to make people uncomfortable, including yourself. But keep in mind that your potential to disturb other people is also a measure of the power inherent in those simple acts of challenging the status quo.

Some will say that it isn't nice to make people uncomfortable. But systems of privilege do far worse than that, and there isn't anything nice about allowing them to continue. Besides, I've never heard of a process of change that really mattered that wasn't also hard, that did not challenge basic assumptions and take us to the edge of our competencies and safety, where we are likely to run into all kinds of difficult feelings, including doubt and fear. But if we cannot tolerate such things, we will never get beneath superficial appearances or learn or change anything of much value, including ourselves.

And if history is any guide, discomfort—to put it mildly—is unavoidable in changing systems. "The meek don't make it," writes William Gamson in his study of social movements.[14] Movements succeed to the extent to which they are willing to disrupt business as usual and make those in power uncomfortable enough to act. Women did not win the right to vote by reasoning with men and showing them the merits of their position, but by risking ridicule and ostracism, not to mention jail and hunger strikes that brought on forced feeding through tubes run down their throats.[15] Nor have black people made a dent in segregation, discrimination, or police violence without sit-ins, marches, demonstrations, confrontations, and civil disobedience, to which whites have often responded with violence and intimidation.[16] As Doug McAdam shows in his study of the civil rights era, the Federal government intervened and enacted civil rights laws only when white violence against demonstrators became so extreme that the government was compelled to act.[17]

It is no different today, with Occupy Wall Street, Black Lives Matter, Dream Defenders, Water Protectors at the Standing Rock Sioux Reservation, and protests and strikes organized in communities and on campuses. Mass demonstrations have been instrumental, for example, in bringing national attention to police violence against people of color. And in 2015, when students at the University of Missouri demonstrated against racist incidents on campus, the administration's failure to act prompted students to organize a strike that demanded, and got, the resignation of the university president and the attention of the state's governor and legislature.[18]

In similar ways, when campus activists organized protests and filed formal complaints about the long history of systematic mishandling of incidents of sexual assault, federal authorities launched an investigation that provoked awareness and prompted reforms on campuses across the country.

As Frederick Douglass put it, "Power concedes nothing without a demand. It never has and it never will."[19] As much as anyone else, I would like to believe Douglass is wrong, that all it takes to end injustice and unnecessary suffering is to point out the reality of oppression. But history gives us no reason to believe that is true.

Be clear in naming the problem. Words matter. Try substituting "equity" and "justice" for "diversity" and notice how it changes the conversation. It's easier to focus on a numbers game, or to assume that difference itself is the problem, than it is to confront the reality of privilege and oppression.

Insist on clarity about the meaning of words such as "privilege" or "racism," critical terms that are often misunderstood and become the occasion for arguments that serve only to distract from the real problem.

Find ways to keep in front of you the relationship between systems and individuals described in the figure in Chapter 6. This basic sociological model is an *essential* tool for avoiding the cultural trap of individualistic thinking by which everything comes down to nothing more than personal experience, identity, or rights, or how good or bad we are, a trap into which systems of privilege disappear in the endless variety of individual experience.[20] To counter this, I have made a practice of beginning every class by having someone draw the model on the board as a continuing reminder of how the world actually works, always at hand to bring us back to reality. You might do some version of this for yourself. Draw it on a piece of paper, tack it on the wall.

Openly model alternative paths. Paths of least resistance become more visible when we choose alternatives, like rules that are broken. Modeling new paths creates tension in a system, which always wants to move toward resolution (like the irritated oyster). We don't have to convince anyone of anything. As Gandhi puts it, the work begins with us trying to be the change we want to see in the world. If you think this has no effect, watch how people react to the slightest departures from established paths and how much they try to ignore or explain away or challenge those who choose something else.

In choosing different paths, we may not know if we're affecting other people, but it's safe to assume that we are. When people are aware that alternatives exist and have the chance to witness other people choosing them, things become possible that were not before. They must now reconcile their choice with what they've seen us do, something they didn't have to deal with before, which increases the resistance around established paths. There is no way to predict how this will play out in the long run, but there is certainly no good reason to think it won't make a difference.

Actively promote change in how systems are organized around privilege. The possibilities here are almost endless, because social life is complicated and privilege is everywhere. You can, for example, join with others to:

- Speak out for equity in your workplace, for equal pay for equal work, for a minimum wage that is a living wage, for fair hiring and promotion practices for everyone.

- Promote awareness and training around issues of privilege, including safeguards and procedures for minimizing the effects of implicit bias, in everything from work and school to health care and policing.

- Oppose the devaluing of women, people of color, and people with disabilities, and the work they do, from dead-end jobs to glass ceilings.

- Support the struggle of Native Americans to recover from centuries of violence and systematic efforts to destroy their cultures, land, and ways of life, efforts that continue to this day.

- Support the well-being of mothers, children, and people with disabilities, including their right to control their bodies and their lives.

- Do not support businesses that are inaccessible to people with disabilities.

- Do not support businesses that engage in unfair labor practices, including low wages and union-busting. Although the labor movement has a long history of racism, sexism, and ableism, unions are currently one of the few organized efforts to protect workers from the excesses of capitalism.

■ Become aware of how class divisions happen in workplaces and schools, and how this oppresses all working people. College students, for example, can investigate if staff are paid a living wage, and speak up if they are not. There is a great silence in this country around issues of class, in part because the dominant ideology presents the United States as a classless society.[21] Break the silence.

■ Oppose the concentration of wealth and power in the United States and globally. The lower, working, and middle classes are the last to benefit from economic upturns and the first to suffer from downturns. Demand that politicians and candidates for public office take a stand on issues of class, starting with the acknowledgment that they exist and cannot be separated from the capitalist political economy.

■ Educate yourself about how the capitalist system works and alternatives to it, such as democratic socialism. Gather with others to try this thought experiment: if you had to design an economic system that would work for everyone, and assuming that your own life would be among the *least* fortunate, what would you want that system to look like? How would it work? And how would it differ from what we have today?

■ Apply what you know about privilege and oppression to stop the human exploitation and devastation of the earth and its non-human species, which is a direct consequence of systems of privilege and their guiding ideology of domination and control.

■ Object to the punitive dismantling of welfare programs and attempts to limit women's access to reproductive health services.

■ Speak out against violence and harassment wherever they occur, whether at home, at work, or on the street.

■ Support services for women who are victimized by men's violence. Volunteer at the local rape crisis center or battered women's shelter. Join and support groups that intervene with violent men.

■ Advocate for clear and effective anti-harassment policies in workplaces, unions, schools, professional associations, religious institutions, and political parties, as well as public spaces such as parks, sidewalks, and malls.

■ Object to theaters and online sites that carry violent pornography, and to people you know who make use of them. This does not require a debate about censorship—just the exercise of freedom of speech to articulate pornography's role in the oppression of women.

- Ask questions about how work, education, religion, and family are shaped by core values and principles that support privilege. It is a path of least resistance, for example, to think of women's entry into military combat roles or the upper reaches of corporate power as a form of progress. But you can also raise questions about what happens to people and societies when political and economic institutions are organized around control and domination, and, by extension, competition and the use of violence. Is it progress when dominant groups share control of oppressive systems of privilege with selected members of subordinate groups, such as white women and people of color?

- Openly support those who step off the path of least resistance. When you witness someone taking a risk, don't wait until later to tell them in private that you're glad they did. Waiting until you're alone makes it safer for you but does the other person little good. Support is most needed when the risk is being taken, not later on, so don't put it off. Make your support as visible and public as the courageous behavior that you are supporting.[22]

- *Support the right of LGBT people to be who they are and move freely and unmolested in the world.* Raise awareness of homophobia, transphobia, and heterosexism. Ask school officials and teachers about what is happening to LGBT students. If they do not know, ask them to find out, since it's likely these students are being harassed, bullied, suppressed, and oppressed by others at one of the most vulnerable stages of life. When gender identity and sexual orientation are discussed, raise questions about their relation to male privilege. Remember that it isn't necessary to have answers to questions in order to ask them.

Throughout this process, try to remember to:

Pay attention to issues of intersectionality—how different forms of privilege combine and interact with one another. There has been a great deal of struggle within various women's movements, for example, about the relationship between male privilege and race, class, gender identity, and sexual orientation.[23] White middle- and upper-middle-class heterosexual feminists have been criticized for pursuing their own agenda to the detriment of other women. Raising concerns about glass ceilings that keep women out of top corporate and professional positions, for example, does little to help working- or lower-class women. There has also been debate over whether some forms of oppression are more important to attack first, or produce more oppressive consequences than others.

One way out of this conflict is to realize that male privilege is problematic not only for emphasizing *male* dominance, but for valuing and promoting dominance and control as ends in themselves. In this sense, all forms of oppression draw support from common roots, and calling attention to those roots undermines *all* forms of privilege. Enabling a small minority of women or people of color to get a bigger piece of the pie will not end gender or racial oppression for the vast majority. But if we identify the core problem as *any* society organized around principles of domination and privilege, then change requires us to focus on all the forms of privilege those principles promote. Whether we begin with gender or disability or race or class or capitalism, if we name the problem correctly, then we'll wind up going in the same direction.

Work with other people. It bears repeating that not doing it alone is an essential part of working for change. From expanding consciousness to taking risks, joining with others who share a commitment to what you're trying to do makes a world of difference. For starters, you can read and talk about books and issues and just hang out with other people who want to understand and make a difference. The roots of the modern women's movement were in small consciousness-raising groups where women got together to try to figure out how their lives were shaped by a patriarchal society. It may not have looked like much at the time, but it laid the foundation for what came after. In the same way, campus protestors have begun using the internet and social media to create a national network through which to share strategies, including manuals for how to be most effective in agitating for change.[24]

One step on this path is to share this book with someone and then talk about it. Or ask around about local groups and organizations that focus on issues of privilege. If you belong to a church, synagogue, or mosque, start a study group, if there isn't one already that you can join. Attend a meeting and introduce yourself. Find out what they're doing to inform the membership about the reality of privilege and oppression.

Or after reading a book or an article that you like, send an e-mail to the author or write in care of the publisher. Don't be stopped by the common belief that authors don't want to be bothered by readers, because the truth is that they usually welcome it and respond (I do). Make contact. Go online. Connect with other people engaged in the same work. Do whatever makes you part of something larger than yourself. *Organize, organize, organize.*

At some point, it is important to develop the skills and knowledge necessary to form alliances across difference. As Paul Kivel argues, one of the keys to being a good ally is a willingness to listen and to give credence to what people say about their own experience.[25] This is not easy to do, since members of dominant groups may not like what they hear about privilege from those who are most harmed by it. It is difficult to hear anger and not take it personally, to think it's all about you, but that is what allies must be ready to do. It is also difficult for members of dominant groups to realize how mistrusted they often are by subordinate groups and not to take that personally as well. Kivel offers the following list pertaining to race to give an idea of what effective allies need to keep in mind:

"respect"	"put your body on the line"
"support"	"don't take it personally"
"find out about us"	"make mistakes"
"listen"	"understanding"
"don't take over"	"honesty"
"don't make assumptions"	"teach your children about racism"
"provide information"	"talk to other white people"
"stand by my side"	"interrupt jokes and comments"
"resources"	"speak up"
"don't assume you know what's	"don't be scared of my anger"
best for me"	"don't ask me to speak for my
"money"	people"
"take risks"	

One of the most important items on Kivel's list is for members of dominants groups to talk to one another rather than rushing in to help members of subordinate groups. What is needed first from men and whites, for example, is to form alliances among themselves as a base from which to educate and challenge other men and whites about sexist and racist behavior and the reality of how systems of privilege work. The same can be said about nondisabled people and those who are heterosexual or cisgender. For members of privileged groups to become allies, they must recall that "power concedes nothing without a demand" and add their weight to that demand. When dominant groups work against privilege, they do more than add their voices. They also make it more difficult for others to dismiss calls for change as being simply the actions of narrow special interest groups, trying to better their position.

Making alliances of all kinds is crucial for managing the risks that come with challenging systems of privilege, no matter how we are located in relation to them. Subordinate groups are the most vulnerable, but men, whites, and others in dominant groups are not immune to retaliation, if only by being ostracized and marginalized.

Don't keep it to yourself. A corollary of joining with others is not to make yourself the sole focus of change. It's not enough to work out private solutions that you keep to yourself, to clean up your act and walk away, to find ways to avoid the worst consequences of privilege and oppression at home and inside yourself and then believe that you have taken responsibility. Privilege and oppression are more than a personal problem that can be solved through personal solutions. At some point, taking responsibility means acting in a larger context, even if it's letting one other person know what you are doing. It makes sense to start with yourself, but it's equally important not to end with yourself.

A good way to convert personal change into something larger is to join and support an organization dedicated to changing systems of privilege. Most college and university campuses, for example, have groups that advocate for change on issues of gender, race, sexual orientation, and disability. There are also national organizations with local and statewide branches. Consider, for example, The American-Arab Anti-Discrimination Committee; the American Association of Disabled Persons (AADP); American Disabled for Attendant Programs Today (ADAPT); the American Indian Movement; Black Lives Matter; the Council on American-Islamic Relations; Dream Defenders; the Feminist Majority; GLAAD (formerly Gay & Lesbian Alliance against Defamation); Gay, Lesbian, and Straight Education Network (GLSEN); Idle No More; Jobs with Justice; the Leading Change Network; the League of United Latin American Citizens (LULAC); Men Engage; the Mexican American Legal and Educational Defense Fund; the National

Abortion Rights Action League; the National Association for the Advancement of Colored People (NAACP); the National Center for Race Amity; the National Conference for Community and Justice; the National Council of La Raza; the National Gay and Lesbian Task Force; the National Organization for Women (NOW); the National Urban League; Not Dead Yet; Showing Up for Racial Justice (SURJ); the Southern Christian Leadership Conference; the Southern Poverty Law Center.[26] And, of course, it you don't find the group you need, you can join with others to start your own.

If all this sounds overwhelming, find ways to remind yourself that you do not have to deal with everything or do it alone. You don't have to set yourself the impossible task of transforming society or even yourself. We *all* need help and support. All we can do is what we can *manage* to do, depending on our situation and resources, with the knowledge that we are making it easier for other people—now and in the future—to see and do what *they* can do. So, rather than defeat yourself before you start, think small, humble, and doable rather than large, heroic, and impossible. Try not to paralyze yourself with expectations you can never meet. It takes surprisingly little to make a difference. Small acts can have radical implications. If, as Edmund Burke writes, the main requirement for the perpetuation of evil is that good people do nothing, then the choice is not between all or nothing, but between nothing and *something*.

Practice humility. For dominant groups in particular, resist the temptation to consider yourself better than people who behave badly around issues of privilege, or whose understanding and analysis of the issues are not as far along as your own. Be alert to the arrogance of self righteousness that comes from thinking you know the way. And don't expect applause for stepping off the path of least resistance and doing the right thing. This is not a competition, or an opportunity to demonstrate what good people we are. There is nothing we can do that will make us not part of the problem.

Dare to make mistakes, to feel awkward and wrong and clueless and confused, out of your depth and full of doubt as you look over the edge of your competency. You have lots of company.

And don't expect an automatic benefit of the doubt based solely on your good intentions. It is too much to ask. Trust is something to be earned. Earn it.

Pay attention to the power of fear. Living in systems of privilege teaches us to be afraid of one another. Oppression depends on fear, whether it's police violence or rape or seeing "those people" as criminals or terrorists or out to get our jobs or to take over the neighborhood. We have also been taught to be afraid of our own power to stand up, to speak out, and to withdraw our consent. It is a fear often masked to not look like fear at all, all those excuses for not showing up—too busy or not enough money in the budget or too little staff or all the rest of the bureaucratic red tape and organizational priorities—"It's not the right time"—that put working for justice out of reach.[27]

There will always be occasions for fear, which means that every act calls for courage. And for that we must look to who we are—not only as individuals of a certain gender and race and class and disability status and sexual orientation, but as human beings—and why we are doing this. "When I dare to be powerful," writes Audre Lorde, "to use my strength in the service of my vision, then it becomes less and less important whether I am afraid."[28]

Don't let other people set the standard for you. Start where you are and work from there. Make lists of all the things you can imagine doing, from reading another book about privilege to joining or starting a group to suggesting policy changes at school or work to protesting against capitalism to raising questions about who cleans the bathroom at home. Then rank them from the most risky to the least. Start with the least risky and set reasonable goals ("What risk for change will I take *today?*"). As you get more experienced at taking risks and forming alliances with others, you can move up your list. You can commit yourself to whatever the next steps are for you, the tolerable risks, the contributions that offer some way to help balance the scales. As long as you do *some*thing, it counts.

In the end, taking responsibility does not have to involve guilt and blame. It means taking on the obligation to help find a way out of the trouble we are all in and to discover constructive ways to act on that obligation. Change does not require that we do anything dramatic or earth-shaking. As powerful as systems of privilege are, they cannot stand the strain of many people coming together to do something about it, beginning with the simplest act of daring to name the system and its consequences out loud.

Never, never give up. There is a story about a woman who moves into a house and is standing at the kitchen sink one day when she notices a small metal bowl wedged in the branches of a bush just outside the window. Whose it is or how it got there, she has no idea, but she winds up leaving it there, where it stays year after year, through winter snow and summer thunderstorms. Until one day she is standing at the sink, the air outside the open window absolutely still, and she happens to look at the bowl, and she is thinking how amazing it is to still be there when, suddenly, for no reason that she can see, it falls. And then it comes to her that, over all those years, there were things at work that she could not see, that culminated in a sudden moment of change that wasn't really sudden at all.

The story reminds me of the many years that I and others have spent trying to shift the understanding of privilege and oppression away from a cultural fixation on the individual to the kind of larger and more comprehensive view I have tried to describe in these pages. And for decades we have watched as nothing seemed to change, as if all that we were doing was having no effect. When, out of the blue, it seemed, just a few years ago, in a televised discussion of police violence in Ferguson, Missouri, I heard a young man speak of the *systemic* nature of race and racism. And then there was the young woman at the University of Missouri who challenged its president to define *systematic* racism. At first I was surprised, having waited so long and at a loss to explain why this should be happening now, until I reminded myself that we never know when the bowl will fall.

Which, of course, can be a long time coming.

I once spoke at a university on the subject of men's violence against women, an event organized by students who were impassioned and dedicated but didn't know how to turn out a crowd. The auditorium was huge, the turnout sparse, even for a much smaller room, people scattered about the hall making for an empty feeling that was difficult to face, much less to fill with my voice. But I was determined to speak to whoever showed up.

When this happens, I make a point of focusing on people in the crowd who are leaning in, making it clear that they've come for something and have something to give in return. Early on, I noticed an elderly man in an aisle seat beside an empty wheelchair, a dozen rows back from the stage. He listened, thoughtful, and during the Q & A, asked about sons and what we can do to save them from patriarchy and to spare those they might harm if we fail. At the end, as people left the hall, he stood, using canes to hold him up, and made his way to the stage and up the stairs and to the podium where I was signing books.

And then it was just the two of us. He thanked me for what I'd said and for coming all this way, and then we talked for a while about the work, the need for men to take a stand. He spoke with difficulty, the words coming out rounded and slurred and I wondered if it was a stroke that brought him down. He was about to leave when he leaned in as much as he could and still hold himself up, and looked into my face and spoke, as only a true elder can to someone younger, with a kind of earnest intensity that comes of being aware of limits to time and what it takes to put one foot in front of the other.

"You keep going," he said. And then, as he turned to walk away, I said after him, "You keep going too."

He paused before turning his head, and I could see from his face that he was thinking about it, working the idea in his mind as he gathered intention behind the words.

And then he said, "I think I will."

I will not forget the stillness in the air as if no one else was in the hall, the look on his face as he made up his mind yet again. And now it comes to me what I saw in his eyes as he made a little nod before saying the words, a sense of clarity, resolution, and calm.

No one knows enough to be either a pessimist or an optimist, to be able to tell whether we are having an effect or not.[29] What we can have is faith, by which I mean our capacity to not become the fear we will encounter along the way, to never doubt our potential to join with others in ways that make a difference. It is all we have. And it is enough.

Keep going.

Epilogue

A Worldview Is Hard to Change

I once received an email from a reader who wrote that anyone who believed as I did "must be either an idiot or a moron."[*] This sort of thing doesn't happen very often, but enough to show how issues of privilege and oppression can provoke strong feelings and personal attacks, as if the only way to understand someone who takes an opposing view is to assume there must be something wrong with them, that no sane, intelligent, decent person could see reality as I appeared to him to do. And, I must confess, when I read his email, I found it hard to imagine how he could fail to get what *I* was trying to say. Unless, of course, there was something wrong with *him*.

So, here we are, limited by our failures of imagination, which makes me wonder, what do I use to imagine him and he to imagine me?

What we imagine depends in part on what we already think we know, our worldview, a collection of beliefs, values, images, and assumptions we use to construct a taken-for-granted reality that shapes how we perceive and make sense of everything from the cosmos to why people do what they do. Mine, for example, includes a belief in gravity, which is supported by science and confirmed by everyday experience and, as far as I can tell, universally accepted as a matter of established fact and therefore not open to debate (all of which is also in my worldview). As a result, I don't question its existence or effect and I live accordingly.

Other perceptions are less certain. If I see the world as a dangerous place, I'll feel the need to protect myself from things that haven't happened and possibly never will, while if I see the world as relatively safe, I will not. When women, for example, are asked to name daily precautions they take to ensure their safety from sexual assault, they typically produce lists whose length surprises many men, whose own lists are much shorter if not altogether empty, reflecting a striking difference in worldviews.

Worldview differences are especially common in perceptions of social reality, including issues of privilege and oppression, and are often occasions

---

[*]It should be noted that 'moron' and 'idiot' are terms that are routinely used without awareness of the role they play in the oppression of people who have cognitive disabilities.

for conflict, as you may already have discovered in reading this book. Consider, for example, how you would respond to the following:

- To what degree are individuals responsible for the quality of their lives? Do people living in poverty, for example, have only themselves to blame? Are the wealthy the sole cause of their own abundance?

- Does every citizen of the United States count equally as a "real" American? Are some more "real" than others?

- What is capitalism? What is socialism? In what ways does each contribute to or interfere with democracy?

- Are corporations people?

- Is it possible for a group or individual to have too much wealth?

- Why is there poverty? Why is there wealth?

- Are sexual orientation and gender identity matters of individual choice?

- What is marriage? Does it matter how it is defined? If so, why? To whom?

- Should social life be organized so that people can participate regardless of whether they have disabilities?

- Does a woman have the right to control her own body, including when she is pregnant?

- Is a human fetus a citizen protected by the U.S. Constitution?

- Why is most violence perpetrated by men?

- What does it mean to love your country when it does things you believe are wrong?

- Is race a biological fact or a cultural idea with no basis in biology?

- Are people of color and white people equally likely to break the law?

- Are things that happened in the past—such as slavery and genocide in the United States—only matters of history, or do they continue to shape social life today?

Our answers to such questions can appear to us as so self-evident and beyond doubt that when we encounter opposing views, we may experience what is known as cognitive dissonance, the discomfort brought on by a mismatch between new information and what we have assumed was true. The more invested we are in the view we hold—the more central it is to our reality and our sense of who we are—the more upset we tend to be.

One way to remove the dissonance is to discredit the new information and the people associated with it, including their motivation and character. In doing this, we rely on our worldviews to imagine "those people" whose reality is so different from our own. It is a kind of imagining that we do all the time as a way to create important information that we lack, including what's going on inside other people, which of course we have no way to observe and know for sure. We make up reality as a way to fill in the gaps left by all the things we cannot know, and to lessen the anxiety that may come from uncertainty. Where it goes wrong is when we believe that what we've created in our minds is the actual thing or person or group that we're dealing with, and not just our idea of them. And then we are prone to the kind of attacks driven by anger, outrage, disbelief, and fear that have become commonplace in this society, especially in the aftermath of the 2016 presidential election—I'm right, you're wrong; I'm good, you're bad; I'm sane, you're sick; I'm smart and you're a fool.

And so it goes until we find a way to step back and see what's really happening, and then imagine something different. This is not an easy thing to do, which is why I try to keep a few things in mind when I feel my own worldview being disturbed or challenged.

First, the many things that a worldview does *not* include tend to slip into the realm of the unthinkable, making us vulnerable to possibilities we haven't even considered. Before the 2012 massacre of children at the elementary school in Newtown, Connecticut, for example, it never occurred to me that such a thing might happen. Nor, apparently, did it occur to anyone else, including police and parents and teachers, who were totally unprepared. The shock produced such a change in worldviews that mass murder in schools is now perceived as likely enough to require elaborate measures of prevention.

Second, we rarely think up the contents of a worldview on our own or adopt them by conscious choice. As a white man, for example, my belief that I am safe from the excessive use of force by police is something I came by from living in a society where that belief is reinforced every day. I don't hear stories on the news about people who look like me being beaten or gunned down by police for no good reason. Nor do I experience my perception as mere opinion or belief, but as the way things *are*, what "everybody knows," not a personal version of reality or point of view, but reality *itself.*

Third, the authority behind widely shared perceptions and beliefs is based in something larger than ourselves, a culture, which increases the tendency not only to experience them as true, but to be unaware of them, as such, in the first place. Which then sets us up to see those who hold different views as having something wrong with them that would make them unable to live in reality.

This is what happened in the aftermath of the Newtown massacre as responses diverged from a shared sense of shock, horror, and grief to a polarizing debate about whether to control access to the kind of guns used to carry out the murders. Both sides accused the other of caring not about the safety of children but only for a narrow political agenda—to promote the unrestricted right to own weapons on the one hand or to destroy the second amendment to the Constitution on the other.

This happened in part because the points of conflict have always been there. Worldviews overlap—everyone is horrified by the murder of children but then in other ways they don't—we disagree about why it happens and what's to be done about it. This country has always been home to various worldviews that get along some of the time but also erupt in conflict when we're confronted with their differences.

Another reason is that a worldview consists of countless interconnecting parts, and disturbing one will touch on many others. The issue of gun control, for example, along with the militarization of police and the role of race in how policing is done, is not simply about guns or social control or even race. It is also connected to what it means to be an American, the cultural definition of manhood, how safe we feel in the world and what we feel entitled to do when that sense of safety is gone; the role of government and authority in the lives of citizens, the belief in the use of violence as the cause of a problem or its solution, the fear of strangers and groups identified as not like 'us,' and the view of government power as a means to ensure the common good or as a threat to individual liberty, including the use of violence against citizens; the masculine ideal of the rugged individual, the degree to which we feel accountable to other people, the meaning of civil rights, of freedom, and the Constitution—to name just a few. And a worldview shapes not only how we perceive such things outside ourselves, but also our identities as individuals, and who we think we are in relation to all of that.

The result of this complexity is that worldviews are highly resistant to critical examination and doubt. It's why we dig in to defend one belief or another, not simply out of habit or because we like what we consider to be the facts, but because we depend on them for our sense of reality—who we are and how to tell the difference between what is true and what is not—making it difficult to separate ourselves from the worldview we've come to have.

In writing this book, for example, I draw on a sociological worldview by which nothing in human life comes down to just a matter of isolated individuals, that, in fact, there is no such thing, because we live our lives as participants in social systems, and what we think and feel and do results from the dynamic relation between the two. I acquired this view over many years, such that I cannot pinpoint exactly where I got it. I also cannot say just how I know for a fact that it's true. I can make an argument, I can cite evidence, but, in the final analysis, it comes down to what I believe.

A reader who shares a sociological perspective will understand that when I use a phrase such as "men's violence," I am not accusing all individual men of being violent people. And that when I point to the reality of white privilege, I am not accusing white people of being bad or suggesting they all benefit to the same degree or don't have obstacles to overcome and burdens to carry in their own lives. In contrast, a reader who does not accept the worldview on which this book is based, may conclude that I must have some kind of personal animosity toward men or white people (or myself) or that I'm out of touch with reality, or all of the above.

When debates turn ugly and accusations and personal attacks fly back and forth, we can be sure that what's at stake is something larger and deeper than the issue at hand. Even more important—given how these things usually go—it's unlikely that the worldview differences that are actually driving the conflict will ever be named, much less examined or discussed, which is why such debates are so unproductive and keep coming back. This is also why, over the past several decades, the United States has become an increasingly polarized society, as people have chosen communities where they are less likely to encounter worldviews that differ from their own.[1]

Whether you find this book illuminating or infuriating, the content of our worldviews is the most likely cause, and it is useful to step back and ask ourselves some critical questions about what is going on:

- What is the basis for believing that a worldview is true? Is it based on a careful study of a comprehensive body of evidence? A collection of stories and impressions? A personal experience? An article of faith? The gut feeling that it must be true? The inability to imagine that it could not?

- What happens if we assume the person we disagree with is every bit as intelligent, thoughtful, and well-intentioned as we are, if not more? How does that affect our understanding of the disagreement and our part in it?

- What does it mean to seriously consider that a view that contradicts our own might be true? What does that consideration require of us?

- Is it possible that *both* opposing views have some element of truth, rather than it having to be all one or the other? If so, how would our worldview have to change to accommodate that possibility?

- What if what we believe turns out not to be true? What else about our worldview would have to change as a result? In other words, what is at stake for us, what is our investment in being right, and what do we stand to lose if we're not?

- And what are the social consequences of adopting one worldview or another? What difference does it make, for example, how the questions posed earlier are answered in the culture at large? What effects will that produce, and for whom?

Such questions focus attention on differences that need to be recognized and reconciled, beginning with basic assumptions about the reality of social life and who we are to one another and what it means to be a human being. This can be confusing, threatening, even frightening work, but it's our only alternative to angry refusals to compromise or even listen to one another. Finding a way out doesn't mean making our worldviews all the same, which I doubt is possible or even desirable. But it does mean opening ourselves to the reality that our worldviews are just that, and they are not the only ones, and those who see things differently are not crazy or stupid or bad. Then we can talk about evidence and consequences and in what kind of society could multiple worldviews coexist without us being at one another's throats.

The United States fought the Civil War—by some measures the bloodiest conflict in our history—from a failure to recognize how worldviews can provoke hostility, fear, and violence, to step back and consider how we perceive and understand ourselves and the world, to strive to understand the worldview of others. We can do better than this, and given how divided this country has become over so many issues, I would say we must, and it is never too soon to begin.

Acknowledgments

As this book goes to press, I'm mindful of people who have played an important part in the work that led to the writing of it. My thanks go to my sister, Annalee Johnson, who introduced me to training work around issues of privilege and encouraged me to take a chance. I'm especially grateful to Jane Tuohy (to whom this book is dedicated) who, more than anyone, provided me with a vision of how I might use what I know in nonacademic settings, along with many opportunities to do so. She has been a role model, a source of affirmation and support, and, at times, a worthy and thoughtful adversary in the heated discussions through which we continue to work through our understanding of these difficult issues as they play out in the real world of people's lives.

I'm also grateful to Shirley Harrell, Ed Hudner, Deat LaCour, Larry Mack, Robin Brown-Manning, and Helen Turnbull for all that I learned in working with them, and to Leslie Brett, Kim Cromwell, Carolyn Gabel, and Anne Menard for how effectively they model lives dedicated to change. I'm especially grateful to my Race in America teaching partner, Fredrica Gray, for her strength and wisdom, her extraordinary breadth of knowledge, and her unfailing sense of humor when we needed it most.

I give my thanks for the thoughtful feedback and suggestions offered by the several reviewers of the manuscript for the first edition including Leon F. Burrell, Joan L. Griscom, Betsy Lucal, Tracy Ore, Fred L. Pincus, Sherwood Smith, and Robert L. Walsh. I'm especially thankful to Estelle Disch, Paula Rothenberg, and Michael Schwalbe for challenging me in all the right places.

I am also indebted to reviewers and others who made valuable suggestions as I prepared the second edition. My thanks go to Joanne Callahan, Kathy Castania, Tracy Citeroni, Jane Marantz Connor, Monica D'Antonio, Rachel David, Ann Fischer, Nicole Grant, Lori Handrahan, Andrea Herrera, Brenda Hubbard, Stuart Johnston, Elizabeth Locke, Betty Garcia Mathewson, Ted McNeilsmith, Joan Morris, V. Spike Peterson, Robert A. Principe, Dena Samuels, Carole Sheffield, Laura Szalacha, Susan L. Thomas, Helen Turnbull, Leah Ulansey, and Janice R. Welsch. I am especially grateful to Michael Schwalbe and Marshall Mitchell for their careful reading of the revised manuscript and, in addition, to Marshall for doing so much to open my eyes to nondisability privilege.

For the third edition, I want to thank Alyssa Beauchamp, Sharon E. Davis, Joseph Henderson, Ramon Jimenez, Lon Jones, Denny McCabe, Ann McCloskey, David. J. Paul, Richard Quinones, Nena Tahil, Christine Webster, and Daniel Zuckergood for their feedback and suggestions. I am especially grateful to Andrea Herrera, Cate Monaghan, Dena Samuels, and Michael Schwalbe for their generous reading of parts of the revision; and to Sybol Anderson, Andrea Herrera, Francie Kendall, Cate Monaghan, Rob Okun, and Jabali Stewart, for all those heartfelt, illuminating, and provocative conversations about difficult things. I am also grateful to the readers, audience members, and workshop participants whose questions, struggles, and insights have pushed me toward a deeper and more nuanced understanding of complex and difficult issues. What I have made of all this, of course, is entirely my own doing and responsibility.

I also want to express my profound debt to the generations of activists, scholars, and writers whose courage and vision and hard work have given us the basis for most of what we know about these issues. And to those authors whose work I encountered so long ago that their insights have inadvertently slipped into my store of common knowledge, I can offer only my appreciation and my apologies for being unable to give them proper attribution.

I thank Serina Beauparlant for her faith that first got the book into print At McGraw-Hill, I want to thank, Sherith Pankratz, for her support for my work and Jamie Laferrera for overseeing the third edition.

My deepest gratitude is reserved for my comrade, soul mate, and most beloved partner in life, Nora L. Jamieson, for all that she does to nurture and challenge and support not only the writer and thinker in me, but the human being. Where would I be without all those moments when you held the vision I'd lost sight of, and the example of your courage and wisdom in the face of a world in such desperate need of both?

Glossary

Words in italics will be found as entries elsewhere in the glossary.

ableism   Anything that has the social consequence of enforcing, enacting, or perpetuating nondisability *privilege*.

ascribed status   A position in a social *system* that is assigned at birth, such as sex or *race*.

attitude   A positive or negative evaluation of people, objects, or situations that predisposes those who hold it to feel and behave in positive or negative ways.

belief   A statement about reality, about what is regarded as true or false, such as, "Male privilege does (or does not) exist."

capitalism   A form of political economy in which the means of production are privately owned by some but used by others (workers) who sell their time to produce goods and services in return for wages.

cissexual   A person whose internal sense of themselves as biologically male or female matches the sex they were assigned at birth. *See also* transsexual.

class *See* social class.

category, social   *See* social category.

centeredness   The feature of social *systems* of *privilege* that makes it a *path of least resistance* to focus attention on members of dominant groups.

cisgender   The condition in which a person's *gender* identity matches the biological sex they were assigned at birth. *See also* transgender.

conferred dominance   A feature of *systems* of *privilege* by which *dominance* by members of privileged groups is socially expected, supported, and normalized.

culture   The collection of *beliefs*, *values*, *norms*, *attitudes*, and material objects associated with a social *system*.

democratic socialism   A form of *political economy* that combines political democracy with government regulation of private business and/or collective ownership of the means of production, such as public utilities by government, or businesses owned by workers.

disability status   A set of *social categories* used to distinguish among people according to *cultural* ideas that define the range of what are regarded as *normal* human abilities.

144

discrimination   The positive or negative treatment of people because they happen to belong to a particular *social category*.

diversity   A term referring to the relative mix of different *social statuses* in a population (e.g., the relative number of whites and people of color, women and men, etc.).

dominance   A principle of *systems* of *privilege* by which the default is for power to be held by members of the privileged *social category*. *See also* male dominance, white dominance.

double bind   A situation in which someone cannot avoid negative outcomes no matter what they do.

ecosystem   All the forms of life that live in relation to one another in a shared place.

entitlement   *See* unearned entitlement.

environmental racism   Policies and practices that favor the concentration of environmental degradation, pollution, and toxicity in or near communities or societies inhabited primarily by people of color.

epistemic privilege   *See* luxury of obliviousness.

femininity   A set of *cultural* ideas used to define the ideal and essential nature of women.

feminism   An *ideology* and framework for the analysis of human life based on the belief that *gender* inequality is real and problematic.

gender   *Cultural* ideas used to construct images and expectations of those identified as female or male.

genderqueer   A person who gender-identifies as neither a man nor a woman (genderless) or as some combination of the two.

heteronormativity   A *cultural* standard by which heterosexuality is defined and enforced as the *normal* sexual orientation.

heterosexism   Anything that has the consequence of enforcing, enacting, or perpetuating heterosexual *privilege*.

heterosexual centeredness   An organizing principle of the *system* of heterosexual *privilege* by which the *path of least resistance* is to place heterosexual people and what they do at the center of attention.

heterosexual dominance   An organizing principle of the *system* of heterosexual *privilege* by which the default condition is for positions of power to be held by heterosexual people.

heterosexual identification   An organizing principle of the *system* of heterosexual *privilege* by which heterosexual people are taken to be the standard for human beings and are thereby regarded as superior to people who are lesbian, gay, or bisexual.

homophobia   Fear of or aversion to same-sex sexual attraction.

identification   The feature of *systems* of *privilege* by which the dominant group is *culturally* defined as the standard for human beings in general, and is therefore regarded as superior or of greater value.

identity   The sum total of who we think we are in relation to other people and *social systems*.

ideology   A set of *cultural* ideas used to explain and justify the status quo or movements for social change.

imperialism   The practice of one nation seeking to dominate others for its own gain.

implicit bias   Unconscious bias either for or against a category of people.

income   Resources, especially in the form of money, received as a result of work, investments, etc. and that may be converted to wealth.

individualism   A way of thinking based on the idea that everything that happens in social life results solely from the thoughts and feelings of individuals without reference to their participation in social *systems*.

intersectionality   A concept that refers to the fact that we live our lives as occupants of a combination of *social statuses* that locate us in relation to social *systems—gender*, *race*, *social class*, and many others—and that to understand our experience and behavior, we have to consider how those combine and interact with one another, often in complicated ways.

intersex   A condition in which someone is born with a combination of what are culturally defined as female and male sex characteristics.

Islamophobia   Prejudice and hostility directed at Muslims and, by extension, anyone who appears to be of Arab or Middle Eastern origin.

LGBTQ   An acronym standing for lesbian, gay, bisexual, *transgender*, and *queer*.

luxury of obliviousness   An aspect of *systems* of *privilege* by which members of dominant groups have the option of choosing whether to be aware of the true extent, causes, and consequences of *privilege* and *oppression*. Also known as *epistemic privilege*.

male centeredness   An organizing principle of the *system* of male *privilege* by which the *path of least resistance* is to place males and what they do at the center of attention.

male dominance   An organizing principle of the *system* of male *privilege* by which the default condition is for positions of power to be held by men.

male identification   An organizing principle of the *system* of male *privilege* by which males are taken to be the standard for human beings and are thereby regarded as superior to females and of greater value.

Manifest Destiny   Originating in the 19th-century, an *ideology* by which the United States was chosen by God to expand across the continent and spread its influence and culture to peoples regarded as "uncivilized" and thereby inferior.

masculinity   A set of cultural ideas used to define the ideal and essential nature of men.

matrix of domination   The interconnection of different forms of *privilege* and *oppression* and the complex ways in which people's standing in relation to one affects their position and experience in relation to another. Also known as *matrix of privilege. See also* intersectionality.

matrix of privilege   *See* matrix of domination.

microaggression   Behaviors that, although often considered harmless by dominant groups, have the consequence of enacting privilege by excluding, degrading, demeaning, insulting, or dismissing others.

model minority   A term applied to subordinate groups, whose achievements are used by dominant groups to disparage and assign responsibility to other subordinate groups for their own *oppression* in a *system* of *privilege*.

nadle   A word used among the Diné (Navaho) tribe of the American Southwest to designate people born with a mixture of female and male characteristics.

nondisability centeredness   An organizing principle of the *system* of nondisability *privilege* by which the *path of least resistance* is to place people without disabilities and what they do at the center of attention.

nondisability dominance   An organizing principle of the *system* of nondisability *privilege* by which the default condition is for positions of power to be held by people without disabilities.

nondisability identification   An organizing principle of the *system* of nondisability *privilege* by which people without disabilities are taken to be the standard for human beings and are thereby regarded as superior to people with disabilities and of greater value.

norm   A *cultural* rule that links appearance or behavior with reward or punishment.

normal   What is *culturally* defined as the socially acceptable range for human beings, including behavior, appearance, cognition, emotion, and physical ability.

obliviousness   *See* luxury of obliviousness.

one drop rule   A way of defining race in the United States by which a person was held to be black if their lineage contained any black ancestors, regardless of their personal appearance or self identification.

oppression   The *systemic* subordination, exploitation, and mistreatment of one group by another as an assertion and defense of *privilege*.

organization   A complex *system* organized around specific goals, and usually consisting of several interrelated groups or subsystems.

other   A marginalized or excluded *social category* of people who are recognized as having no valid point of view regarding themselves or the dominant groups who benefit from their *oppression* and exclusion, and whose experience has meaning and value only in relation to the dominant group.

paradigm   A framework of guiding assumptions, theories, and methods that define a particular approach to observing, interpreting, and understanding reality.

paradox   Two statements that appear to contradict each other when both, in fact, are true.

passive oppression   The perpetuation of *privilege* and *oppression* through inattention, insensitivity, neglect, or lack of awareness.

path of least resistance   In a social *system*, the behavior or appearance that is expected of participants based on their position in a particular situation.

patriarchy   A social *system* organized around the principles of *male dominance*, *male centeredness*, *male identification*, and an obsession with control that is gendered as *masculine*.

political correctness   Originally, a standard used by social activists as a way to monitor their behavior and speech to ensure that it was consistent with their *values*, *beliefs*, and political principles.

political economy   A concept that refers to the interdependent workings and interests of political and economic *systems* and elites, making it impossible to understand the one without taking into account its relation to the other.

prejudice   A positive or negative *attitude* directed at people simply because they occupy a particular *social status*.

privilege   An advantage that is unearned, exclusive to a particular group or *social category*, and socially conferred by others.

queer A general term for those who, in various ways, reject, test, or otherwise transgress the boundaries of what is culturally regarded as *normal* in relation to *gender*, sexual identity, or *sexual orientation* and expression.

race A socially constructed set of categories based on physical appearance, especially skin color, used primarily as a basis for *privilege* and economic exploitation.

racism Anything that has the consequence of enacting, enforcing, or perpetuating a *system* of *privilege* based on *race*.

reference group A group used by others as a standard against which to measure such qualities as appearance, behavior, ability, or achievement.

segregation The physical separation of different groups from one another.

sexism Anything that has the effect of enacting, enforcing, or perpetuating *privilege* based on *gender*.

social category The collection of all people who occupy a particular *social status* (e.g, "college students" or "women").

social class In general, distinctions and divisions resulting from the unequal distribution of resources and rewards such as wealth, power, and prestige in a social *system*. A Marxist approach focuses on how relationships among capitalists, workers, and the means of production create and perpetuate inequality. More mainstream approaches focus on people's ability to satisfy wants and needs, especially through income and the use of prestige and power.

social construction of reality The process of using language and other symbols to construct perceptions of what is considered to be real.

social mobility The movement of people from one social *class* position to another.

social status A position occupied by one or more people in a social *system*, such as employee, sister, or man.

system (social) An interconnected collection of *socially structural* relationships, *ecological* arrangements, *cultural* symbols, ideas, and objects, and population dynamics and conditions that combine to form a whole. Complex systems are comprised of smaller systems that are related to one another and the larger system through cultural, structural, ecological, and population arrangements and dynamics.

status *See* social status.

stereotype A rigid, over-simplified, positive or negative belief that is attached to all members of a particular group or *social category*.

transgender A transgender person is someone whose experience of themselves does not match the sex they were assigned at birth. S*ee also* cisgender.

transsexual A transsexual person is someone who either has or wants to undergo a medically assisted transition to bring their body into alignment with how they experience themselves in terms of *gender*. S*ee also* cissexual.

trans man A person who was sex-assigned as female at birth and who *gender*-identifies as a man.

trans woman A person who was sex-assigned as male at birth and who *gender*-identifies as a woman.

unearned advantage A desirable feature of social life that should be available to all as an *unearned entitlement*, but that has become a form of *privilege* available only to members of dominant groups (such as being treated with respect).

unearned entitlement A desirable feature of social life that should be available to all.

value An idea about relative worth, goodness, or desirability used in choosing among alternatives. In a *patriarchy*, for example, maleness is valued above femaleness, and being in control is valued above not being in control.

white centeredness An organizing principle of the *system* of white *privilege* by which the *path of least resistance* is to place white people and what they do at the center of attention.

white dominance An organizing principle of the *system* of white *privilege* by which the default condition is for positions of power to be held by white people.

white identification An organizing principle of the *system* of white *privilege* by which white people are taken to be the standard for human beings and regarded as superior to people of color and of greater value.

white privilege A general term for unearned advantages available exclusively to those who are socially identified as white.

worldview The collection of interconnected *beliefs*, *values*, *attitudes*, images, stories, and memories out of which a sense of reality is constructed and maintained. S*ee also* social construction of reality; paradigm.

zero-sum society A social *system* in which every gain by some is offset by a corresponding loss for others.

Notes

INTRODUCTION

1. Lorraine Hansberry, *A Raisin in the Sun*. New York: Random House, 1950.
2. See the National Center on Disability and Journalism's "Style Guide" at http://ncdj.org/style-guide/. As the third edition goes to press in 2016, I'm aware that among disability rights activists views may be changing about the language used to describe people with disabilities, with some arguing that to *not* use the word 'disabled' can have the effect of making disability invisible, as if it were socially and personally irrelevant. See Barbara J. King, for example, "'Disabled:' Just #SayTheWord." *National Public Radio*, Feb. 25, 2016. Online at http://www.npr.org/sections/13.7/2016/02/25/468073722/disabled-just-saytheword.
3. One of the most effective explanations of the myth of biological race is found in a PBS video series, *Race: the Power of an Illusion*. For more, go to http://www.pbs.org/race/000_General/000_00-Home.htm. See also Daniel J. Fairbanks, *Everyone Is African: How Science Explodes the Myth of Race*. New York: Prometheus Books, 2015; Jacqueline Jones, *A Dreadful Deceit: The Myth of Race from the Colonial Era to Obama's America*. New York: Basic Books, 2015.
4. See Theodore W. Allen, *The Invention of the White Race*, vols. 1 & 2, 2nd ed. New York: Verso, 2012; Audrey Smedley and Brian Smedley, *Race in North America: Origin and Evolution of a Worldview*, 4th ed. Boulder, CO: Westview Press, 2011; Nell Irvin Painter, *The History of White* People. New York: W. W. Norton, 2010; and Basil Davidson, *The African Slave Trade*, rev. and exp. edition. New York: Atlantic Monthly Press, 1980.
5. See Derald Wing Sue, *Microaggressions in Everyday Life: Race, Gender, and Sexual Orientation*. New York: Wiley, 2010.

CHAPTER 1: WE'RE IN TROUBLE

1. See Ryan Gabrielson, Ryann Grochowski, and Eric Sagara, "Deadly Force, in Black and White." *ProPublica*, Oct. 10, 2014, available online at http://www.propublica.org/article/deadly-force-in-black-and-white.
2. W. E. B. Du Bois, *The Souls of Black Folk*. New York: Penguin, 1989. First published in 1903.
3. See, for example, Eduardo Bonilla-Silva, *Racism without Racists: Color-Blind Racism and the Persistence of Racial Inequality in the United States*, 4th ed. Lanham, MD: Rowman and Littlefield, 2013; and *White Supremacy and Racism in the Post–Civil Rights Era*. Boulder, CO: Lynne Rienner, 2001; Ta-Nehisi Coates, *Between the World and Me*. New York: Spiegel and Grau, 2015; George Horse Capture, Duane Champagne, and Chandler C. Jackson. *American Indian Nations: Yesterday, Today, and Tomorrow*. Lanham, MD: AltaMira Press, 2007; Moon-Kie Jung, Joao Costa Vargas, and Eduardo Bonilla-Silva, *State of White*

Supremacy: Racism, Governance, and the United States. Stanford, CA: Stanford University Press, 2011; James H. Carr and Nandinee Kutty (eds.), *Segregation: The Rising Costs for America*. New York: Routledge, 2008; and Donald A. Barr, *Health Disparities in the United States: Social Class, Race, Ethnicity, and Health*, 2nd ed. Baltimore, MD. Johns Hopkins University Press, 2014.

4. See Michele Alexander, *The New Jim Crow: Mass Incarceration in the Age of Colorblindness*. New York: New Press, 2012.

5. See Sean F. Reardon and Ann Owens, "60 Years after Brown: Trends and Consequences of School Segregation," *Annual Review of Sociology*, 40, 2014; Gary Orfield, "Schools More Separate: Consequences of a Decade of Resegregation," The Civil Rights Project, Harvard University, 2001. Online at http://www.civilrightsproject.harvard.edu/research/deseg/Schools_More_Separate.pdf.

6. See Edward N. Wolff, *The Asset Price Meltdown and the Wealth of the Middle Class*. New York: National Bureau of Economic Research, Working Paper 18599, Nov. 2012. See also G. William Domhoff, "Who Rules America?" Feb. 2013. Accessed online at http://whorulesamerica.net/power/wealth.html.

7. See Sylvia A. Allegretto, "The State of Working America's Wealth, 2011." Washington, DC: Economic Policy Institute, 2011; Beverly Moran, *Race and Wealth Disparities: A Multidisciplinary Discourse*. Lanham, MD: Rowman and Littlefield, 2008; U.S. Census Bureau, *Current Population Reports, Series P-60, Money Income in the United States*, 2012. Washington, DC: U.S. Government Printing Office, 2013; and *Statistical Abstract of the United States, 2012*. Washington, DC: U.S. Government Printing Office, 2013; Valerie Wilson and William M. Rodgers III, "Black-White Wage Gaps Expand with Rising Wage Inequality." Washington, D.C.: Economic Policy Institute, 2016; Roland G. Fryer, Devah Pager, and Jörg L. Spenkuch, "Racial Disparities in Job Finding and Offered Wages." *Journal of Law and Economics*, 56(3), 633–689, 2013.

8. See, for example, Bryce Covert, "Getting a College Degree Won't Protect Black Workers from the Economy's Racial Barriers," in *ThinkProgress*, May 20, 2014. Available online at http://thinkprogress.org/economy/2014/05/20/3439739/black-college-graduates-unemployment/.

9. See Celia Ridgeway, *Framed by Gender: The Persistence of Gender Inequality in the Modern World*. New York: Oxford, 2011; Susan J. Douglas, *Enlightened Sexism: The Seductive Message that Feminism's Work Is Done*. New York: Henry Holt, 2010; Barbara J. Berg, *Sexism in America: Alive, Well, and Ruining Our Future*. Chicago: Lawrence Hill, 2009; David Cotter, Joan Hermsen, and Reeve Vanneman, "The End of the Gender Revolution? Gender Role Attitudes from 1977–2008." *American Journal of* Sociology (117, 1) Jul. 2011; U.S. Census Bureau, Current Population Survey, Annual Social and Economic (ASEC) Supplement, Table PINC-05, "Work Experience—People 15 Years Old and Over by Total Money Earnings, Age, Race, Hispanic Origin, Sex, and Disability Status." Washington, DC: U.S. Government Printing Office, 2011; Kenneth Chang, "Bias Persists for Women in Science," *The New York Times*, Sep. 24, 2012; Shaila Dewan and Robert Gebeloff, "The New American Job: More Men Enter Fields Dominated by Women," *The New York Times*, May 20, 2012; "Women in Elective Office 2013," Center for American Women and Politics,

Eagleton Institute of Politics, Rutgers University, 2013; Shira Offer and Barbara Schneider, "Revisiting the Gender Gap in Time-Use Patterns: Multitasking and Well-Being among Mothers and Fathers in Dual-Earner Families," *American Sociological Review*, Dec. 2011; and Judith Treas and Sonja Drobnic, *Dividing the Domestic: Men, Women, and Household Work in Cross-National Perspective.* Stanford, CA: Stanford University Press, 2010.

10. See Sanja Bahun-Radunović, *Violence and Gender in the Globalized World.* Burlington, VT: Ashgate, 2008; "Unholy Alliance," *The New York Times*, Mar. 11, 2013; and Siddharth Kara, *Sex Trafficking: Inside the Business of Modern Slavery.* New York: Columbia University Press, 2010.

11. See Associated Press, "One Third of Women Assaulted by a Partner, Global Report Says," *The New York Times*, Jun. 20, 2013.

12. See Anya Kamenetz, "The History of Campus Sexual Assault," Feb. 2, 2015, available on the National Public Radio website at http://www.npr.org/sections/ed/2014/11/30/366348383/the-history-of-campus-sexual-assault?sc=ipad&f=1001; data on risks to servicewomen reported on PBS *Newshour*, Jul. 30, 2013.

13. See Pam Fessler, "Why Disability and Poverty Still go Hand in Hand 25 Years After Landmark Law." National Public Radio, Jul. 26, 2015. Available online at http://www.npr.org/sections/health-shots/2015/07/23/424990474/why-disability-and-poverty-still-go-hand-in-hand-25-years-after-landmark-law; Brewster Thackeray, "State of the Union for People with Disabilities," National Organization on Disability (www.comstocknod.org), 2003; Lennard J. Davis, *The Disability Studies Reader,* 4th ed. New York: Routledge, 2013; Harris & Associates, "N.O.D./Harris Survey of Americans with Disabilities." Washington, DC: National Organization on Disabilities, 2000; and U.S. Census Bureau (2006), American Community Survey: Selected economic characteristics. Available online at http://www.census.gov/acs/www/index.html.

14. For a fuller picture of what she is up against (and I am not), see Peggy McIntosh, "White Privilege and Male Privilege: A Personal Account of Coming to See Correspondences Through Work in Women's Studies." Wellesley, MA: Wellesley Centers for Research on Women, 1988; and Joe R. Feagin and Karyn D. McKinney, *The Many Costs of Racism.* Lanham, MD: Rowman and Littlefield, 2003.

15. See, for example, Carol Brooks Gardner, *Passing By: Gender and Public Harassment.* Berkeley: University of California Press, 1995; and "Why Telling a Woman to Smile Makes Her Want to Scream." National Public Radio, Apr. 9, 2016, available online at http://www.npr.org/sections/goatsandsoda/2016/04/09/473433505/why-telling-a-woman-to-smile-makes-her-want-to-scream.

CHAPTER 2: PRIVILEGE, OPPRESSION, AND DIFFERENCE

1. See, for example, Michael Kimmel, *Angry White Men: American Masculinity at the End of an Era.* New York: Nation Books, 2015.

2. See Audrey Smedley and Brian Smedley, *Race in North America: Origin and Evolution of a Worldview*, 4th ed. Boulder, CO: Westview, 2011.

3. Personal correspondence, Feb. 27, 2004.

4. Marilyn Loden and Judy B. Rosener, *Workforce America: Managing Employee Diversity as a Vital Resource.* New York: McGraw-Hill, 1991, p. 20.

5. See Anne Fausto-Sterling, *Sexing the Body: Gender Politics and the Construction of* Sexuality. New York: Basic Books, 2000; Michel Foucault, *History of Sexuality.* New York: Vintage, 1980; and M. Kay Martin and Barbara Voorhies, *Female of the Species.* New York: Columbia University Press, 1975; see also Anne Fausto-Sterling, "The Five Sexes: Why Male and Female Are Not Enough," *The Sciences* (Mar./Apr. 1993), pp. 20–24; and Jamison Green, *Becoming a Visible Man.* Nashville: Vanderbilt University Press, 2004.

6. See Jonathan Ned Katz, "The Invention of Heterosexuality." *Socialist Review* 20 (Jan.–Mar., 1990): 7–34; and Neil Miller, *Out of the Past: Gay and Lesbian History from 1869 to the Present.* New York: Vintage, 1995.

7. The sections that follow are organized around types of behavior that are discussed in terms of racism by Joe R. Feagin and Melvin P. Sikes, *Living with Racism: The Black Middle-Class Experience.* Boston: Beacon Press, 1994, pp. 21–22. I apply them more broadly here.

8. James Baldwin, "On Being 'White' . . . and Other Lies," *Essence,* 1984. Reprinted in David R. Roediger (ed.), *Black on White: Black Writers on What It Means to Be White.* New York: Schocken, 1999, pp. 177–80.

9. See Michael Omi and Howard Winant, *Racial Formations in the United States.* London: Routledge, 1986.

10. For a classic statement about the social construction of reality, see Peter L. Berger and Thomas Luckmann, *The Social Construction of Reality: A Treatise in the Sociology of Knowledge*, rev. ed. London: Allen Lane, 1967.

11. For more on the social construction of whiteness, see Theodore W. Allen, *The Invention of the White Race,* vols. 1 & 2, 2nd ed. New York: Verso, 2012; Charles Gallagher, "White Racial Formation: Into the Twenty-First Century," in Richard Delgado and Jean Stefancic (eds.), *Critical White Studies.* Philadelphia: Temple University Press, 1997, pp. 6–11; Christopher Wills, "The Skin We're In," in Delgado and Stefancic, pp. 12–14; Reginald Horsman, "Race and Manifest Destiny: The Origins of American Racial Anglo-Saxonism," in Delgado and Stefancic, pp. 139–44; and Kathleen Neal Cleaver, "The Antidemocratic Power of Whiteness," in Delgado and Stefancic, pp. 157–63.

12. See Eli Clare, "Stolen Bodies, Reclaimed Bodies." *Public Culture* 13(3), 2001, pp. 359–65; Susan Wendell, *The Rejected Body.* New York: Routledge, 1996; and Paul Jaeger and Cynthia Ann Bowman, *Understanding Disability: Inclusion, Access, Diversity, and Civil Rights.* Wesport, CT: Praeger, 2005.

13. See Adrian Piper, "Passing for White, Passing for Black," in *Critical White Studies,* in Delgado and Stefancic (eds.) Philadelphia: Temple University Press, 1997, pp. 425–31.

14. For her classic statement on the concept of privilege, see Peggy McIntosh, "White Privilege and Male Privilege: A Personal Account of Coming to See Correspondences Through Work in Women's Studies." Wellesley, MA: Wellesley Centers for Research on Women, 1988.

15. Ibid., p. 35.

16. See Michell Fine and Adrienne Asch, "Disability beyond Stigma: Social Interaction, Discrimination, and Activism," in *Readings for Diversity and Social Justice,* Maurianne Adams, Warren J. Blumenfeld, Rosie Castañeda, Heather W. Hackman, Madeline L. Peters, and Ximena Zúñiga (eds.). New York: Routledge, 2000, pp. 330–39.

17. See Robert Terry, "The Negative Impact of White Values," in Benjamin P. Bowser and Raymond Hunt (eds.), *Impacts of Racism on White Americans.* Newbury Park, CA: Sage Publications, 1981, p. 120; and Jean Baker Miller, who makes a similar observation in relation to gender in *Toward a New Psychology of Women,* 2nd ed. Boston: Beacon Press, 1987.

18. James Baldwin, "On Being 'White' . . . and Other Lies," *Essence,* 1984. Reprinted in David R. Roediger (ed.), *Black on White: Black Writers on What It Means to Be White.* New York: Schocken Books, 1999, pp. 177–80.

19. See Ellis Cose, *Rage of a Privileged Class.* New York: HarperCollins, 1993, p. 48.

20. See Lisa Heldke, "A Du Boisian Proposal for Persistently White Colleges." *Journal of Speculative Philosophy*, Vol. 18, No. 3, 2004, pp. 224–38; and George Lipsitz, *The Possessive Investment in Whiteness: How White People Benefit from Identity Politics*, rev. ed. Philadelphia: Temple University Press, 2006.

21. Charlotte Bunch, "Not for Lesbians Only," *Quest* 11, no. 2 (Fall 1975).

22. Harry Brod, "Work Clothes and Leisure Suits: The Class Basis and Bias of the Men's Movement," in *Men's Lives,* Michael Kimmel and Michael A. Messner (eds.). New York: Macmillan, 1989, p. 280. Italics in original.

23. See, for example, Ilana Yurkiewicz, "Study Shows Gender Bias in Science is Real," *Scientific American*, Sep. 23, 2012. Available online at http://blogs.scientificamerican.com/unofficial-prognosis/study-shows-gender-bias-in-science-is-real-heres-why-it-matters.

24. See Michael Schwalbe, *Manhood Acts: Gender and the Practices of Domination.* Boulder, CO: Paradigm, 2014.

25. Peggy McIntosh , "White Privilege and Male Privilege: A Personal Account of Coming to See Correspondences through Work in Women's Studies." Wellesley, MA: Wellesley Centers for Research on Women, 1988.

26. In addition to the sources cited in this section, see the Resources appendix.

27. See "The Racial Dimension of New York Police's Use of Force," National Public Radio, Oct. 1, 2015, online at http://www.npr.org/sections/thetwo-way/2015/10/01/445026910/the-racial-dimension-of-new-york-polices-use-of-force-in-1-graphic; Michele Alexander, *The New Jim Crow: Mass Incarceration in the Age of Colorblindness.* New York: New Press, 2012; and Ryan Gabrielson, Ryann Grochowski, and Eric Sagara, "Deadly Force, in Black and White." *ProPublica*, Oct. 10, 2014, available online at http://www.propublica.org/article/deadly-force-in-black-and-white.

28. See Celia Ridgeway , *Framed by Gender: The Persistence of Gender Inequality in the Modern World.* New York: Oxford, 2011; Kenneth Chang, "Bias Persists for Women in Science." *The New York Times*, Sep. 24, 2012; Roland G. Fryer, Devah Pager, and Jörg L. Spenkuch, "Racial Disparities in Job Finding and Offered Wages." *Journal of Law and Economics*, 56(3), 633–689, 2013; M. arianne Bertrand and Sendhil Mullainathan, "Are Emily and Greg More Employable Than

Lakisha and Jamal? A Field Experiment on Labor Market Discrimination." *American Economic Review*, 94, 2004, pp. 991–1013; and András Tilcsik, "Pride and Prejudice: Employment Discrimination against Openly Gay Men in the United States." *American Journal of Sociology*, Sep. 2011.

29. See Kevin Hylton, *"Race" and Sport: Critical Race Theory*. New York: Routledge, 2009.
30. See Ridgeway, *Framed by Gender: The Persistence of Gender Inequality in the Modern World*. New York: Oxford, 2011.
31. See Vincent Roscigno, *The Face of Discrimination: How Race and Gender Impact Work and Home Lives*. Lanham, MD: Rowan and Littlefield, 2007.
32. See Algernon Austin, "Whiter Jobs, Higher Wages. Occupational Segregation and the Lower Wages of Black Men." Economic Policy Institute, briefing paper 288, Feb. 25, 2011; Ariane Hegewisch, Hannah Liepmann, Jeffrey Hayes, and Heidi Hartmann, "Separate and Not Equal? Gender Segregation in the Labor Market and the Gender Wage Gap." Institute for Women's Policy Research, Sep. 2010; and Rosalind S. Chou and Joe R. Feagin, *The Myth of the Model Minority: Asian Americans Facing Racism*. Boulder, CO; Paradigm, 2008.
33. See Renea Merle, "Minority Homeowners More Affected by Home Foreclosures than Whites." *The Washington Post*, Jun. 18, 2010; Tara Seigel Bernard, "Blacks Face Bias in Bankruptcy," *The New York Times*, Jan. 20, 2012; Jacob Rugh and Douglas S. Massey, "Racial Segregation and the American Foreclosure Crisis." *American Sociological Review*, Oct. 2010.
34. See Ian Ayres and Peter Siegelman, "Race and Gender Discrimination in Bargaining for a New Car," *American Economic* Review, Jun. 1995; James H. Carr and Nandinee Kutty, *Segregation: The Rising Costs for America*. New York: Routledge, 2008; and D. Henriques, "Review of Nissan Car Loans Explains Why Blacks Pay More." *The New York Times*, Jul. 4, 2001, p. 1.
35. Blacks, by contrast, have been found to be less likely than whites to receive state of the art treatment even when they can afford it. See Augustus A. White, *Seeing Patients: Unconscious Bias in Health Care*. Cambridge: Harvard University Press, 2011.
36. See Donald A. Barr, *Health Disparities in the United States: Social Class, Race, Ethnicity, and Health*, 2nd ed. Baltimore, MD: Johns Hopkins University Press, 2014; and Augustus A. White, *Seeing Patients: Unconscious Bias in Health Care*. Cambridge: Harvard University Press, 2011.
37. See, for example, Robert D. Bullard, "Confronting Environmental Racism in the Twenty-First Century," *Global* Dialogue, 4, 1, Winter 2002; Dorceta Taylor, *Toxic Communities: Environmental Racism, Industrial Pollution, and Residential Mobility*. New York: New York University Press, 2014; and Carl Zimring, *Clean and White: A History of Environmental Racism in the United States*. New York: New York University Press, 2016.
38. See, for example, "2015 Hollywood Diversity Report." Bunch Center for African American Studies, University of California at Los Angeles, Feb. 25, 2015. Available online at http://www.bunchecenter.ucla.edu/index.php/2015/02/2015-hollywood-diversity-report.
39. See, for example, Mary M Talbot, *Language and Gender: An Introduction,* 2nd ed. Cambridge: Polity Press, 2010; and Laurie P. Arliss, *Women and Men*

Communicating: Challenges and Changes, 2nd ed. Prospect Heights, IL: Waveland, 2000.

40. Many of the examples of cisgender privilege are taken from the website, "Everyday Feminism," found online at www.everydayfeminism.com.
41. See, for example, Amanda K. Sesko and Monica Biernat, "Prototypes of Race and Gender: The Invisibility of Black Women," *Journal of Experimental Social Psychology* 46 (2010), 356–60; and Michael Welp, "Vanilla Voices: Researching White Men's Diversity Learning Journeys," *American Behavioral Scientist* 45 (8), Apr. 2002.
42. Paul Kivel, *Uprooting Racism: How White People Can Work for Racial Justice,* rev. ed. Gabriola Island, BC: New Society Publishers, 2002, p. 122.
43. See Ruth Frankenberg, *The Social Construction of Whiteness: White Women, Race Matters.* Minneapolis: University of Minnesota Press, 1993.
44. See, for example, Naomi Klein, "Why #BlackLivesMatter Should Transform the Climate Debate." *The Nation*, Dec. 12, 2014.
45. For her classic discussion of the meaning of oppression, see Marilyn Frye, *The Politics of Reality: Essays in Feminist Theory.* Trumansburg, NY: Crossing Press, 1983, pp. 1–16. See also Alison Bailey, "Privilege: Expanding on Marilyn Frye's 'Oppression,'" *Journal of Social Philosophy*, Winter 1998, pp 104 –19.

CHAPTER 3: CAPITALISM, CLASS, AND THE MATRIX OF DOMINATION

1. See Theodore W. Allen, *The Invention of the White Race,* vols. 1 & 2, 2nd ed. New York: Verso, 2012; Audrey Smedley and Brian Smedley, *Race in North America: Origin and Evolution of a Worldview*, 4th ed. Boulder, CO: Westview, 2011; and Basil Davidson, *The African Slave Trade*, rev. and exp. edition. New York: Atlantic Monthly Press, 1980.
2. See Basil Davidson, *The African Slave Trade*, rev. and exp. edition. New York: Atlantic Monthly Press, 1980. See also Audrey Smedley and Brian Smedley, *Race in North America: Origin and Evolution of a Worldview*, 4th ed. Boulder, CO: Westview Press, 2011.
3. For more about capitalism and how it works, see Richard C. Edwards, Michael Reich, and Thomas E. Weisskopf, *The Capitalist System,* 3rd ed. Englewood Cliffs, NJ: Prentice Hall, 1986, and Joan Smith, *Social Issues and the Social Order: The Contradictions of Capitalism.* Cambridge, MA: Winthrop, 1981. See also Peter Saunders, *Capitalism.* Minneapolis: University of Minnesota Press, 1995. And for a more whimsical (but no less informative) view, try David Smith and Phil Evans, *Marx's "Kapital" for Beginners.* New York: Pantheon, 1982.
4. See Thomas Piketty, *Capital in the 21st Century.* Cambridge: Belknap Press, 2014.
5. See "The Families Funding the 2016 Presidential Election." *The New York Times*, Oct. 10, 2015. Online at http://www.nytimes.com/interactive/2015/10/11/us/politics/2016-presidential-election-super-pac-donors.html?_r=0.
6. See Martin Gilens and Benjamin I. Page, "Testing Theories of American Politics: Elites, Interest Groups, and Average Citizens." *Perspectives on Politics*, 12, 3 (Sep. 2014), pp. 557–62.

7. See, for example, David A. Stockman, *The Great Deformation: The Corruption of Capitalism in America.* New York: Public Affairs Books, 2013.

8. See "House Passes Physician Bargaining Bill," Reuter's Online, Jun. 30, 2000; and Robert A. Brooks, *Cheaper by the Hour: Temporary Lawyers and the Deprofessionalization of the Law.* Philadelphia, PA: Temple University Press, 2012.

9. See Charles C. Ragin and Y. W. Bradshaw, "International Economic Dependence and Human Misery: 1938–1980: A Global Perspective," *Sociological Perspectives* 35 (2), 1992, pp. 217–47. See also Harold R. Kerbo, *Social Stratification and Inequality,* 8th ed. New York: McGraw-Hill, 2012, chps 14–16.

10. See Edward N. Wolff, *The Asset Price Meltdown and the Wealth of the Middle Class.* New York: National Bureau of Economic Research, Working Paper 18599, Nov. 2012. Online at G. William Domhoff, "Who Rules America?" http://whorulesamerica.net/power/wealth.html.

11. For more on class, see Stanley Aronowitz, *How Class Works: Power and Social Movement.* New Haven: Yale University Press, 2004; Benjamin I. Cage and Lawrence R. Jacobs. *Class War? What Americans Really Think about Class Inequality.* Chicago: University of Chicago Press, 2009; Harold Kerbo, *Social Stratification and Inequality,* 8th ed. New York: McGraw-Hill, 2011, Chapters 6–9, and E. O. Wright, *Classes.* New York: Schocken, 1985. See also the "Social Class" in the Resources section in this book.

12. See, for example, Leonard Beeghley, *Living Poorly in America: The Reality of Poverty and Pauperism.* New York: Praeger, 1983; Frances Fox Piven and Richard A. Cloward, *Regulating the Poor: The Functions of Public Welfare,* updated ed. New York: Vintage Books, 1993; and Jeffrey Reiman, *The Rich Get Richer and the Poor Get Prison: Ideology, Class, and Criminal Justice,* 10th ed. New York: Macmillan, 2012.

13. See, for example, Martha R. Burt, *Over the Edge: The Growth of Homelessness in the 1980s.* New York: Russell Sage Foundation, 1992; and Peter H. Rossi, *Down and Out in America: The Origins of Homelessness.* Chicago: University of Chicago Press, 1989. See also Jacob Rugh and Douglas S. Massey, "Racial Segregation and the American Foreclosure Crisis." *American Sociological Review,* Oct. 2010.

14. For more on social mobility, see Harold R. Kerbo, *Social Stratification and Inequality,* 8th ed. New York: McGraw-Hill, 2012, Chapter 11.

15. See Sheldon Danziger and Peter Gottschalk, *Uneven Tides: Rising Inequality in America.* New York: Russell Sage Foundation, 1993.

16. In 2014, for example, the breakdown was lower class, 9%; working class, 46%; middle class, 42%; upper class, 3% (less than 1% gave no answer). Source: National Opinion Research Center, University of Chicago. See http://gssdataexplorer.norc.org/variables/568/vshow.

17. See, for example, Barbara Ehrenreich, *Fear of Falling: The Inner Life of the Middle Class.* New York: HarperCollins, 1989; and *Nickel and Dimed: On (Not) Getting By in America.* New York: Metropolitan Books, 2001. See also Juliet B. Schor, *The Overworked American: The Unexpected Decline of Leisure.* New York: Basic Books, 1993.

18. See Lester C. Thurow, *The Zero-Sum Society: Distribution and the Possibilities for Economic Change.* New York: Basic Books, 2001.

19. See Edward E. Baptist, *The Half Has Never Been Told: Slavery and the Making of American Capitalism.* New York: Basic Books, 2014.

20. See U.S. Census Bureau, *Negro Population: 1790–1915.* Washington, DC: U.S. Government Printing Office, 1918.

21. See Theodore W. Allen, *The Invention of the White Race,* 2nd edition. New York: Verso, 2012.

22. For a vivid description and analysis of this, see W. E. B. Du Bois, *The Souls of Black Folk.* New York: Penguin, 1989 (originally published in 1903), Ch. 8.

23. See Ronald Takaki, *Iron Cages: Race and Culture in 19th-Century America,* rev. ed. New York: Oxford, 2000; and *Strangers from a Different Shore,* rev. ed. Boston: Back Bay Books, 1998.

24. See the following by Immanuel Wallerstein: *The Modern World System.* New York: Academic Press, 1976; *The Capitalist World-Economy.* Cambridge: Cambridge University Press, 1979; *The Modern World System II: Mercantilism and the Consolidation of the European World Economy, 1600–1750.* New York: Academic Press, 1980; and *The Modern World System III: The Second Era of Great Expansion of the Capitalist World-Economy, 1730–1840.* New York: Academic Press, 1989. See also Howard Zinn, *A People's History of the United States,* 20th anniv. ed. New York: Perennial, 2003.

25. See, for example, Dee Brown, *Bury My Heart at Wounded Knee: An Indian History of the American West.* New York: Henry Holt, 1991; and Jack D. Forbes, *Columbus and Other Cannibals,* rev. ed. New York: Seven Stories Press, 1992.

26. See Theodore Allen, *Racial Oppression and Social Control* and *The Origin of Racial Oppression in Anglo-America.* New York, Verso, 2002; Charles Gallagher, "White Racial Formation: Into the Twenty-First Century," in Richard Delgado and Jean Stefancic (eds.), *Critical White Studies,* pp. 6–11. Philadelphia: Temple University Press, 1997; Kathleen Neal Cleaver, "The Antidemocratic Power of Whiteness," in Delgado and Stefancic, pp. 157–63; Baldwin, "On Being 'White' . . . and Other Lies." in *Essence,* 1984. Reprinted in David R. Roediger (ed.), *Black on White: Black Writers on What It Means to Be White,* pp. 177–80. New York: Schocken Books, 1999.

27. See Reginald Horsman, "Race and Manifest Destiny: The Origins of American Racial Anglo-Saxonism," in Delgado and Stefancic, pp. 139–44.

28. See David R. Roediger, *The Wages of Whiteness: Race and the Making of the American Working Class,* new ed. London and New York: Verso, 2007.

29. A powerful example of a situation in which this strategy ultimately failed is the great coal mine strike early in the twentieth century, dramatized in the film *Matewan.* See also Rebecca J. Bailey, *Matewan Before the Massacre.* Morgantown, WV: West Virginia University Press, 2008.

30. Reich, Michael. "The Political-Economic Effects of Racism," in Richard C. Edwards, Michael Reich, and Thomas E. Weisskopf (eds.), *The Capitalist System,* 3rd ed. Englewood Cliffs, NJ: Prentice Hall, 1986, pp. 304–11.

31. See Pam Fessler, "Why Disability and Poverty Still go Hand in Hand 25 Years After Landmark Law." National Public Radio, Jul. 26, 2015. Available online at http://www.npr.org/sections/health-shots/2015/07/23/424990474/why-disability-and-poverty-still-go-hand-in-hand-25-years-after-landmark-law;

Brewster Thackeray, "State of the Union for People with Disabilities," National Organization on Disability (www.nod.org), 2003; and Oliver Friedman, *Review of Situation of Goodwill Industries in Connection with Fair Labor Standards Act.* Goodwill Industries International, Inc., Archives, Feb. 25, 1940.

32. See, for example, Heidi I. Hartmann, "The Family as the Locus of Gender, Class, and Political Struggle: The Example of Housework," in *Signs: Journal of Women in Culture and Society* 6 (Spring 1981), pp. 366–94; Eli Zaretsky, *Capitalism, the Family, and Personal Life.* New York: Harper & Row, 1986; and Rosemary Tong, *Feminist Thought: A More Comprehensive Introduction,* 4th ed. Boulder, CO: Westview Press, 2013.

33. See Barbara Reskin, "Bringing the Men Back In: Sex Differentiation and the Devaluation of Women's Work," *Gender and Society* 2, no. 1 (Mar. 1988); Irene Tinker, *Persistent Inequalities: Women and World Development.* New York: Oxford, 1990; and Sharon Ann Navarro, "Las Mujeres Invisibles/The Invisible Women," in *Women's Activism and Globalization: Linking Local Struggle and Transnational Politics.* Nancy A. Naples and Manisha Desai (eds.) New York: Routledge, 2002.

34. See Marilyn Waring, *If Women Counted: A New Feminist Economics.* San Francisco: HarperCollins, 1990.

35. See Cecila L. Ridgeway, *Framed by Gender: How Gender Inequality Persists in the Modern World.* New York: Oxford, 2011.

36. See Patricia Hill Collins, *Black Feminist Thought: Knowledge, Consciousness, and the Politics of Empowerment,* 2nd ed. New York: Routledge, 2008, Ch. 11; Estelle Disch, *Reconstructing Gender: A Multicultural Anthology,* 5th ed. New York: McGraw-Hill, 2008. See also bell hooks, *Talking Back: Thinking Feminist, Thinking Black.* Boston: South End Press, 1989; Judith Lorber, *Paradoxes of Gender.* New Haven, CT: Yale University Press, 1995; Audre Lorde, *Sister Outsider: Essays and Speeches.* Freedom, CA: Crossing Press, 1984, especially pp. 114–23; and Gerda Lerner, "Reconceptualizing Differences Among Women," in Alison M. Jagger and Paula S. Rothenberg (eds.), *Feminist Frameworks,* 3rd ed. New York: McGraw-Hill, 1993, pp. 237–48.

37. See Rosalind S. Chou and Joe R. Feagin, *The Myth of the Model Minority: Asian Americans Facing Racism.* Boulder, CO; Paradigm, 2008; and Ronald Takaki, *Strangers from a Different Shore: A History of Asian-Americans.* Boston: Little, Brown and Company, 1998, p. 474.

38. See Kivel, *Uprooting Racism: How White People Can Work for Racial Justice,* rev. ed. Gabriola Island, BC: New Society Publishers, 2002, pp. 143–46.

CHAPTER 4: MAKING PRIVILEGE AND OPPRESSION HAPPEN

1. See John F. Dovidio and Samuel L. Gaertner (eds.), *Prejudice, Discrimination, and Racism.* Orlando, FL: Academic Press, 1986.

2. See Claudia Goldin and Cecelia Rouse. "Orchestrating Impartiality: The Impact of "Blind" Auditions on Female Musicians." *The American Economic Review* 90, no. 4 (2000): 715–41.

3. The classic work on prejudice is Gordon W. Allport, *The Nature of Prejudice.* New York: Anchor, 1958. See also Dovidio and Gaertner, *Prejudice, Discrimination, and Racism;* and Daniela Gioseffi (ed.), *On Prejudice: A Global Perspective.* New York: Anchor, 1993.

4. There is a huge literature on the effects of privilege and oppression on people's lives. See the Resources appendix at the end of this book. For more on microaggression, see Derald Wing Sue, *Microaggressions in Everyday Life: Race, Gender, and Sexual Orientation.* New York: Wiley, 2010.

5. See Joe R. Feagin and Melvin P. Sikes, *Living with Racism: The Black Middle-Class Experience.* Boston: Beacon Press, 1994, pp. 15–17. See also Ta-Nehisi Coates, *Between the World and Me.* New York: Spiegel and Grau, 2015; and Edward E. Telles and Vilma Ortiz, *Generations of Exclusion: Mexican Americans, Assimilation, and Race.* New York: Russell Sage Foundation, 2008.

6. Banaji, Mahzarin R., *Blindspot: Hidden Biases of Good People.* New York: Delacorte, 2013. See also Barbara Trepagnier, *Silent Racism: How Well-Meaning People Perpetuate the Racial Divide*, 2nd ed. Boudler, CO: Paradigm Publishers, 2010.

7. See "When Whites Get a Free Pass: Research Shows White Privilege Is Real." *The New York Times*, Febr. 24, 2015, p. A23.

8. For more on microaggression, see Derald Wing Sue, *Microaggressions in Everyday Life: Race, Gender, and Sexual Orientation.* New York: Wiley, 2010.

9. See Yara Mekawi and Konrad Bresin, "Is the Evidence from Racial Bias Shooting Task Studies a Smoking Gun?" *Journal of Experimental Social Psychology*, Vol. 61, Nov. 2015, pp. 120–30.

10. See Walt Harrington, "On the Road with the President of Black America," *The Washington Post Magazine,* Jan. 25, 1987, p. W14.

11. See Douglas S. Massey and Nancy A. Denton, *American Apartheid: Segregation and the Making of the Underclass.* Cambridge, MA: Harvard University Press, 1998; Kenya Downs, "Why Is Milwaukee So Bad for Black People?" National Public Radio, Mar. 5, 2015, available online at http://www.npr.org/sections/codeswitch/2015/03/05/390723644/why-is-milwaukee-so-bad-for-black-people; and James H. Carr and Nandinee Kutty (eds.), *Segregation: The Rising Costs for America.* New York: Routledge, 2008.

12. See, for example, "The Disproportionate Risks of Driving While Black." *The New York Times*, Oct. 24, 2015, p. A1.

13. See Abby Goodnough, "Harvard Professor Jailed; Officer Is Accused of Bias." *The New York Times*, Jul. 20, 2009.

14. Claude M. Steele, "Race and the Schooling of Black Americans," *Atlantic Monthly,* Apr. 1992, p. 73.

15. See Benjamin, *Black Elite,* p. 20; and Joe R. Feagin and Melvin P. Sikes, *Living with Racism: The Black Middle-Class Experience.* Boston: Beacon Press, 1994, p. 25.

16. See the Associated Press, "U.S. Majority Have Prejudice Against Blacks." Oct. 27, 2012.

17. Marian Wright Edelman, *The Measure of Our Success: A Letter to My Children and Yours.* Boston: Beacon Press, 1992.

18. Quoted in Joe R. Feagin and Melvin P. Sikes , *Living with Racism: The Black Middle-Class Experience.* Boston: Beacon Press, 1994, pp. 23–24.

19. See Michelle L. Meloy and Susan L. Miller, *The Victimization of Women: Law, Policies, and Politics.* New York: Oxford University Press, 2011; Laura L. O'Toole, Jessica R. Schiffman, and Margie L. Kiter Edwards, *Gender Violence: Interdisciplinary* Perspectives, 2nd ed. New York: New York University Press, 2007; C. Bohmer and A. Parrot, *Sexual Assault on Campus.* New York: Lexington, 1993; Carol Brooks Gardner. *Passing By: Gender and Public Harassment.* Berkeley: University of California Press, 1995; Marilyn French, *The War Against Women.* New York: Ballatine Books, 1992; Allan G. Johnson, "On the Prevalence of Rape in the United States," in *Signs: Journal of Women in Culture and Society* 6, no. 1 (1980), pp. 136–46; and Diana E. H. Russell, *Sexual Exploitation: Rape, Child Sexual Abuse, and Workplace Harassment.* Beverly Hills, CA: Sage, 1984.

20. See Joe R. Feagin and Melvin P. Sikes, *Living with Racism: The Black Middle-Class Experience.* Boston: Beacon Press, 1994, p. 213; and Ellis Cose, *The Rage of a Privileged Class.* New York: HarperCollins, 1993, pp. 31, 32–33.

21. See the Bureau of Labor Statistics, "2016 Employment and Earnings Online," accessed at http://www.bls.gov/opub/ee/2016/cps/annual.htm#empstat.

22. See the U.S. Bureau of the Census, *Statistical Abstract of the United States, 2012.* Washington, DC: U.S. Government Printing Office, 2013), Table 627.

23. See the U.S. Bureau of the Census, *Statistical Abstract of the United States, 2012.* Washington, DC: U.S. Government Printing Office, 2013), Table 703; and the Bureau of Labor Statistics and U.S. Census Bureau, *Current Population Survey,* "2014 Person Income Statistics" Online at https://www.census.gov/hhes/www/cpstables/032015/perinc/pinc03_000.htm.

24. See Harris & Associates, "N.O.D./Harris Survey of Americans with Disabilities." Washington, DC: National Organization on Disabilities, 2000; U.S. Census Bureau, American Community Survey: Selected economic characteristics, 2006. Online at http://www.census.gov/acs/www/index.html

25. See Harris and Associates, *ibid.*

26. See Gary David Comstock, *Violence Against Lesbians and Gay Men.* New York: Columbia University Press, 1995; Brian McNaught, *Gay Issues in the Workplace.* New York: St. Martins Griffin, 1994; Suzanne Pharr, *Homophobia A Weapon of Sexism.* New York: Women's Project, 1997; and James Woods and Jay H. Lucas, *The Corporate Closet: The Professional Lives of Gay Men in America.* New York: Free Press, 1993.

27. See Suzanne Pharr, *Homophobia A Weapon of Sexism.* New York: Women's Project, 1997, pp. 19, 23–24.

28. See Barbara Perry, "Doing Gender and Doing Gender Inappropriately: Violence Against Women, Gay Men and Lesbians." in *In the Name of Hate: Understanding Hate Crimes.* New York: Routledge, 2001; Michelle L. Meloy and Susan L. Miller. *The Victimization of Women: Law, Policies, and Politics.* New York: Oxford University Press, 2011; Laura L. O'Toole, Jessica R. Schiffman, and Margie L. Kiter Edwards, *Gender Violence: Interdisciplinary* Perspectives, 2nd ed. New York: New York University Press, 2007; Diana E. H. Russell, *Sexual*

Exploitation: Rape, Child Sexual Abuse, and Workplace Harassment. Beverly Hills, CA: Sage, 1984; Peggy Reeves Sanday, *A Woman Scorned: Acquaintance Rape on Trial.* New York: Doubleday, 1996.

29. See Suzanne Pharr, *Homophobia A Weapon of Sexism.* New York: Women's Project, 1997, p. 26.
30. Much of this discussion is based on Joseph Barndt, *Dismantling Racism: The Continuing Challenge to White America.* Minneapolis: Augsburg, 1991, Ch. 3; and Paul Kivel, *Uprooting Racism: How White People Can Work for Racial Justice,* rev. ed. Gabriola Island, BC: New Society Publishers, 2002, pp. 46–71.
31. See Ruth Frankenberg, *The Social Construction of Whiteness: White Women, Race Matters.* Minneapolis: University of Minnesota Press, 1993, pp. 60–61.
32. Joseph Barndt, *Dismantling Racism: The Continuing Challenge to White America.* Minneapolis: Augsburg, 1991, pp. 51–52; Cornel West, *Race Matters.* New York: Vintage, 1993, p.19.
33. See Anya Kamenetz, "The History of Campus Sexual Assault," National Public Radio, Feb. 2, 2015, online at http://www.npr.org/sections/ed/2014/11/30/366348383/the-history-of-campus-sexual-assault?sc=ipad&f=1001; and data on risks to servicewomen reported on PBS Newshour, Jul. 30, 2013.
34. See Joe R. Feagin and Melvin P. Sikes, *Living with Racism: The Black Middle-Class Experience.* Boston: Beacon Press, 1994, p. 53.

CHAPTER 5: THE TROUBLE WITH THE TROUBLE

1. For more on this idea, see Richard Delgado and Jean Stefancic, "Imposition," in Richard Delgado and Jean Stefancic (eds.), *Critical White Studies: Looking Behind the Mirror.* Philadelphia: Temple University Press, 1997, pp. 98–105.
2. R. Roosevelt Thomas, *Beyond Race and Gender: Unleashing the Power of Your Total Work Force by Managing Diversity.* New York: AMACOM, 1991, p. 41.
3. Most companies that have earned a reputation for "diversity" work have succeeded primarily around issues of sexual orientation and gender identity. Those who've effectively engaged with male and white privilege are much harder to find.

CHAPTER 6: WHAT IT HAS TO DO WITH US

1. Kivel, *Uprooting Racism: How White People Can Work for Racial Justice,* rev. ed. Gabriola Island, BC: New Society Publishers, 2002, p. 91.
2. See David Thomas, "Racial Dynamics in Cross-Race Developmental Relationships," *Administrative Science Quarterly,* June 1993, pp. 169–94.
3. See "Interview with Franklin McCain," in Clayborne Carson, David J. Garrow, Gerald Gill, Vincent Harding, and Darlene Clark Hine (eds.), *The Eyes on the Prize Civil Rights Reader.* New York: Penguin, 1991, pp. 114–16.
4. See Kenneth Chang, "Bias Persists for Women of Science, A Study Finds." *The New York Times,* Sep. 24, 2012.
5. See Charles Duhigg and David Barboza, "In China, Human Costs Are Built Into an iPad." *The New York Times,* Jan. 25, 2012, p. A1.

CHAPTER 7: HOW SYSTEMS OF PRIVILEGE WORK

1. For more on patriarchy and how it works, see Allan G. Johnson, *The Gender Knot: Unraveling Our Patriarchal Legacy,* 3rd ed. Philadelphia: Temple University Press, 2014. The general model for systems of privilege found there and in the present book derives from Marilyn French's monumental work on patriarchy, *Beyond Power: Men, Women, and Morals.* New York: Summit Books, 1985.

2. See Cecelia L. Ridgeway, *Framed by Gender: How Gender Inequality Persists in the Modern World.* New York: Oxford University Press, 2011, pp. 80–82; Erik Voeten, "Student Evaluations of Teaching Are Probably Biased. Does It Matter?" *Washington* Post, Oct. 2, 2013; and Bernice Sandler et al., *The Chilly Classroom Climate: A Guide to Improve the Education of Women.* Washington, DC: National Association for Women in Education, 1996, part 4.

3. Quoted in Sandler, ibid., p. 60.

4. See Katharine Q. Seelye and Julie Bosman, "Media Charged with Sexism in Clinton Coverage." *The New York Times*, Jun. 13, 2008. See also Sam Sanders, "#MemeoftheWeek: Megyn Kelly's Body Politic." National Public Radio, Jan. 29, 2016, online at http://www.npr.org/2016/01/29/464719435/-memeoftheweek-megyn-kellys-body-politic.

5. See Michael Schwalbe, *Manhood Acts: Gender and the Practices of Domination.* Boulder, CO: Paradigm, 2014.

6. See Deborah Tannen, *You Just Don't Understand: Women and Men in Conversation.* New York: Morrow, 1990, and *Talking from 9 to 5.* New York: Morrow, 1994.

7. See Joe R. Feagin and Melvin P. Sikes, *Living with Racism: The Black Middle-Class Experience.* Boston: Beacon Press, 1994, p. 94.

8. See, for example, R.L.G., "How Black to Be?" *The Economist*, Apr. 10, 2013, online at http://www.economist.com/blogs/johnson/2013/04/code-switching.

9. See Joe R. Feagin and Melvin P. Sikes , *Living with Racism: The Black Middle-Class Experience.* Boston: Beacon Press, 1994, p. 229.

10. "America the Beautiful," by Katharine Lee Bates, 1893.

11. Although an alum of all-women Wellesley College (that counts the composer of "America the Beautiful" among its graduates) informs me that students have rewritten the lyrics more than once, including the use of "sisterhood."

12. See Cynthia Leifer, et. al. "Gender Bias Plagues Academia." *The New* Republic, Aug. 5, 2015; and Erik Voeten, "Student Evaluations: of Teaching Are Probably Biased. Does It Matter?" *Washington* Post, Oct. 2, 2013. For an excellent discussion of double binds, see Marilyn Frye, "Oppression," in *The Politics of Reality: Essays in Feminist Theory.* Trumansburg, NY: Crossing Press, 1983.

13. For more on how this works, see Arlie Hochschild, *The Second Shift: Working Parents and the Revolution at Home,* rev. ed. New York: Viking/Penguin, 2012; Ridgeway, Cecila L., *Framed by Gender: How Gender Inequality Persists in the Modern World.* New York: Oxford University Press, 2011.

14. See, for example, Bunch Center for African American Studies, University of California at Los Angeles, "2015 Hollywood Diversity Report." February 25, 2015. Online at http://www.bunchecenter.ucla.edu/index.php/2015/02/2015-hollywood-diversity-report/; Jesse Washington, "Less Than 5% of actors in top films are Hispanic, new study finds." *The Washington Post*, Aug. 9, 2014.

15. See, for example, Richard Butsch, "Class and Gender in Four Decades of Television Situation Comedy," *Critical Studies in Mass Communications* 9 (1992), pp. 387–99; Gregory Mantsios, "Media Magic: Making Class Invisible." In Paul Rothenberg (ed.), *Race, Class, and Gender in the United States.* New York: Worth Publishers, 2013, pp. 510–19.
16. See Parul Sehgal, "Memory Lapse." *The New York Times* Magazine, Feb. 2, 2016, pp. 15–17.
17. See American Association of University Women, *How Schools Shortchange Girls.* Washington, DC: American Association of University Women, 1992; David M. Sadker and Karen Zittleman, *Still Failing at Fairness: How Gender Bias Cheats Girls and Boys in School and What We Can Do about It.* New York: Charles Scribner's Sons, 2009; and Bernice Sandler et al., *The Chilly Classroom Climate: A Guide to Improve the Education of Women.* Washington, DC: National Association for Women in Education, 1996.
18. See Kenneth Chang, "Bias Persists for Women in Science." *The New York Times,* Sep. 24, 2012; Bystydzienski, Jill M. and Sharon R. Bird. *Removing Barriers: Women in Academic Science, Technology, Engineering, and Mathematics.* Bloomington, IN: Indiana University Press, 2006; and American Association of University Women, *How Schools Shortchange Girls;* and Sadker and Zittleman, *Still Failing at Fairness.*
19. See, for example, Beverly Daniel Tatum, *Why Are All the Black Kids Sitting Together in the Cafeteria?* 5th ed. New York: Basic Books, 2003.
20. See David T. Wellman, *Portraits of White Racism,* 2nd ed. New York: Cambridge University Press, 2012.
21. See Jessie P. Guzman (ed.), *1952 Negro Yearbook.* New York: William H. Wise Co., 1952, pp. 275–79.
22. See Amy Louise Wood, *Lynching and Spectacle: Witnessing Racial Violence in America, 1890–1940.* Chapel Hill: University of North Carolina Press, 2011; and the Equal Justice Initiative, *Lynching in America: Confronting the Legacy of Racial Terror.* Washington, DC, Equal Justice Initiative, 2015. Online at http://www.eji.org/lynchinginamerica.
23. See Paula J. Giddings, *Ida: A Sword among Lions: Ida B. Wells and the Campaign against Lynching.* New York: Amistad, 2008.
24. See David T. Wellman, *Portraits of White Racism,* 2nd ed. New York: Cambridge University Press, 2012, p. 222.
25. Joel Kovel, *White Racism: A Psychohistory.* New York: Pantheon, 1970, p. 212.
26. See Alexander Thomas and Samuel Sillen, *The Theory and Application of Symbolic Interactionism.* Boston: Houghton-Mifflin, 1977.

CHAPTER 8: GETTING OFF THE HOOK: DENIAL AND RESISTANCE

1. This chapter owes much to Paul Kivel's *Uprooting Racism: How White People Can Work for Racial Justice,* rev. ed. Gabriola Island, BC: New Society Publishers, 2002, pp. 50–62; and David T. Wellman's *Portraits of White Racism.* 2nd ed. New York: Cambridge University Press, 2012, pp. 207–09.
2. Christina Hoff Sommers, "The War Against Boys," *Atlantic Monthly,* May 2000, pp. 59–74.

3. See Jonathan Haidt, *The Righteous Mind: Why Good People Are Divided by Politics and Religion*. New York: Vintage, 2013.
4. See Stanley Cohen, *States of Denial: Knowing About Atrocity and Suffering*. Cambridge, UK: Polity Press, 2001.
5. See William Ryan's classic book on this subject, *Blaming the Victim*. New York: Vintage, 1976.
6. For an in-depth look at sexual harassment, see Carol Brooks Gardner. *Passing By: Gender and Public Harassment*. Berkeley: University of California Press, 1995; see also "Why Telling a Woman to Smile Makes Her Want to Scream." National Public Radio, Apr. 9, 2016, online at http://www.npr.org/sections/goatsandsoda/2016/04/09/473433505/why-telling-a-woman-to-smile-makes-her-want-to-scream.
7. See Barrett A. Lee et. al. "Beyond the Census Tract: Patterns and Determinants of Racial Segregation at Multiple Geographical Sites." *American Sociological Review* 73 (Oct. 2008); James H. Carr and Nandinee Kutty, eds. *Segregation: The Rising Costs for America*. New York: Routledge, 2008; Douglas S. Massey and Nancy A. Denton, *American Apartheid: Segregation and the Making of the Underclass*. Cambridge, MA: Harvard University Press, 1998.
8. See Allan G. Johnson, *The Gender Knot: Unraveling Our Patriarchal Legacy*, 3rd edition. Philadelphia: Temple University Press, 2014.
9. For an insightful discussion of this, see Beverly Daniel Tatum, *Why Are All the Black Kids Sitting Together in the Cafeteria?* 5th ed. New York: Basic Books, 2003.
10. Ruth Frankenberg, *Social Construction of Whiteness: White Women, Race Matters*. Minneapolis: University of Minnesota Press, 1993, p.49. Italics in original.
11. For more on this idea, see Richard Delgado and Jean Stefancic, "Imposition," in Richard Delgado and Jean Stefancic (eds.), *Critical White Studies: Looking Behind the Mirror*. Philadelphia: Temple University Press, 1997, pp. 98–105.
12. Marian Wright Edelman, *The Measure of Our Success: A Letter to My Children and Yours*. Boston: Beacon Press, 1992.

CHAPTER 9: WHAT CAN WE DO?

1. See Elizabeth Fisher, *Woman's Creation: Sexual Evolution and the Shaping of Society*. New York: McGraw-Hill, 1979; and Gerda Lerner, *The Creation of Patriarchy*. New York: Oxford University Press, 1986.
2. This is what Warren Farrell means when he describes male power as mythical. In this case, he's right: See *The Myth of Male Power*. New York: Berkley Books, 1993. See also Michael Schwalbe, *Manhood Acts: Gender and the Practices of Domination*. Boulder, CO: Paradigm, 2014.
3. See Michael Kimmel, *Angry White Men: American Masculinity at the End of an Era*. New York: Nation Books, 2015.
4. I don't know of a published source for this idea attributed to Gandhi. I came across it years ago. It is true that wise sayings are often misattributed to famous people such as Gandhi or Albert Einstein, and that may be the case here.
5. See J. R. Wilkie, "Changes in U.S. Men's Attitudes Towards the Family Provider Role, 1972–1989," *Gender and Society* 7, no. 2 (1993): 261–79.

6. See "A Survey of LGBT Americans: Attitudes, Experiences and Values in Changing Times," Pew Research Center, Jun. 13, 2013, found online at http://www.pew-socialtrends.org/2013/06/13/a-survey-of-lgbt-americans/; and "In Gay Marriage Debate, Both Supporters and Opponents See Legal Recognition as 'Inevitable,'" Pew Research Center, Jun. 6, 2013, found online at http://www.people-press.org/2013/06/06/in-gay-marriage-debate-both-supporters-and-opponents-see-legal-recognition-as-inevitable.
7. The classic statement of how this happens is by Thomas S. Kuhn, *The Structure of Scientific Revolutions.* Chicago: University of Chicago Press, 1970.
8. Bonaro W. Overstreet, *Hands Laid Upon the Wind.* New York: Norton, 1955, p. 15.
9. Chris Crass calls this "decolonizing your mind." See *Towards the "Other America": Anti-Racist Resources for White People Taking Action for Black Lives Matter.* St. Louis: Chalice Press, 2015, p. 46.
10. My thanks to Joanne Callahan for suggesting the addition of this section.
11. For more on silence, see Dena Samuels, "Sounds and Silences of Language," in Amy L. Ferber, Christina M. Jiménez, Andrea O'Reilly Herrera, and Dena R. Samuels (eds.) *The Matrix Reader: Examining the Dynamics of Oppression and Privilege.* New York: McGraw-Hill, 2009, pp.502–8; and Beverly Daniel Tatum, *Why Are All the Black Kids Sitting Together in the Cafeteria?* 5th ed. New York: Basic Books, 2003.
12. See Audre Lorde, "The Transformation of Silence into Language and Action," in *"Sister Outsider: Essays and Speeches."* Berkeley: The Crossing Press, 1984.
13. For more on this, see Ward Churchill, "Crimes Against Humanity," *Z Magazine* 6 (Mar. 1993), pp. 43–47.
14. See William A. Gamson, "Violence and Political Power: The Meek Don't Make It," *Psychology Today* 8 (Jul. 1974), pp. 35–41.
15. See, for example, Alice Echols, *Daring to Be Bad: Radical Feminism in America 1967–1975.* Minneapolis: University of Minnesota Press, 1989.
16. For more on this, see the excellent PBS documentary of the civil rights movement, *Eyes on the Prize.*
17. See Doug McAdam, *Political Process and the Development of Black Insurgency 1930–1970.* Chicago: University of Chicago Press, 1982.
18. "University of Missouri Protests Spur a Day of Change." *The New York Times*, Nov. 10, 2015, p. A1.
19. Frederick Douglass, speech before the West Indian Emancipation Society (Aug. 4, 1857), in *The Life and Writings of Frederick Douglass,* ed. Philip S. Foner. New York: International Publishers, 1950, p. 437.
20. See Eileen T. Walsh, "Ideology of the Multiracial Movement: Dismantling the Color Line and Disguising White Supremacy?" in *The Politics of Multiracialism: Challenging Racial Thinking*, Heather M. Dalmage (ed.) New York: SUNY Press, 2004.
21. See Gregory Mantsios, "Media Magic: Making Class Invisible," in Paul Rothenberg (ed.), *Race, Class, and Gender in the United States.* New York: Worth Publishers, 2013, pp. 510–19.
22. My thanks to Joanne Callahan for making me aware of this issue.
23. See Estelle B. Freedman, *No Turning Back.* New York: Ballantine, 2002.
24. See, for example, Ibby Caputo, "Campus Protestors Across the Country Swap Ideas, Information." National Public Radio (WBUR), Dec. 13, 2015, online at

http://www.wbur.org/npr/459514516/campus-protesters-across-the-country-swap-ideas-information.

25. See Paul Kivel, *Uprooting Racism: How White People Can Work for Racial Justice,* rev. ed. Gabriola Island, BC: New Society Publishers, 2002, part 3, "Being Allies."

26. You'll find an excellent compilation of local, national, and international organizations of men working for change in Rob Okun's book, *Voice Male: The Untold Story of the Pro-Feminist Men's Movement.* Amherst: Interlink Publishing Group, 2014.

27. For this and much more, see Chris Crass, *Towards the "Other America": Anti-Racist Resources for White People Taking Action for Black Lives Matter.* St. Louis: Chalice Press, 2015.

28. Audre Lorde, *The Cancer Journals.* San Francisco: Aunt Lute Books, 1997, p. 13.

29. I first heard this from Wayne W. Dyer during a discussion he led on public television.

EPILOGUE

1. See Jonathan Haidt, *The Righteous Mind: Why Good People Are Divided by Politics and Religion.* New York: Pantheon, 2012.

Resources

PRIVILEGE AND OPPRESSION ACROSS
TWO OR MORE DIMENSIONS

Adams, Maurianne, Warren J. Blumenfeld, Rosie Castañeda, Heather W. Hackman, Madeline L. Peters, and Ximena Zúñiga (eds.) *Readings for Diversity and Social Justice,* 3rd ed. New York: Routledge, 2013.

Amott, Teresa L., and Julie A. Matthaei. *Race, Gender, and Work: A Multicultural Economic History of Women in the United States,* rev. ed. Boston: South End Press, 1996.

Andersen, Margaret L., and Patricia Hill Collins (eds.) *Race, Class, and Gender: An Anthology,* 9th ed. Belmont, CA: Wadsworth, 2015.

Anzaldúa, Gloria (ed.) *Making Face, Making Soul/Haciendo Caras: Creative and Critical Perspectives by Feminists of Color.* San Francisco: Aunt Lute Books, 1990.

Collins, Patricia Hill. *Black Feminist Thought: Knowledge, Consciousness, and the Politics of Empowermen,.* 2nd ed. New York: Routledge, 2008.

Davis, Angela. *Women, Race, and Class.* New York: Random House, 1981.

Disch, Estelle. *Reconstructing Gender: A Multicultural Anthology,* 5th ed. New York: McGraw-Hill, 2008.

Esty, Katharine, Richard Griffin, and Marcie Schorr Hirsch. *Workplace Diversity: A Manager's Guide to Solving Problems and Turning Diversity into a Competitive Advantage.* Holbrook, MA: Adams, 1995.

Ferber, Amy L., Christina M. Jiménez, Andrea O'Reilly Herrera, and Dena R. Samuels (eds.) *The Matrix Reader: Examining the Dynamics of Oppression and Privilege.* New York: McGraw-Hill, 2009.

Ganz, Marshall. *Why David Sometimes Wins: Leadership, Organization, and Strategy in the California Farm Worker Movement.* Oxford: 2009.

Gioseffi, Daniela (ed.) *On Prejudice: A Global Perspective.* New York: Anchor Books, 1993.

Harro, Bobbie. "The Cycle of Liberation," in *Readings for Diversity and Social Justice,* Maurianne Adams, Warren J. Blumenfeld, Rosie Castañeda, Heather W. Hackman, Madeline L. Peters, and Ximena Zúñiga (eds.) New York: Routledge, 2000, pp. 463–69.

Higginbotham, Elizabeth. "Black Professional Women: Job Ceilings and Employment Sectors," in *Workplace/Women's Place,* Dana Dunn (ed.) Los Angeles: Roxbury, 1997, pp. 234–46.

hooks, bell. *Ain't I a Woman: Black Women and Feminism.* Boston: South End Press, 1981.

———. *Feminist Theory: From Margin to Center.* Boston: South End Press, 1984.

———. *Sisters of the Yam: Black Women and Self-Recovery.* Boston: South End Press, 1993.

————. *Talking Back: Thinking Feminism, Thinking Black.* Boston: South End Press, 1989.

James, Stanlie M., Francis Smith Foster, and Beverly Guy-Sheftall (eds.) *Still Brave: The Evolution of Black Women's Studies.* New York: The Feminist Press, 2009.

Johnson, Allan G. *The Forest and the Trees: Sociology as Life, Practice, and Promise,* 3rd ed. Philadelphia: Temple University Press, 2014.

Kimmel, Michael S. and Amy L. Ferber (eds.). *Privilege: A Reader,* 3rd ed. Boulder: Westview, 2013.

Lerner, Gerda. "Reconceptualizing Differences Among Women," in Alison M. Jaggar and Paula S. Rothenberg (eds.), *Feminist Frameworks,* 3rd ed. New York: McGraw-Hill, 1993, pp. 237–48.

Loden, Marilyn, and Judy B. Rosener. *Workforce America: Managing Employee Diversity as a Vital Resource.* Homewood, IL: Business One Irwin, 1991.

Lorde, Audre. *Sister Outsider: Essays and Speeches.* Freedom, CA: Crossing Press, 1984.

Love, Barbara J. "Developing a Liberatory Consciousness," in Maurianne Adams, Warren J. Blumenfeld, Rosie Castañeda, Heather W. Hackman, Madeline L. Peters, and Ximena Zúñiga (eds.) *Readings for Diversity and Social Justice.* New York: Routledge, 2000, pp. 470–74.

McIntosh, Peggy. "White Privilege and Male Privilege: A Personal Account of Coming to See Correspondences Through Work in Women's Studies," in Anne Minas (ed.) *Gender Basics: Feminist Perspectives on Women and Men,* 2nd ed. Belmont, CA: Wadsworth, 2000. This classic article is widely reprinted in anthologies.

Mills, Nicholas (ed.) *Debating Affirmative Action.* New York: Dell, 1994.

Moraga, Cherríe, and Gloria Anzaldúa (eds.) *This Bridge Called My Back: Writings by Radical Women of Color,* 4th ed. New York: Third Woman Press, 2015.

Ore, Tracy E. *The Social Construction of Difference and Inequality: Race, Class, Gender, and Sexuality,* 6th ed. New York: McGraw-Hill, 2013.

Pascale, Celine-Marie. *Making Sense of Race, Class, and Gender: Commonsense, Power, and Privilege in the United States.* New York: Routledge, 2006.

Potter, Hillary. *Battle Cries: Black Women and Intimate Partner Abuse.* New York: New York University Press, 2008.

Roediger, David R. *The Wages of Whiteness: Race and the Making of the American Working Class,* new ed. New York: Verso, 2007.

Roscigno, Vincent. *The Face of Discrimination: How Race and Gender Impact Work and Home Lives.* Lanham, MD: Rowan and Littlefield, 2007.

Rosenblum, Karen E., and Toni-Michelle C. Travis (eds.) *The Meaning of Difference: American Constructions of Race, Sex and Gender, Social Class, and Sexual Orientation,* 7th ed. New York: McGraw-Hill, 2015.

Rothenberg, Paula S. (ed.) *Race, Class, and Gender: An Integrated Study,* 9th ed. New York: St. Martin's Press, 2013.

————. *Invisible Privilege: A Memoir About Race, Class, and Gender.* Lawrence, KS: University Press of Kansas, 2000.

Ryan, William. *Blaming the Victim.* New York: Vintage, 1976.

St. Jean, Yanick, and Joe R. Feagin. *Double Burden: Black Women and Everyday Racism.* Armonk, NY: M. E. Sharpe, 1999.

Sue, Derald Wing. *Microaggressions in Everyday Life: Race, Gender, and Sexual Orientation.* New York: Wiley, 2010.

U.S. Census Bureau. *Current Population Reports, Series P-60, Money Income in the United States.* Washington, DC: U.S. Government Printing Office. These reports are issued regularly with the latest data.

———. *Statistical Abstract of the United States.* Washington, DC: U.S. Government Printing Office. This volume is issued annually and is a readily available source of information on occupation, employment status, poverty, the distribution of wealth, educational attainment, etc.

Zinn, Howard. *A People's History of the United States.* New York: Perennial, 2005.

GENDER

Abramson, Joan. *Old Boys—New Women: Sexual Harassment in the Workplace.* New York: Praeger, 1993.

American Association of University Women. *How Schools Shortchange Girls.* Washington, DC: American Association of University Women, 1992.

Andersen, Margaret L. *Thinking about Women: Sociological Perspectives on Sex and Gender,* 10th ed. New York: Macmillan, 2014.

Bahun-Radunovis, Sanja (ed.) *Violence and Gender in the Globalized World.* Burlington, VT: Ashgate, 2008.

Benokraitis, Nijole V. "Sex Discrimination in the 21st Century," in Nijole V. Benokraitis (ed.) *Subtle Sexism: Current Practice and Prospects for Change.* Thousand Oaks, CA: Sage, 1997, pp. 5–33.

———, and Joe R. Feagin. *Modern Sexism: Blatant, Subtle, and Covert Discrimination,* New York: Pearson, 2009.

Blau, Francine S., Marianne A. Ferber, and Anne E. Winkler. *The Economics of Women, Men, and Work,* 7th ed. Englewood Cliffs, NJ: Prentice-Hall, 2014.

Bohmer, Carol, and Andrea Parrot. *Sexual Assault on Campus.* New York: Lexington, 1993.

Brod, Harry. "Work Clothes and Leisure Suits: The Class Basis and Bias of the Men's Movement," in Michael Kimmel and Michael A. Messner (eds.) *Men's Lives.* New York: Macmillan, 1989, p. 289.

Browne, A., and K. R. Williams. "Gender Intimacy and Legal Violence: Trends From 1976 Through 1987," in *Gender and Society* 7, no. 1(1993): 78–98.

Bunch, Charlotte. "Not for Lesbians Only." *Quest* 11, no. 2 (Fall 1975).

Burn, Shawn Meghan. *Women across Cultures: A Global Perspective*, 3th ed. New York: McGraw-Hill, 2010.

Bystydzienski, Jill M. and Sharon R. Bird. *Removing Barriers: Women in Academic Science, Technology, Engineering, and Mathematics.* Bloomington, IN: Indiana University Press, 2006.

Center for Research on Women. *Secrets in Public: Sexual Harassment in Our Schools.* Wellesley, MA: Wellesley College Center for Research on Women, 1993.

Chernin, Kim. *The Obsession: Reflections on the Tyranny of Slenderness.* New York: Harper & Row, 1981.

Chesney-Lind, Meda, and Nikki Jones. *Fighting for Girls: New Perspectives on Gender and Violence.* Albany, NY: State University of New York, 2010.

Colwill, Nina L. "Women in Management: Power and Powerlessness," in Dana Dunn (ed.) *Workplace/Women's Place.* Los Angeles: Roxbury, 1997, pp. 186–97.

Corcoran-Nantes, Yvonne, and Ken Roberts. "'We've Got One of Those': The Peripheral Status of Women in Male-Dominated Industries," in Dana Dunn (ed.) *Workplace/Women's Place.* Los Angeles: Roxbury, 1997, pp. 271–87.

Crittenden, Ann. *The Price of Motherhood: Why the Most Important Job in the World Is Still the Least Valued.* New York: Owl Books, 2010.

Dagiewicz, Molly. *Equality with a Vengeance: Men's Rights Groups, Battered Women, and Antifeminist Backlash.* Boston: Northeastern University Press, 2011.

Douglas, Susan J., *Enlightened Sexism: The Seductive Message that Feminism's Work Is* Done. New York: Henry Holt, 2010.

Dunn, Dana (ed.) *Workplace/Women's Place,* 3rd ed. New York: Oxford University Press, 2006.

Dworkin, Andrea. *Woman Hating.* New York: Dutton, 1974.

Ehrenreich, Barbara, and Deidre English. *For Her Own Good: 150 Years of Experts' Advice to Women,* 2nd ed. New York: Anchor Books/Doubleday, 2005.

———, and Arlie Russell Hochschild. *Global Woman.* New York: Owl Books, 2004.

Epstein, Cynthia Fuchs. *Deceptive Distinctions: Sex, Gender, and the Social Order.* New Haven, CT: Yale University Press, 1990.

Faludi, Susan. *Backlash: The Undeclared War Against American Women,* 15th anniv. ed. New York: Crown, 2006.

Fausto-Sterling, Anne. "The Five Sexes: Why Male and Female Are Not Enough." *Sciences* 33 (Mar./Apr. 1993): 20–24.

———. *Myths of Gender: Biological Theories about Women and Men,* 2nd rev. ed. New York: Basic Books, 1992.

Federal Glass Ceiling Commission. *A Solid Investment: Making Full Use of the Nation's Human Capital.* Washington, DC: Federal Glass Ceiling Commission, 1995.

Fenstermaker, S., and C. West (eds.) *Doing Gender, Doing Difference: Inequality, Power, and Institutional Change.* New York: Routledge, 2002.

French, Marilyn. *Beyond Power: On Men, Women, and Morals.* New York: Summit Books, 1985.

———. *The War Against Women.* New York: Summit Books, 1992.

Frye, Marilyn. *The Politics of Reality: Essays in Feminist Theory.* Trumansburg, NY: Crossing Press, 1983.

Gardner, Carol Brooks. *Passing By: Gender and Public Harassment.* Berkeley: University of California Press, 1995.

Gilbert, Paula Ruth, and Kimberly K. Eby (eds.) *Violence and Gender: An Interdisciplinary Reader,* 2nd ed. Englewood Cliffs, NJ: Prentice Hall, 2007.

Grewal, Inderpal, and Caren Kaplan (eds.) *Introduction to Women's Studies: Gender in a Transnational World,* 2nd ed. New York: McGraw-Hill, 2005.

Haslett, Beth Bonniwell, and Susan Lipman. "Micro Inequities: Up Close and Personal," in Nijole V. Benokraitis (ed.) *Subtle Sexism: Current Practice and Prospects for Change.* Thousand Oaks, CA: Sage, 1997, pp. 34–53.

Helgesen, Sally. "Women's Ways of Leading," in Dana Dunn (ed.) *Workplace/ Women's Place.* Los Angeles: Roxbury, 1997, pp. 181–85.

Hernandez, Daisy and Bushra Rehman, (eds.) *Colonize This! Young Women of Color on Today's Feminism.* Seattle, WA: Seal Press, 2002.

Hochschild, Arlie. *The Second Shift: Working Parents and the Revolution at Home,* rev. ed. New York: Viking/Penguin, 2012.

Hosken, Fran P. *The Hosken Report: Genital and Sexual Mutilation of Females,* 4th rev. ed. Lexington, MA: Women's International Network News, 1994.

Jaggar, Alison M., and Paul Rothenberg (eds.) *Feminist Framework,*. 3rd ed. New York: McGraw-Hill, 1993.

Jahren, Hope. *Lab Girl.* New York: Knopf, 2016.

Johnson, Allan G. *The Gender Knot: Unraveling Our Patriarchal Legacy,* 3rd ed. Philadelphia: Temple University Press, 2014.

———. "On the Prevalence of Rape in the United States." *Signs: Journal of Women in Culture and Society* 6, no. 1 (1980).

Jones, Ann. *Next Time She'll Be Dead: Battering and How to Stop It.* Boston: Beacon Press, 2000.

Kaufman, Michael (ed.) *Beyond Patriarchy.* New York: Oxford, 1987.

Kerber, Linda K., and Jane Sherron De Hart (eds.) *Women's America: Refocusing the Past,* 8th ed. New York: Oxford University Press, 2015.

Kimmel, Michael. *Angry White Men: American Masculinity at the End of an Era.* New York: Nation Books, 2013.

———. *Manhood in America: A Cultural History,* 3rd ed. New York: Free Press, 2011.

———, and Amy Aronson (eds.) *The Gendered Society Reader*, 5th ed. New York: Oxford, 2013.

———, R. W. Connell, and Jeff Hearn (eds.) *Handbook on Studies of Men and Masculinities.* Thousand Oaks, CA: Sage, 2004.

———, and Michael Messner (eds.) *Men's Lives,* 9th ed. Boston: Allyn & Bacon, 2012.

Lederer, Laura (ed.) *Take Back the Night: Women on Pornography.* New York: Morrow, 1980.

Loden, Marilyn. *Feminine Leadership.* New York: Random House, 1985.

Lorber, Judith. *Gender Inequality: Feminist Theories and Politics,* 5th ed. Los Angeles: Roxbury, 2011.

———. *Paradoxes of Gender.* New Haven, CT: Yale University Press, 1995.

MacKinnon, Catharine A. *Only Words.* Cambridge, MA: Harvard University Press, 1993.

Meloy, Michelle L. and Susan L. Miller. *The Victimization of Women: Law, Policies, and Politics*. New York: Oxford University Press, 2011.

Miller, Jean Baker. *Toward a New Psychology of Women.* 2nd ed. Boston: Beacon Press, 1987.

Minas, Anne (ed.) *Gender Basics: Feminist Perspectives on Women and Men,* 2nd ed. Belmont, CA: Wadsworth, 2000.

Moore, Lynda L. *Not As Far As You Think: The Realities of Working Women.* Lexington, MA: Lexington Books, 1986.

Morgan, Robin (ed.) *Sisterhood Is Global.* New York: Feminist Press, 1996.

Okun, Rob (ed.) *Voice Male: The Untold Story of the Profeminist Men's Movement.* Amherst, MA: Interlink, 2013.

O'Toole, Laura L., Jessica R. Schiffman, and Margie L. Kiter Edwards. *Gender Violence: Interdisciplinary Perspectives,* 2nd ed. New York: New York University Press, 2007.

Paludi, Michele A. *Sexual Harassment on College Campuses.* Albany: State University of New York Press, 1996.

Peterson, V. Spike, and Anne Sisson Runyan. *Global Gender Issues,* 4th ed. Boulder, CO: Westview Press, 2013.

Pharr, Suzanne. *Homophobia: A Weapon of Sexism,* expanded ed. Inverness, CA: Women's Project, 1997.

Reardon, Kathleen Kelley. "Dysfunctional Communication Patterns in the Workplace: Closing the Gap Between Women and Men," in *Workplace/Women's Place,* Dana Dunn, ed. Los Angeles: Roxbury, 1997, pp. 165–80.

———. *They Don't Get It, Do They?* Boston: Little, Brown, 1995.

Rhode, Deborah L. *Speaking of Sex: The Denial of Gender Inequality.* Cambridge, MA: Harvard University Press, 1999.

Rich, Adrienne. *Of Woman Born.* New York: Norton, 1995.

Richardson, Laurel, Verta Taylor, and Nancy Whittier (eds.) *Feminist Frontiers,* 9th ed. New York: McGraw-Hill, 2011.

Ridgeway, Cecila L., *Framed by Gender: How Gender Inequality Persists in the Modern World.* New York: Oxford University Press, 2011.

Rosenberg, Janet, Harry Perlstadt, and William R. F. Phillips. "'Now That We Are Here': Discrimination, Disparagement, and Harassment at Work and the Experience of Women Lawyers," in *Workplace/Women's Place,* Dana Dunn (ed.) Los Angeles: Roxbury, 1997, pp. 247–59.

Rotundo, Anthony. *American Manhood: Transformations in Masculinity from the Revolution to the Modern Era.* New York: Basic Books, 1993.

Russell, Diana E. H. *Sexual Exploitation: Rape, Child Sexual Abuse, and Workplace Harassment.* Beverly Hills, CA: Sage, 1984.

——— (ed.) *Making Violence Sexy: Feminist Views on Pornography.* New York: Teachers College Press, 1993.

———, and Roberta A. Harmes. *Femicide in Global Perspective.* New York: Teachers College Press, 2001.

Sadker, David M. and Karen Zittleman, *Still Failing at Fairness: How Gender Bias Cheats Girls and Boys in School and What We Can Do about It.* New York: Charles Scribner's Sons, 2009.

Sanday, Peggy Reeves. *A Woman Scorned: Acquaintance Rape on Trial.* New York: Doubleday, 1996.

Sandler, Bernice, Lisa A. Silverberg, and Roberta M. Hall. *The Chilly Classroom Climate: A Guide to Improve the Education of Women.* Washington, DC: National Association for Women in Education, 1996.

Sapiro, Virginia. *Women in American Society: An Introduction to Women's Studies,* 5th ed. New York: McGraw-Hill, 2003.

Schultz, Vicki. "Reconceptualizing Sexual Harassment." *Yale Law Journal,* April 1998, pp. 1683–1805.

Schwalbe, Michael. *Manhood Acts: Gender and the Practices of Domination.* Boulder, CO: Paradigm, 2014.

Stone, Pamela. *Opting Out? Why Women Really Quit Careers and Head for Home.* Berkeley, CA: University of California Press, 2007.

Stoltenberg, John. *Refusing to Be a Man.* New York: Meridian, 1989.

———. *The End of Manhood: A Book for Men of Conscience.* New York: Dutton, 1993.

Swerdlow, Marian. "Men's Accommodations to Women Entering a Nontraditional Occupation: A Case of Rapid Transit Operatives," in *Workplace/Women's Place,* Dana Dunn (ed.) Los Angeles: Roxbury, 1997, pp. 260–70.

Thistle, Susan. *From Marriage to Market: The Transformation of Women's Lives and Work.* Berkeley: University of California Press, 2006.

Thorne, Barrie. *Gender Play: Girls and Boys in School.* New Brunswick, NJ: Rutgers University Press, 1993.

Tong, Rosemarie. *Feminist Thought: A More Comprehensive Introduction*, 4th ed. Boulder, CO.: Westview Press, 2013.

Treas, Judith and Sonja Drobnic. *Dividing the Domestic: Men, Women, and Household Work in Cross-National Perspective.* (Stanford, CA: Stanford University Press, 2010.

Waring, Marilyn. *If Women Counted: A New Feminist Economics.* San Francisco: HarperCollins, 1990.

Wilkie, J. R. "Changes in U.S. Men's Attitudes Towards the Family Provider Role, 1972–1989." *Gender and Society* 7, no. 2 (1993): 261–79.

Williams, Christine L. *Still a Man's World: Men Who Do Women's Work.* Berkeley: University of California Press, 1995.

Wolf, Naomi. *The Beauty Myth: How Images of Beauty Are Used Against Women.* New York: Morrow, 1991.

RACE

Alexander, Michele. *The New Jim* Crow. New York: New Press, 2012.

Allen, Theodore W. *The Invention of the White Race,* vols. 1–2, 2nd ed. New York: Verso, 2012.

Allport, Gordon W. *The Nature of Prejudice.* New York: Anchor, 1958.

Baldwin, James. "On Being 'White'. . . and Other Lies." *Essence* 14 (April 1984): 90–92.

Barndt, Joseph. *Dismantling Racism: The Continuing Challenge to White America.* Minneapolis: Augsburg, 1991.

Barr, Donald A. *Health Disparities in the United States: Social Class, Race, Ethnicity, and Health,* 2nd ed. Baltimore, MD. Johns Hopkins University Press, 2014.

Barrett, James R., and David Roediger. "How White People Became White," in *Critical White Studies,* Richard Delgado and Jean Stefancic (eds.) Philadelphia: Temple University Press, 1997, pp. 402–06.

Bell, Derrick. *And We Are Not Saved: The Elusive Quest for Racial Justice.* New York: Basic Books, 1987.

———. *Faces at the Bottom of the Well: The Permanence of Racism.* New York: Basic Books, 1992.

Benjamin, Lois. *The Black Elite: Facing the Color Line in the Twilight of the Twentieth Century.* Chicago: Nelson-Hall, 1991.

Better, Shirley Jean. *Institutional Racism, A Primer on Theory and Strategies for Social Change,* 2nd ed. Chicago: Burnham, 2007.

Bonilla-Silva, Eduardo. *Racism without Racists: Color-Blind Racism and the Persistence of Racial Inequality in the United States,* 4th ed. Lanham, MD: Rowman and Littlefield, 2013.

————. *White Supremacy and Racism in the Post–Civil Rights Era.* Boulder, CO: Lynne Rienner Publishers, 2001.

Brown, Dee. *Bury My Heart at Wounded Knee: An Indian History of the American West.* New York: Bantam, 1972.

Capture, George Horse, Duane Champagne, and Chandler C. Jackson. *American Indian Nations: Yesterday, Today, and Tomorrow.* Lanham, MD: AltaMira Press, 2007.

Carr, James H., and Nandinee Kutty (eds.) *Segregation: The Rising Costs for America.* (New York: Routledge, 2008.

Carson, Clayborne, David J. Garrow, Gerald Gill, Vincent Harding, and Darlene Clark Hine (eds.) *The Eyes on the Prize Civil Rights Reader.* New York: Penguin, 1991.

Champagne, Duane. *Social Change and Cultural Continuity among Native Nations.* Lanham, MD: AltaMira Press, 2008.

Chou, Rosalind S. and Joe R. Feagin. *The Myth of the Model Minority: Asian Americans Facing Racism.* Boulder, CO; Paradigm, 2008.

Churchill, Ward. "Crimes Against Humanity." *Z Magazine* 6, Mar. 1993: 43–47. Reprinted in Margaret L. Andersen and Patricia Hill Collins (eds.) *Race, Class, and Gender,* 3rd ed. Belmont, CA: Wadsworth, 1998, pp. 413–20.

Coates, Ta-Nehisi. *Between the World and* Me. New York: Spiegel and Grau, 2015.

Collins, Patricia Hill. *Black Feminist Thought: Knowledge, Consciousness, and the Politics of Empowerment,* 2nd ed. New York: Routledge, 2008.

Correspondents of *The New York Times. How Race is Lived in America.* New York: Times Books, 2001.

Cose, Ellis. *The Rage of a Privileged Class.* New York: HarperCollins, 1993.

Crass, Chris. *Towards the "Other America": Anti-Racist Resources for White People Taking Action for Black Lives Matter.* St. Louis: Chalice Press, 2015.

Davis, Angela Y. *Women, Race, and Class.* New York: Random House, 1981.

Delgado, Richard, and Jean Stefancic (eds.) *Critical White Studies.* Philadelphia: Temple University Press, 1997.

Doane, Ashley W., and Eduardo Bonilla-Silva (eds.) *White Out: The Continuing Significance of Racism.* New York: Routledge, 2003.

Dovidio, John F., and Samuel L. Gaertner (eds.) *Prejudice, Discrimination, and Racism.* Orlando, FL: Academic Press, 1986.

Du Bois, W. E. B. *The Souls of Black Folk.* New York: Penguin, 1996.

Edelman, Marian Wright. *The Measure of Our Success: A Letter to My Children and Yours.* Boston: Beacon Press, 1992.

Farrow, Anne, Joel Lang, and Jenifer Frank. *Complicity: How the North Promoted, Prolonged, and Profited from Slavery.* New York: Ballantine, 2006.

Feagin, Joe R. *Systemic Racism: A Theory of Oppression.* New York: Routledge, 2006.

_____, and Karyn D. McKinney. *The Many Costs of Racism.* Lanham, MD: Rowman and Littlefield, 2003.

———, and Eileen O'Brien. *White Men on Race.* Boston: Beacon Press, 2004.

———, and Melvin P. Sikes. *Living with Racism: The Black Middle-Class Experience.* Boston: Beacon Press, 1995.

Frankenberg, Ruth. *The Social Construction of Whiteness: White Women, Race Matters.* Minneapolis: University of Minnesota Press, 1993.

Evelyn Nakano Glenn. *Shades of Difference: Why Skin Color Matters.* Stanford, CA: Stanford University Press, 2009.

Forbes, Jack D. *Columbus and Other Cannibals*, rev. ed. New York: Seven Stories Press, 1992.

Gomez, Laura E. *Manifest Destinies: The Making of the Mexican American Race.* New York: New York University Press, 2007.

Hacker, Andrew. *Two Nations: Black and White, Separate, Hostile, Unequal.* New York: Scribner, 1992.

Hartman, Chester and Gregory D. Squires (eds.) *The Integration Debate: Competing Futures for American Cities.* New York: Routledge, 2010.

Howard, Gary. *We Can't Teach What We Don't Know: White Teachers, Multiracial Schools,* 3rd ed. New York: Teachers College Press, 2016.

Hurtado, Aida. *The Color of Privilege.* Ann Arbor: University of Michigan Press, 1999.

Hylton, Kevin. *"Race" and Sport: Critical Race Theory.* New York: Routledge, 2009.

Johnson, Allan G. "Sociology as Worldview: Where White Privilege Came From," in *The Forest and the Trees: Sociology as Life, Practice, and Promise,* 3rd ed. Philadelphia: Temple University Press, 2014, pp.147–57.

Jung, Moon-Kie, Joao Costa Vargas, Eduardo Bonilla-Silva. *State of White Supremacy: Racism, Governance, and the United States.* Stanford, CA: Stanford University Press, 2011.

Katznelson, Ira. When Affirmative Action Was White: The Untold History of Racial Inequality in Twentieth Century America. New York: W. W. Norton, 2006.

Kendi, Ibram X. Stamped *from the Beginning: The Definitive History of Racist Ideas in America.* New York: Nation Books, 2016.

Kivel, Paul. *Uprooting Racism: How White People Can Work for Racial Justice,* 3rd ed. Philadelphia: New Society Publishers, 2011.

Kovel, Joel. *White Racism: A Psychohistory.* New York: Pantheon, 1970.

Lewis, Amanda. *Race in the Schoolyard.* Piscataway, NJ: Rutgers University Press, 2003.

Lipsitz, George. *The Possessive Investment in Whiteness: How White People Profit from Identity Politics,* rev. & exp. ed. Philadelphia: Temple University Press, 2006.

Lynch, Michael J., E. Britt Patterson, and Kristina A. Childs. *Racial Divide: Racial and Ethnic Bias in the Criminal Justice System.* New York: Criminal Justice Press, 2008.

MacLeod, Jay. *Ain't No Makin' It*, 3rd ed. Boulder: Westview, 2009.

Marable, Manning, and Leith Mullings (eds.) *Let Nobody Turn Us Around: Voices of Resistance, Reform, and Renewal.* Lanham, MD: Rowman and Littlefield, 2000.

———. "Racism, Prisons, and the Future of Black America," in *Along the Color Line: Explorations in the Black Experience,* August Meier and Elliot Rudwick (eds.) Chicago: University of Illinois Press, Nov. 2002.

Massey, Douglas S., and Nancy A. Denton. *American Apartheid: Segregation and the Making of the Underclass.* Cambridge, MA: Harvard University Press, 1998.

Moran, Beverly. *Race and Wealth Disparities: A Multidisciplinary Discourse.* Lanham, MD: Rowman and Littlefield, 2008.

Muhammad, Khalil Gibran. *The Condemnation of Blackness: Race, Crime, and the Making of Modern Urban America.* Cambridge, MA: Harvard University Press, 2010.

"On Views of Race and Inequality, Blacks and Whites Are Worlds Apart." Pew Research Center, June 27, 2016. Found online at http://www.pewsocialtrends.org/files/2016/06/ST_2016.06.27_Race-Inequality-Final.pdf

Painter, Nell Irvin. *The History of White People.* New York: W. W. Norton, 2010.

Peek, Lori. *Behind the Backlash: Muslim Americans after 9/11.* Philadelphia: Temple University Press, 2011.

Perry, Imani. *More Beautiful and More Terrible: The Embrace and Transcendence of Racial Inequality in the United States.* New York: New York University Press, 2011.

Piper, Adrian. "Passing for White, Passing for Black," in Richard Delgado and Jean Stefancic (eds.) *Critical White Studies,* Philadelphia: Temple University Press, 1997, pp. 425–31.

Prager, Devah. *Marked: Race, Crime, and Finding Work in the Era of Mass Incarceration.* Chicago: University of Chicago Press, 2007.

Reséndez, Andrés. *The Other Slavery: The Uncovered Story of Indian Enslavement in America.* New York: Houghton Mifflin Harcourt, 2016.

Rothenberg, Paula (ed.) *White Privilege: Essential Readings on the Other Side of Racism,* 5th ed. New York: Worth, 2015.

Shapiro, Thomas M. *The Hidden Cost of Being African-American: How Wealth Perpetuates Inequality.* New York: Oxford University Press, 2005.

Shrag, Peter. *Not Fit for Our Society: Immigration and Nativism in America.* Berkeley: University of California Press, 2010.

Smedley, Audrey, and Brian Smedley. *Race in North America: Origin and Evolution of a Worldview,* 4th ed. Boulder, CO: Westview, 2011.

Smedley, Brian, Adrienne Y. Smith, and Alan R. Nelson (eds.) *Unequal Treatment: Confronting Racial and Ethnic Disparities in Health Care.* Washington, DC: The National Academies Press, 2003.

Steele, Claude M. "Race and the Schooling of Black Americans." *Atlantic Monthly,* Apr. 1992, p. 73.

Suarez, Ray. *Latino Americans: The 500-Year Legacy that Shaped a Nation.* New York: Celebra Trade, 2013.

Sullivan, Shannon. *Good White People: The Problem with Middle-Class White Anti-Racism.* State University of New York Press, 2014.

Takaki, Ronald. *Strangers from a Different Shore: A History of Asian-Americans,* rev. ed. Boston: Back Bay Books, 1998.

Tatum, Beverly Daniel. *Why Are All the Black Kids Sitting Together in the Cafeteria?* 5th ed. New York: Basic Books, 2003.

Telles, Edward E. and Vilma Ortiz. *Generations of Exclusion: Mexican Americans, Assimilation, and Race.* New York: Russell Sage Foundation, 2008.

Terry, Robert. "The Negative Impact on White Values," in *Impacts of Racism on White Americans,* Benjamin P. Bowser and Raymond Hunt (eds.) Newbury Park, CA: Sage, 1981.

Thomas, Alexander, and Samuel Sillen. *Racism and Psychiatry.* New York: Brunner/Mazel, 1972.

Thomas, David. "Racial Dynamics in Cross-Race Developmental Relationships." *Administrative Science Quarterly,* Jun. 1993, pp.169–94.

Thomas, Roosevelt R. *Beyond Race and Gender: Unleashing the Power of Your Total Work Force by Managing Diversity.* New York: AMACOM, 1991.

Trepagnier, Barbara. *Silent Racism: How Well-Meaning People Perpetuate the Racial Divide,* 2nd ed. Boudler, CO: Paradigm Publishers, 2010.

Van Ausdale, Debra, and Joe R. Feagin. *The First R: How Children Learn Race and Racism.* Lanham, MD: Rowman and Littlefield, 2002.

Wellman, David T. *Portraits of White Racism,* 2nd ed. New York: Cambridge University Press, 2012.

West, Cornel. *Race Matters.* New York: Vintage, 1993.

Western Prison Project. "The Prison Index." Online at http://www.safetyandjustice.org/story/prison-index-fact-sheet-disenfranchisement.

Yancy, George. *Look, a White! Philosophical Essays on Whiteness.* Philadelphia: Temple University Press, 2012.

Zimring, Carl. *Clean and White: A History of Environmental Racism in the United States.* New York: New York University Press, 2016.

GENDER IDENTITY AND SEXUAL ORIENTATION

Abelove, Henry, Michele Aina Barale, and David M. Halperin (eds.) *The Lesbian and Gay Studies Reader.* New York: Routledge, 1993.

Baker, Dan, and Sean Strub. *Cracking the Corporate Closet.* New York: HarperCollins, 1993.

Blumenfeld, Warren. *Homophobia: How We All Pay the Price.* Boston: Beacon Press, 1992.

Bornstein, Kate, and S. Bear Bergman, *Gender Outlaws.* New York: Seal Press, 2010.

Comstock, David Gary. *Violence Against Lesbians and Gay Men.* New York: Columbia University Press, 1991.

Elliot, Patricia, ed. *Debates in Transgender, Queer, and Feminist Theory.* Burlington, VT: Ashgate Publishing Company, 2010.

Fausto-Sterling, Anne. *Sexing the Body: Gender Politics and the Construction of Sexuality.* New York: Basic Books, 2000.

Galupo, M. Paz, ed. *Bisexuality and Same-Sex Marriage.* New York: Routledge, 2009.

Gilreath, Shannon. *The End of Straight Supremacy.* New York: Cambridge University Press, 2011.

Girshick, Lori B. *Transgender Voices: Beyond Women and Men.* Hanover, NH: University Press of New England, 2009.

Gross, Larry P., and James D. Woods (eds.) *The Columbia Reader on Gays and Lesbians in Politics, Society, and the Media.* New York: Columbia University Press, 1999.

Heath, Melanie, *One Marriage under God: The Campaign to Promote Marriage in America.* New York: NYU Press, 2012.

Holmes, Morgan (ed.) *Critical Intersex.* Burlington, VT: Ashgate, 2009.

McNaught, Brian. *Gay Issues in the Workplace.* New York: St. Martin's, 1993.

Miller, Neil. *Out of the Past: Gay and Lesbian History from 1869 to the Present,* rev. ed. New York: Vintage, 2008.

Pascoe, C. J. *Dude, You're a Fag: Masculinity and Sexuality in High School.* Berkeley, CA; University of California Press, 2007.

Pharr, Suzanne. *Homophobia: A Weapon of Sexism,* expanded ed. Inverness, CA: Women's Project, 1998.

Schilt, Kristen. *Just One of the Guys? Transgender Men and the Persistence of Gender Inequality.* Chicago: University of Chicago Press, 2011.

Shrage, Laurie J. *"You've Changed": Sex Reassignment and Personal Identity.* New York: Oxford, 2009.

Warner, Michael. *The Trouble with Normal.* Cambridge, MA: Harvard University Press, 2000.

Woods, James, and Jay H. Lucas. *The Corporate Closet: The Professional Lives of Gay Men in America.* New York: Free Press, 1993.

SOCIAL CLASS

Aronowitz, Stanley. *How Class Works: Power and Social Movement.* New Haven, CT: Yale University Press, 2004.

Cage, Benjamin I. and Lawrence R. Jacobs. *Class War? What Americans Really Think about Class Inequality.* Chicago, IL: University of Chicago Press, 2009.

Danziger, Sheldon, and Peter Gottschalk. *Uneven Tides: Rising Inequality in America.* New York: Russell Sage Foundation, 1993.

Domhoff, G. William. *Who Rules America?* 7th ed. New York: McGraw-Hill, 2013.

Ehrenreich, Barbara. *Fear of Falling: The Inner Life of the Middle Class.* New York: HarperCollins, 1990.

———. *Nickel and Dimed: On (Not) Getting By in America.* New York: Metropolitan Books, 2001.

Gilbert, Dennis. *The American Class Structure in an Age of Growing Inequality.* 9th ed. Belmont, CA: Wadsworth, 2014.

Halpern, Greg. *Harvard Works Because We Do.* New York: W. W. Norton, 2003.

hooks, bell. *Where We Stand: Class Matters.* New York: Routledge, 2000.

Johnson, Allan G. "Why Is There Poverty: Putting the 'Social' Back into Social Problems," in *The Forest and the Trees: Sociology as Life, Practice, and Promise,* 3rd ed. Philadelphia: Temple University Press, 2014, pp. 134–141.

Kerbo, Harold R. *Social Stratification and Inequality,* 8th ed. New York: McGraw-Hill, 2012.

Neubeck, Kenneth J., and Noel A. Cazenave. *Welfare Racism: Playing the Race Card Against America's Poor.* New York: Routledge, 2001.

Reiman, Jeffrey. *The Rich Get Richer and the Poor Get Prison: Ideology, Class, and Criminal Justice,* 10th ed. Upper Saddle River, NJ: Routledge, 2012.

Roediger, David R. *The Wages of Whiteness: Race and the Making of the American Working Class,* new ed. New York: Verso, 2007.

Royce, Edward. *Poverty and Power: The Problem of Structural Inequality,* 2nd ed. Lanham, MD: Rowman and Littlefield, 2015.

Schor, Juliet B. *The Overworked American: The Unexpected Decline of Leisure.* New York: Basic Books, 1993.

Sennett, Richard, and Jonathan Cobb. *The Hidden Injuries of Class.* New York: W. W. Norton, 1993.

Shipler, David K. *The Working Poor: Invisible in America.* New York: Knopf, 2005.

DISABILITY STATUS

Charlton, James I. *Nothing About Us Without Us: Disability Oppression and Empowerment.* Berkeley: University of California Press, 2000.

Condeluci, A. *Interdependence: The Route to Community,* 2nd ed. New York: St. Lucie Press, 1995.

Davis, Lennard J. *The Disability Studies Reader,* 4th ed. New York: Routledge, 2013.

Fine, Michelle, and Adrienne Asch. "Disability beyond Stigma: Social Interaction, Discrimination, and Activism," in *Readings for Diversity and Social Justice,* Maurianne Adams, Warren J. Blumenfeld, Rosie Castañeda, Heather W. Hackman, Madeline L. Peters, and Ximena Zúñiga (eds.) New York: Routledge, 2000, pp. 330–39.

Jaeger, Paul, and Cynthia Ann Bowman. *Understanding Disability: Inclusion, Access, Diversity, and Civil Rights.* Wesport, CT: Praeger, 2005.

Johnson, Mary. *Make Them Go Away: Clint Eastwood, Christopher Reeve and the Case Against Disability Rights.* The Advocado Press, 2003.

Lane, Harlan L. *The Mask of Benevolence: Disabling the Deaf Community.* Chicago: Independent Publishers Group, 2000.

National Women's Studies Association Journal 14 (3), Fall 2002, issue devoted to Feminist Disability Studies.

Shapiro, Joseph. *No Pity.* New York: Three Rivers Press, 1993.

Smith, Bonnie, and Beth Hutchinson (eds.) *Gendering Disability.* Piscataway, NJ: Rutgers University Press, 2004.

Wendell, Susan. *The Rejected Body: Feminist Philosophical Reflections on Disability.* New York: Routledge, 1996.

Credits

Chapter 9 is excerpted and adapted from the chapter entitled "Unraveling the Gender Knot" from *The Gender Knot: Unraveling our Patriarchal Legacy* by Allan G. Johnson. Used by permission of Temple University Press. © 2014 by Allan G. Johnson. All Rights Reserved.

Index